ROYAL HISTORICAL SOCIETY

STUDIES IN HISTORY

New Series

LLOYD GEORGE, LIBERALISM AND THE LAND

LLOYD GEORGE, LIBERALISM AND THE LAND

THE LAND ISSUE AND PARTY POLITICS IN ENGLAND, 1906–1914

Ian Packer

THE ROYAL HISTORICAL SOCIETY
THE BOYDELL PRESS

First published 2001

A Royal Historical Society publication
Published by The Boydell Press
an imprint of Boydell & Brewer Ltd
PO Box 9, Woodbridge, Suffolk IP12 3DF, UK
and of Boydell & Brewer Inc.
PO Box 41026, Rochester, NY 14604–4126, USA
website: http://www.boydell.co.uk

ISBN 0 86193 252 8

ISSN 0269–2244

A catalogue record for this book is available
from the British Library

Library of Congress Cataloging-in-Publication Data
Packer, Ian, 1962–
    Lloyd George, liberalism and the land : the land issue and party
politics in England, 1906–1914 / Ian Packer.
        p. cm. – (Royal Historical Society studies in history. New series)
    Includes bibliographical references (p.) and index.
    ISBN 0–86193–252–8 (alk. paper)
    1. LLoyd George, David, 1863–1945 – Views on land reform.
2. Land reform – Great Britain – History – 20th century.
3. Liberalism – Great Britain – History – 20th century.   4. Great
Britain – Politics and government – 1901–1910.   5. Great Britain
– Politics and government – 1910–1936.   6. Liberal Party (Great
Britain)   I. Title.   II. Series.
DA566.9.L5 P34 2002
942.082'092 – dc21   2001035334

This book is printed on acid-free paper

Printed in Great Britain by
St Edmundsbury Press, Bury St Edmunds, Suffolk

FOR LYNDA

Contents

		Page
Acknowledgements		ix
Abbreviations		xi
1	The origins of the land issue	1
2	The failure of rural reform, 1906–1910	33
3	The transformation of the urban land issue, 1906–1910	54
4	New directions in rural strategy: the rural land report, 1912–1913	76
5	New wine in old bottles: the urban land report, 1912–1914	95
6	Breaking down the 'relics of feudalism': the rural land campaign, 1913–1914	115
7	The urban land campaign, 1913–1914	138
8	Confusing the enemy: the Unionist Party and the land issue, 1912–1914	156
9	Labour and the land issue, 1912–1914	162
10	The strange death of the land issue	178
Conclusion		194
Appendix		197
Bibliography		203
Index		217

Publication of this volume was aided by a grant from the Scouloudi Foundation, in association with the Institute of Historical Research.

Acknowledgements

This book has undergone a long journey since it started life as an Oxford DPhil. thesis. Lady Margaret Hall, Oxford, the Universities of Exeter and Teesside and Queen's University, Belfast, have all provided congenial and encouraging environments in which to complete my initial research and then to expand and revise it into its current form. My doctoral supervisor, Dr Michael Hart, has been unfailingly helpful and patient, as well as sharing with me his unrivalled knowledge of twentieth-century Liberalism. I have also greatly benefited from Terry Jenkins's expertise on nineteenth-century Liberalism. Miles Taylor and Martin Daunton provided much-appreciated constructive criticism when the book was submitted to the RHS. I owe a particular debt of gratitude for their support to my colleagues at Queen's, especially Peter Jupp, Alvin Jackson, Ian Green and Richard Butterwick. I would also like to thank Christine Linehan, Averill Buchanan and Tony Sheehan for his help in all matters technological. Many other friends in Belfast have enabled me to keep some sense of perspective when dealing with the intricacies of Edwardian politics.

My parents have given me far more help than I can ever repay. My greatest debt, though, is to Lynda. Without her I would never have achieved anything and I dedicate this book to her.

Historians depend on the goodwill and knowledge of librarians, archivists and owners of private papers. I am no exception and I am grateful to the following institutions and individuals for access to and permission to quote from manuscript sources: the National Library of Wales; the University of Birmingham Library; the University of Bristol Library; the Syndics of Cambridge University Library (Crewe papers); the Trustees of the National Library of Scotland (Elibank papers); the Scottish Record Office; Mrs G. Stafford (Steel-Maitland papers); the marquess of Salisbury (4th marquess of Salisbury papers); the University of Keele Library; the Public Record Office; the West Yorkshire Archive Service; Liverpool City Library; the British Library (Balfour papers); the British Library of Political and Economic Science; Friends House; Mr M. Rowntree (A. Rowntree papers); the Clerk of the Records of the House of Lords Record Office (Samuel papers); the Clerk acting on behalf of the Beaverbrook Foundation Trust (Lloyd George papers); Manchester Central Reference Library; the Trustees of the Trevelyan papers at the Robinson Library, University of Newcastle; the Bodleian Library, Oxford; J. Bonham Carter (Asquith papers); J. Ingall (Bryce papers); J. N. Llewellyn Palmer (Carrington papers); the Hon. Mrs C. Gascoigne (Sir W. Harcourt and L. Harcourt papers); the Warden and Fellows of New College,

Oxford (Milner papers); Nuffield College Library; Lord Gainford and Professor Cameron Hazlehurst (J. Pease papers); Rhodes House Library; the Trustees of the Joseph Rowntree Foundation (B. S. Rowntree papers), and the Joseph Rowntree Reform Trust.

Ian Packer
Belfast, 2000

Abbreviations

AgHR	*Agricultural History Review*
AMC	Association of Municipal Corporations
BL	British Library, London
BLPES	British Library of Political and Economic Science
Bod. Lib.	Bodleian Library, Oxford
BSP	British Socialist Party
CD	Carrington diary
CUB	Central Unemployed Body
EHR	*English Historical Review*
HJ	*Historical Journal*
HLRO	House of Lords Record Office
HWJ	*History Workshop Journal*
ILP	Independent Labour Party
IRSH	*International Review of Social History*
JBS	*Journal of British Studies*
LCC	London County Council
LG	Lloyd George papers (HLRO)
LL	*Labour Leader*
LLRA	Land Law Reform Association
LM	*Liberal Magazine*
LNS	Land Nationalisation Society
LTRA	Land Tenure Reform Association
LV	*Land Values*
NFU	National Farmers Union
NLF	National Liberal Federation
NLHC	National Land and Housing Council
NLHL	National Land and Home League
NLS	National Library of Scotland
NLW	National Library of Wales
NR	*National Review*
P&P	*Past and Present*
PRO	Public Record Office
SHR	*Scottish Historical Review*
SRO	Scottish Record Office
TCBH	*Twentieth Century British History*
TRHS	*Transactions of the Royal Historical Society*
UCTLV	United Committee for the Taxation of Land Values
USRC	Unionist Social Reform Committee

VS   *Victorian Studies*
WHR   *Welsh History Review*
WYAS   West Yorkshire Archive Service

1

The Origins of the Land Issue

A forgotten controversy: the English land issue

In the late nineteenth and early twentieth centuries the United Kingdom was one of the most urbanised societies in the world. This book argues that despite this salient fact, land reform remained a central element of its politics. In some ways this was not surprising. In particular, there were specific social, political and national configurations in Ireland, Scotland and Wales that gave the 'land question' a special resonance in those countries and their demands naturally impinged on the wider level of British politics. This situation has been widely studied and has produced a very substantial historiography on land reform in the non-English nations of the United Kingdom.[1]

This book, however, does not retread these well-worn paths, but deals with the less well-known but equally significant English dimension of the 'land question'. Demands for land reform had very different causes and meanings in different parts of the United Kingdom. In Ireland the economic grievances of tenant farmers became inextricably linked to the political demands of Irish nationalism. In Wales dislike of landowners was intimately associated with the unpopularity of the Anglican Church. In Scotland the plight of the crofters and memories of the Highland clearances gave the land issue a particular flavour all of its own. Despite these differences agricultural depression allowed all these issues to come to a head during the 1880s and created a palpable sense of crisis within landed society. But this crisis had an English dimension, too. In a reversal of the usual processes of British historiography, it is this English dimension that is often omitted from the picture and the peculiarities of the English land issue have not been fully explored.

The situation in England was certainly peculiar in the sense that it was

---

[1]   For Ireland see P. Bew, *Land and the national question in Ireland, 1858–82*, Dublin 1978; A. Gailey, *Ireland and the death of kindness: the experience of constructive unionism, 1890–1905*, Cork 1987; W. E. Vaughan, *Landlords and tenants in mid-Victorian Ireland*, Oxford 1994; P. Bull, *Land, politics and nationalism*, Dublin 1996. For Scotland see H. J. Hanham, 'The problem of Highland discontent, 1880–5', *TRHS* 5th ser. xix (1969), 21–65; E. A. Cameron, *Land for the people? The British government and the Scottish Highlands, c. 1880–1925*, East Linton 1996; I. Packer, 'The land issue and the future of Scottish Liberalism in 1914', *SHR* lxxv (1996), 52–71. For Wales see J. P. D. Dunbabin, 'The Welsh "tithe war" ', in J. P. D. Dunbabin (ed.), *Rural discontent in nineteenth-century Britain*, London 1974, 211–31; D. Howell, *Land and people in nineteenth-century Wales*, London 1978; M. Cragoe, *An Anglican aristocracy: the moral economy of the landed estate in Carmarthenshire, 1832–95*, Oxford 1996.

very different from that elsewhere in the United Kingdom. Agricultural depression did not set farmers against landlords but solidified their alliance. Rural land reform in England focused on the agricultural labourer – a notably neglected figure in Scotland, Wales and Ireland. Moreover, the depression was only a background factor in the English land issue, which was fundamentally a matter of political prejudices and manoeuvres, not economic grievances and popular protest. The key events in England in the 1880s were the extension of the urban franchise to the counties in 1884–5, the Liberal Party's search for a formula to win the allegiance of agricultural labourers and the mass defection of landowners to the Unionist camp in 1886. These events allowed the long-standing radical animus against landowners to become the official stance of the Liberal Party and encouraged it to take up previously marginal ideas about allotments and smallholdings in order to gain the rural vote.

Thereafter the rural land issue was a significant part of the English party political struggle down to 1914. But English land reform was also distinctive in acquiring an increasingly significant urban dimension. Radicals came to see 'the land' as the solution for subjects as disparate as the crisis in local government finance, unemployment and housing shortages. What these topics had in common was a conviction in the Liberal Party that landlords must be responsible for many of the ills of urban society, just as they were for the difficulties of rural England. These issues, rural and urban, played a part in British politics that was consistently obtrusive and occasionally crucial: Joseph Chamberlain's campaign to provide agricultural labourers with 'three acres and a cow' in 1885 was only the first skirmish in a long controversy about allotments and smallholdings that reached a crescendo with the Liberals' 1907 Smallholdings Act; land taxation bitterly divided Tories and Liberals from the 1880s onwards and provided the occasion for the great constitutional crisis of 1909–11, when it was included in the People's Budget; the Liberals' plans to win the following general election were centred on a great, new land campaign of Lloyd George's devising, launched in 1913; and Lloyd George returned to 'the land' in the 1920s to revivify Liberalism.

The land issue's importance in British politics did not, therefore, just stem from the situation in Ireland, Wales and Scotland. It had an English element that was crucially significant. Though this has received much less attention than its counterparts, it has been explained in a number of ways. None of these approaches is entirely satisfactory. It has, for instance, become a commonplace of the recent historiography on late Victorian Britain that landowners remained a substantial feature of the British political, economic and social landscape right up to 1914.[2] Land reform was one way of attacking the very basis of landlords' power and identity. But it was only one option,

[2] D. Cannadine, *The decline and fall of the British aristocracy*, London 1990; A. Adonis, *Making aristocracy work: the peerage and the political system in Britain, 1884–1914*, Oxford 1993.

together with extending local and national democracy, reforming the Lords, the system of taxation, the civil service, the law, the army, the Church, the honours system, the governing of the empire or even the monarchy. To some historians, the Liberals' specific interest in the land can only be explained as a sign of the party's inability to grapple with the problems of modern, urban Britain. Most appealingly, Avner Offer argued that the obsession of English Liberals with rural land reform can best be understood as a reflection of the almost universal reverence for nature in English middle-class sensibility. This could be found in all parts of the political spectrum, but serious-minded Liberals, disillusioned with formal religion, seem to have been particularly susceptible to transcendental nature worship.[3] The passion of Sir Edward Grey for his beech trees and the Trevelyan clan for twenty-mile tramps before breakfast is well-known. But it turns out, on closer inspection, that even so unlikely a figure as Asquith was a devotee of the beauties of the Lakes and Herbert Samuel was a fanatical bicyclist and rhapsodist of the charms of southern England. This is interesting in itself and Offer suggests that if we are going to understand the resonance and force of the Liberal interest in the countryside in this period we have to appreciate it as an endeavour to 'revive the latent energies of British romanticism'.

Alun Howkins took a slightly different approach in his essay 'The discovery of rural England'.[4] He claimed that the origins of what he identified as the predominant vision today of 'real' English society as an idealised rural community where economic relations were personal and organic and there was no social conflict can be located in the period from the 1880s to 1914. Liberal politicians were interested in reviving rural life because they saw the countryside as the home of the 'real England', which needed to be nurtured and cared for. These sorts of analyses fit neatly into the overall approach of Martin Wiener in his famous polemic, English culture and the decline of the industrial spirit, in which he argued that, under the influence of a fundamentally anti-entrepreneurial intelligentsia, Edwardian society had turned away from the glorification of industrial enterprise to be captivated by the myth of England as a pre-industrial Garden of Eden.[5] Thus, Liberals' interest in rural land reform can be explained away as part of the English bourgeoisie's obsession with nature and its rosy view of country life.

The land issue's urban dimension, especially Liberals' interest in land taxation, can also be fitted into this picture. To historians like Offer, Bentley Gilbert and George Bernstein this kind of policy was as irrelevant as the Liberals' arcadian view of the countryside.[6] Land taxation represented an

3 A. Offer, Property and politics, 1870–1914: landownership, law, ideology and urban development in England, Cambridge 1981, 328–49.
4 A. Howkins, 'The discovery of rural England', in R. Colls and P. Dodd (eds), Englishness: politics and culture, 1880–1920, Beckenham 1986, 62–88.
5 M. J. Wiener, English culture and the decline of the industrial spirit, Cambridge 1981.
6 Offer, Property and politics; B. Gilbert, 'David Lloyd George: the reform of British land-

utterly impractical radical fallacy, of no interest to most town-dwellers and as unrelated to the problems of urban society as an obsession with rural smallholdings. Liberals' interest in urban land reform was another sign of the party's enfeeblement in the Edwardian era and its failure to connect with the aspirations of the working class.

These views represent the dominant way of analysing the role of the land issue in English politics. Some historians, though, who have charted the development of the New Liberalism from the 1890s to 1914 have taken a more charitable view of the Liberals' involvement with land reform. To Michael Freeden, H. V. Emy and Martin Pugh the Edwardian Liberals' interest in the land was an important example of the party's wider re-orientation towards social reform and state intervention in the economy.[7] This approach goes some way towards rehabilitating the Liberals' approach to land reform as an intellectual enterprise. But the land question was not just an *idée fixe* for Liberals. Both its content and significance fluctuated directly in response to changing political circumstances.

The focus of rural land reform, for instance, switched from the creation of smallholdings to minimum wages and on to agricultural development in little more than a decade. Moreover, while land reform was only one element in the Liberal programme in the 1890s, it became a central plank of the party's appeal in 1909–14, only to fade away after World War One. These developments and their significance can only be fully understood by analysing the role that land reform played in the Liberal Party's political strategy and this book provides the first such detailed examination of the relationship between Liberalism and the English land issue. In particular, the book seeks to explain why land reform became so central to Liberalism in the Edwardian era and argues that this development had profound implications for the party's nature and prospects of future success on the eve of the First World War. In doing so it sheds important new light on the vexed question of the decline of Liberalism.

Landlords, Liberals and Radicals

It is a truism that nineteenth-century England was a society governed by landed gentlemen. As John Stuart Mill said in 1871 to the inaugural meeting of the Land Tenure Reform Association, 'It is a rule, to which history as yet furnishes few exceptions, that nations are governed by their landed propri-

holding and the budget of 1914', *HJ* xxi (1978), 117–41; G. Bernstein, *Liberalism and Liberal politics in Edwardian England*, London 1986, 145–7.
[7] M. Freeden, *The new Liberalism: an ideology of social reform*, Oxford 1978; H. V. Emy, *Liberals, Radicals and social politics, 1892–1914*, Cambridge 1973, esp. pp. 203–34; M. Pugh, *The making of modern British politics, 1867–1939*, Oxford 1982, 127–9.

etors. At all events they have ruled this country.'[8] This judgement has largely been confirmed by twentieth-century historians. As late as 1880, 322 of the 652 MPs owned more than 2,000 acres. The House of Lords remained very much an assembly of great landowners until the 1920s and retained a veto over all legislation until 1911. Even in the period 1885 to 1908, 40 per cent of cabinet ministers were peers. The Justices of the Peace (three-quarters of whom were landowners) ran the counties until 1889 and often afterwards in the guise of county councillors.[9] This was not really a surprising situation. Landowners were the traditional governing elite. In the late Victorian era their dominance of the peaks of wealth-holding and social prestige was only just beginning to be diluted.[10] Whilst they retained the will to rule, they would not easily be dislodged.

The basis of this power was the concentration of landownership in the hands of a relatively small group of people. The parliamentary land survey of 1873 was usually interpreted as having revealed that fewer than 6,000 people owned two-thirds of England and Wales.[11] Moreover, this was a system that was difficult to criticise in the 1860s and 1870s. Landowners had many allies in the rest of society. Professions like the law were intimately connected with the administration of land and, by the early 1900s, there were more than a million owners of urban house property in England who might be disturbed by any move against property in land.[12] In the countryside, large agricultural estates were usually rented out to tenant farmers. They saw landowners as their allies in the production process. While landlords provided the major part of the capital – the land itself and the permanent fixtures – and took a small, but certain, return in the form of rent, farmers provided the working capital and received a higher, but less certain, return from the farm's profits. English farmers had little desire to own their land. They were entrepreneurs, not land-hungry peasants, and had no wish to tie their capital up in land when it could be put to work making a profit from farming. This economic alliance made political co-operation the norm. Landlords monopolised the representation of the counties in parliament and on the magistrates' bench in return for paying close attention to the interests of farmers.[13]

But, just as importantly, landowners and their allies could plausibly claim that the system of great estates had produced a uniquely efficient agriculture

---

8   LTRA, *Report of inaugural public meeting, 15 May 1871*, London 1871, 1.

9   H. J. Hanham, *Elections and party management*, London 1959, p. xv n. 2; Adonis, *Making aristocracy work*, 167–8; C. Zangerl, 'The social composition of the county magistracy in England and Wales, 1831–87', *JBS* xi (1971), 113–25.

10   Cannadine, *Decline and fall*, 88–138, 341–87.

11   The raw data was variously interpreted in A. Arnold, *Free land*, London 1880; G. C. Brodrick, *English land and English landlords*, London 1881; J. Bateman, *The great landowners of Great Britain and Ireland*, 4th edn, London 1883.

12   Offer, *Property and politics*, 18–29, 118–19.

13   See R. J. Olney, *Lincolnshire politics, 1832–85*, Oxford 1973, 32–56, for farmer–landlord relations in one county.

that had been of immense benefit to all of British society. During the period of rapid urbanisation in 1750–1850 agricultural production had risen to meet the demands of the new town population and food imports had never been a serious enough drain on foreign exchange to undermine Britain's economic growth. Landowners had used some of their accumulated wealth to invest in new industries, particularly transport and mining. Moreover, up to 1850 agriculture was able both to absorb some of the growing population as well as to provide workers for new industries. All members of rural society were tied into a cash economy and provided a market for urban produce. British agriculture was even efficient enough to survive the repeal of the corn laws in 1846 and to flourish for thirty years under Free Trade. All these factors made it easy for agriculturists to argue that the British land system was an essential complement to urban society and economic growth. Its economies of scale and labour and superiorities of skill and investment were endlessly compared with those of continental peasantries, to demonstrate the virtues of the landlord/tenant/labourer system.[14]

There were some critics of the *status quo*, most of whom in the 1870s could be found in the Liberal Party. The party's leadership, like that of the Conservatives, was still overwhelmingly made up of great landowners. Not surprisingly, they had no interest in fundamentally reforming the English system of landholding.[15] But the Whigs regarded themselves as rulers by popular consent and had no wish to maintain aristocratic privileges that provoked more trouble than they were worth. They had, after all, accepted the repeal of the corn laws in the 1840s far more readily than the Tories. The Whigs might also be more open to farmers' grievances than the Conservatives, especially if this would drive a wedge between farmers and Tories. However, before the late 1870s this propensity had only manifested itself in Ireland, where Gladstone had produced the 1870 Land Act, rather than in England.

Some radical MPs, however, wished to take up the cause of land reform more seriously. Their leading figure, until his death in 1865, had been Richard Cobden. Disillusioned by the failure of political reform in 1832 or the repeal of the corn laws to challenge the dominance of landowners, Cobden had become an exponent of what he dubbed 'Free Trade in Land'. As he said in his last great speech of November 1864, if he had been younger, 'I would take Adam Smith in hand, and I would have a league for Free Trade in land just as we had a league for Free Trade in corn.'[16] Cobden advocated the abolition of the laws of primogeniture, entail and strict settlement that landowners used to help maintain their estates intact when they passed to the next generation.

[14] See J. Chambers and G. Mingay, *The agricultural revolution*, London 1966, 199–211, and H. Merivale, 'Essays on the tenure of land', *Edinburgh Review* cxxxiv (1874), 449–83, for a typical defence of the land system on these lines.
[15] J. Parry, *The rise and fall of Liberal government in Victorian Britain*, London 1993, best describes the world view of the Liberals' pre-1886 leadership.
[16] J. Morley, *Life of Richard Cobden*, London 1881, 920.

Rather optimistically, he believed that without these laws there would be a much greater variety of landholding. Much more radical was that other patron saint of Victorian Liberalism, John Stuart Mill. Mill helped found the Land Tenure Reform Association in 1871, which urged the state to purchase land on the market and offer it to small cultivators.[17] Later on, the advocacy of Cobden and Mill provided land reform with a respectable Liberal pedigree. But at the time both men saw the acute difficulty of making their concerns relevant and justifiable to an urban audience. Mill realised the crucial importance of contesting the alleged superior efficiency of the system of great estates and spent a good deal of time synthesising the works of writers like Richard Jones and W. T. Thornton to try and rehabilitate the peasant cultivator.[18] But neither Mill nor Cobden was able to show why the Liberal Party should become vitally concerned with the structure of landholding rather than more obtrusive signs of aristocratic privilege and Free Trade in Land remained the hobby of a few radical backbenchers until the late 1870s.[19]

However, the traditions of working-class radicalism inherited by Liberalism in the mid-nineteenth century provided another potential reservoir of support for land reform. Most working-class radicals were far more concerned with immediate struggles for religious equality, democracy and fiscal reform than any aspect of the land question. But behind all these policies lay the assumption that the aristocracy was the enemy of the open, democratic society that they wished to create.[20] They were bound, therefore, to endorse enthusiastically, if vaguely, most forms of land reform. Moreover, working-class radicalism had inherited various strains of thought that saw the land as the common heritage of all the people.[21] This could be justified on a number of grounds. Appeal could be made to the Bible that 'The earth is the Lord's, and the fulness thereof' (1 Corinthians x. 26) rather than being the possession of the landlords. A sort of primitive natural rights theory could be used to assert that everyone had a right to use the land to earn their living, just as they had the right to use their labour. Often history was invoked to claim that the land had been stolen from the people, either when the 'Norman Yoke' was imposed in 1066 or at the time of the enclosures.

These ideas had been turned into concrete plans of action by some of the most illustrious figures in the radical pantheon. In the 1790s Thomas Spence had called for the collective ownership of land by the parishes. Tom Paine described his plan for a tax on the increment in land values in 1797. Robert Owen had wanted the land to be worked by communes, trading with similar

---

17 LTRA, *Report of inaugural meeting*, 37–9.

18 See C. Dewey, 'The rehabilitation of the peasant proprietor in nineteenth-century economic thought', *History of Political Economy* vi (1974), 17–47.

19 F. M. L. Thompson, 'Land and politics in England in the nineteenth century', *TRHS* 5th ser. xv (1965), 23–44.

20 E. Biagini, *Liberty, retrenchment and reform*, Cambridge 1992, esp. pp. 50–60.

21 This is explored in M. Chase, *The people's farm: English radical agrarianism, 1775–1840*, Oxford 1988.

urban ventures. The leading Chartist, Feargus O'Connor, started a land company to plant workers on the land as an alternative to the horrors of industrialisation. Bronterre O'Brien went further and demanded the nationalisation of the land, a demand endorsed by the Chartist Convention of 1851.[22] These ideas were bequeathed to later generations and taken up in the late 1860s by organisations like the Land and Labour League. In particular, settlement on the land was propounded as a solution to urban distress and unemployment.[23] But something was needed to make land reform a political issue, rather than a strand in various sorts of Liberal and radical thought. This missing ingredient was provided by the onset of agricultural depression.

The emergence of the rural land issue

The long period of prosperity enjoyed by Victorian agriculture drew to a close in the mid-1870s under the pressure of foreign imports and a succession of bad harvests. Wheat prices fell from an average of 56s. per quarter in 1866–71 to 17s. 6d. in 1894.[24] The result was a chorus of protest, especially from the farmers of eastern England, who found their light, dry soils difficult to convert from wheat to other crops. Demands for agricultural protection began to resurface. This gave those radicals who were interested in land reform their chance. They argued that agriculture could only be revived by a reform of the structure of landholding, rather than protection. In some ways their case was plausible. Foreign competition could most successfully be combated by producers of fresh food. Market gardening, dairying and poultry farming could all be presented as areas where small-scale production might be more appropriate than the system of great estates and large tenant farms. Radicals scoured the continent for examples of how peasants had weathered the depression better than English farmers.[25] Historical researchers like Thorold Rogers claimed to have demonstrated that only a return to the small farm units of the Middle Ages could restore agricultural prosperity.[26] This propaganda offensive was not without effect on the Whig leadership. Hartington suggested in 1879 that a future Liberal government would make land transfer easier.[27] This was a fairly painless concession to his radical wing and allowed

---

[22] T. Spence, *The rights of infants*, London 1797; T. Paine, *Agrarian justice: opposed to agrarian law and to agrarian monopoly*, London 1797; R. Owen, *The signs of the times: or the approach of the millennium*, London 1841; E. Barry, *Nationalisation in British politics*, London 1965, 28–41.

[23] R. Harrison, 'The Land and Labour League', *Bulletin of the International Institute of Social History* viii (1953), 169–95.

[24] F. M. L. Thompson, *English landed society in the nineteenth century*, London 1963, 308–10.

[25] Revd B. Zincke, 'Peasants of the Limagne', *Fortnightly Review* xxx (1878), 646–60, 821–35.

[26] Rogers's work culminated in his *Six centuries of work and wages*, London 1884.

[27] T. Jenkins, *Gladstone, Whiggery and the Liberal Party, 1874–86*, Oxford 1988, 82–3.

the Liberal leaders to say something about how they would deal with agricultural depression. After a great deal of wrangling, the promise was kept with the Settled Estates Act of 1882. Hard-pressed landowners who wished to sell up were unwilling to die in the last ditch against 'Free Land', when it might be in their own interests.

More importantly, though, agricultural depression focused attention on the institution of landownership by provoking reactions from within rural society. This was most obvious and most serious in Ireland. The Land League's agitation made English radicals more aware that British landowners were not regarded kindly by all their tenants and that landowners could be presented as rack-renters who presided over rural squalor. Their experience of Irish resistance in the 1880s was crucial in shaping the views of many English radicals about the significance of the land issue.[28] Moreover, Gladstone's Irish Land Act of 1881 showed that the state and the Liberal Party, when pressed, could interfere with a landlord's conduct of his estates in the name of social equity.

Irish land legislation also provided an important precedent. Gladstone's reluctant acceptance in 1881 of a system of land courts and security of tenure established a model of how Liberals could use the state to deal with strained relations between landlords and tenants. Despite protestations to the contrary at the time, this blueprint could be extended to other areas of the United Kingdom. Gladstone's brief third government produced the Crofters' Holdings (Scotland) Act of 1886, which contained similar measures in an attempt to quieten the agrarian unrest in the West Highlands in the early 1880s.[29] The royal commission on Welsh land, appointed by the Liberals in 1893, recommended a system of land courts for Wales.[30] Should Liberalism ever wish to undertake a major reorganisation of tenurial conditions in England it had only to refer to its actions in Ireland and the Highlands.

Events in Ireland made explicit another, equally important, facet of the general relationship between land reform and Liberalism. Initially, Liberal governments did not seem hostile to the idea of using state loans to create a class of peasant proprietors in Ireland. The 1870 Land Act contained the 'Bright clauses' to this effect and there were land purchase measures in the 1881 act, too. But when Gladstone proposed a wide-ranging land purchase bill in 1886, as a complement to his Home Rule scheme, most radicals in his party were horrified.[31] They violently objected to a bill that would, as they saw it, make the taxpayer 'pay through the nose for the benefit of Irish land-

---

28 F. Channing, *Memories of Midland politics, 1885–1910*, London 1918, 3.
29 See Cameron, *Land for the people?*, 14–39, for an up-to-date assessment.
30 *Report of the royal commission on Welsh land*, 1896 (C. 8242).
31 G. D. Goodlad, 'The Liberal Party and Gladstone's land purchase bill of 1886', *HJ* xxxii (1989), 627–41.

lords'.[32] The bill did not proceed beyond its first reading and was later denounced by Gladstone himself. Thus, after 1886, Liberalism moved away from the idea of state loans to would-be owner-occupiers anywhere in the United Kingdom, on the grounds that this policy would merely be a form of state subsidy to landlords. Instead, the idea became increasingly associated with Conservatism. Tories had heartily disliked Gladstone's 1881 Irish Land Act as an unwarranted interference with the rights of property.[33] They claimed that the act had deprived landlords of any benefit from their owner-ship of the soil. The logical alternative, therefore, was to provide state credit to allow tenants to buy out their landlords and there was a series of increas-ingly generous Tory land acts to this effect from 1885 to 1903. This policy did not have to be confined to Ireland. The Conservatives' 1897 Congested Districts (Scotland) Act applied it to the crofting areas of the Highlands.[34] Increasingly, some Tories saw benefits in the creation of a (hopefully) conser-vative peasantry to shore up the 'bulwarks of property' and land purchase acquired a positive gloss, rather than being merely an escape route for desperate landowners. In this light, it might even be applicable to English conditions. Thus events in Ireland in the 1880s started to give both major parties distinctive stances on land reform that had implications for the rest of the United Kingdom.

This development in turn helped concentrate attention on the English countryside, which some radicals hoped would soon resemble the state of revolt in Ireland. In the late 1870s some farmers' leaders were increasingly disillusioned with the failure of the Conservatives to combat the depression and with the slowness of landlords in reducing rents. An independent Farmers Alliance was set up in 1879 to articulate their grievances, particu-larly about the inadequacies of the 1875 Agricultural Holdings Act, which had gone a little way towards standardising and putting on a legal footing the compensation farmers could demand at the end of a lease for the improve-ments they had made to a farm.[35] The Liberal leadership began to feel that they might at last wean the farmers away from Toryism and, indeed, in 1880 the Liberals did unusually well in the English counties, winning 50 of 170 seats. This encouraged Harcourt, in particular, to make a serious bid for the farmers' allegiance. The malt tax was repealed in 1880. It was followed by a Ground Game Act the same year and an amended Agricultural Holdings Act in 1883. The Conservatives were disconcerted and divided, with Northcote complaining of 'the audacity with which the Government are putting them-selves forward as the true farmer's friends – and the momentary applause

---

[32] Sir E. Russell to W. Gladstone, 2 May 1886, W. Gladstone papers, BL, MS Add. 44497, fo. 91.

[33] M. O'Callaghan, *British high politics and a nationalist Ireland*, Cork 1994, 95–103, 145–52.

[34] Cameron, *Land for the people?*, 83–101.

[35] J. Fisher, 'The Farmers Alliance: an agricultural protest movement of the 1880s', *AgHR* xxvi (1978), 15–25.

which they are obtaining from the Chambers of Agriculture and other representatives of the farmers interests'.[36] For the first time a Liberal government had made issues connected with land reform a plank in its platform, albeit a minor one.

This initiative was not sustained. The Farmers Alliance faded away in the early 1880s under the impact of revived protectionist sentiment in farming circles and disillusion with the continuing depression under the Liberals. But the land issue did not die with it. The key to this was the gradual emergence into the political limelight of 'Hodge', as the agricultural labourer was usually termed in the patronising political shorthand of late Victorian politics. The spread of agricultural trade unionism, or 'Revolt of the Field', in 1872–4 revealed that forty years of slowly rising wages, together with the spread of literacy and organisations like benefit clubs and Methodist chapels, had allowed the labourers finally to organise themselves against the farmers and landlords.[37] This was a not unwelcome prospect to many radicals and a few like Jesse Collings played some role in the union's affairs, while most radical newspapers applauded the union's efforts.[38] The possibility of new support in the countryside further hastened the Liberal leadership's commitment to extending household franchise to the counties. Gladstone approved the policy in private in 1873 and Hartington made it a public commitment in 1877.[39] From the start the 1880 Liberal government was expected to redeem this pledge at the end of its term and reap a suitable reward from the grateful new voters.

This was a development of fundamental importance for the land issue, for it raised the serious prospect that the Liberals might finally capture the English counties from the Tories, if they could only keep Hodge's gratitude. There were a number of policies the new voters could be enticed with, including the creation of a democratic local government framework, attacks on the Church of England, poor law reform, the defence of cheap food in the face of calls for protection and the development of rural education. But land reform was also an attractive possibility that might both win the labourers' votes and undermine the power of Tory landlords. For instance, the policy of Free Land, as embodied in the 1882 Settled Estates Act, seemed to have done little to hasten the demise of the great estates and a group of Gladstonian loyalists, led by Arthur Arnold, MP for Salford, founded the Free Land League in 1885 to pursue further the 'unfettering' of land transfer.[40]

36 Iddlesleigh diary, entry for 20 June 1880, Iddlesleigh papers, BL, MS Add. 50063A (pt II), fos 347–51.
37 J. Dunbabin, 'The rise and fall of agricultural trades unionism in England', in Dunbabin, *Rural discontent*, 62–84.
38 J. Collings and J. Green, *Life of the Right Hon. Jesse Collings*, London 1920, 113–21.
39 H. C. G. Matthew, *Gladstone, 1809–74*, Oxford 1988, 224; Jenkins, *Gladstone, Whiggery and the Liberal Party*, 81.
40 A. Arnold to W. Gladstone, 7 Sept. 1885, W. Gladstone papers, MS Add. 44095, fos 483–8.

But some radicals in the mid-1880s were calling for Liberals to go further and use the power of local authorities to provide allotments for labourers, so freeing them from poverty and landlord dominance by giving them a means of supplementing their wages. This might have remained merely another radical nostrum. What transformed its significance was the tireless advocacy of Jesse Collings, a Birmingham ironmonger and MP for Ipswich. Collings promoted an Allotments Extension Act in 1882 to allow trustees of lands allotted for the general benefit of the rural poor under the enclosure acts to let their land out as allotments and he founded an Allotments Extension Association the following year to popularise the measure. But this remained an organisation of Birmingham-based radicals.[41] Collings did not in any sense 'represent' the agricultural labourers. Indeed, since the collapse of the National Agricultural Labourers Union in the late 1870s there was no organisation that could remotely claim to speak on behalf of 'Hodge'. Collings's activities were significant because he was a close ally of Joseph Chamberlain, not because he was a tribune of the labourers.

Chamberlain, like many radicals, had shown some interest in Free Land in the 1870s and in legislation to help farmers in the early 1880s.[42] But when he launched his 'Unauthorised Campaign' in August 1885 he seized on Collings's idea for allotments, with free education and graduated taxation, as the main items in a radical platform that would sweep the Liberals to victory and demonstrate the popularity of radical ideas with the new post-Third Reform Act electorate. Chamberlain felt that allotments were an ideal issue because they could appeal to urban as well as rural workers on the grounds that they would stop labourers migrating to the towns.[43] He did not, and could not, know they would be popular with agricultural labourers. Faced with the new electorate enfranchised in 1885 he could only guess and hope.

Chamberlain's advocacy made land reform an important talking-point among the political classes and put it in the front rank of controversial issues for the first time. However, 'Three acres and a cow', as the allotments policy was labelled, probably played a fairly minor role in the constituencies in the 1885 election, even in English country districts. Chamberlain had no organisation to spread his ideas and his programme was not official party policy, so candidates could choose to ignore it entirely. On the other hand, traditional battles over Church disestablishment and Free Trade were particularly fierce and probably mattered more at local level.[44] But this was not how many politicians interpreted the matter. In 1880 the Liberals had performed fairly well in the English counties but in 1885 they did even better, winning 132 of 231

---

[41] Collings and Green, *Life of Collings*, 140–6, 164–5; J. Chamberlain to C. Dilke, 7 Sept. 1885, Dilke papers, BL, MS Add. 43887, fos 162–3.
[42] R. Jay, *Joseph Chamberlain: a political study*, Oxford 1981, 19, 38, 40–1, 49, 72.
[43] See Chamberlain's speech at Hull reported in *Times*, 6 Aug. 1885.
[44] A. Simon, 'Church disestablishment as a factor in the general election of 1885', *HJ* xviii (1975), 791–820.

seats. This was a welcome contrast to the Liberals' relatively poor results in the boroughs, which prevented an overall Liberal majority. Deprived of much else to boast about, radicals were eager to claim that the triumph in the counties was the result of Chamberlain's fearless espousal of a radical programme of land reform. 'Is not the cow working wonders for us?' as Labouchere gleefully wrote to Chamberlain.[45]

This claim appeared plausible because virtually all politicians thought that the results in the English counties would be determined by the votes of the agricultural labourers, so it was natural to assume that a policy designed to appeal to their interests was responsible for the Liberals' good showing. In some ways this wildly over-estimated the significance of the agricultural vote in county seats. As Michael Barker has pointed out, only a shrinking minority of workers were actually employed on the land and nearly half of Liberal gains in the counties in 1885 were in predominantly industrial seats in northern England.[46] But the outlook of late Victorian politicians was dominated by decades of thinking of county seats as synonymous with the interests of agriculture – a view that was reinforced by the prominence of large landowners in the leadership of both parties.[47] In 1885 they just assumed that agricultural labourers had replaced farmers as the most important 'interest' that had to be placated to win the county seats. Moreover, as census and parliamentary boundaries rarely coincided, it was impossible to produce detailed and accurate evidence about the social profile of constituencies that might have challenged the traditional view that agriculture dominated the politics of the counties. Thus it seemed to most politicians that Chamberlain had discovered the key to success in the English counties.

But while contemporaries over-emphasised the importance of agriculture, they were correct to think of it as a crucial factor in the Third Reform Act system. Not only did it still employ one adult in eight in 1881, the redistribution of seats in 1884–5 had deliberately enhanced the significance of the English agricultural vote at the insistence of the Tory leadership. As Dilke wrote to Chamberlain, 'we have been over-generous to some English agricl. counties'.[48] Obvious examples of this included making Rutland a separate seat and giving two MPs each to under-populated counties like Huntingdonshire and Westmorland.[49] In addition, the boundary commissioners were effectively instructed to separate agricultural and industrial

45 H. Labouchere to J. Chamberlain, 3 Dec. 1885, in A. Thorold, *Life of Labouchere*, London 1913, 245.

46 M. Barker, *Gladstone and Radicalism: the reconstruction of Liberal policy in Britain, 1885–94*, Hassocks 1975, 36, 258.

47 D. Brooks, 'Gladstone's fourth ministry, 1892–4: policies and personalities', unpubl. PhD diss. Cambridge 1975, 129–30.

48 Dilke to J. Chamberlain, 22 Nov. 1884, Joseph Chamberlain papers, University of Birmingham Library, Birmingham, MS 5/24/77.

49 In 1885 Rutland had 4,166 electors, the two Hunts seats had 5,655 and 5,989 and the two Westmorland seats 5,630 and 6,022. The average number of voters for a county seat,

populations when drawing the boundaries of county divisions.[50] One effect of this was to prevent agricultural voters being swamped by urban voters in many counties. Although the abolition of small boroughs added about one million new voters (mainly from small towns, often connected with agriculture) to the counties, some 1.2 million urban voters were removed by the creation of new boroughs and the extension of borough boundaries.[51] Everything had been done to ensure that agriculture was more than fairly represented after 1885. Although it is impossible to determine the percentage of adult males in each seat employed in agriculture, an estimate that 111 out of 456 English seats had a significant agricultural population is reasonable.[52] The Liberals won fifty-four of these constituencies in 1885, comprising 41 per cent of their English county victories. Thus while politicians may have exaggerated the importance of the Liberals' success in agricultural areas, the party did make a significant breakthrough in rural England.

However, there is one final point to consider. Not all of those employed on the land were labourers. Politicians' image of agriculture was dominated by the traditional ideal of large arable farms with dozens of labourers. But British agriculture was far more complex and diverse than this, even in southern and eastern England.[53] In northern and western England the predominance of smaller, family-run pastoral farms meant that in some areas there were almost as many farmers and their relatives as there were labourers. But the political significance of labourers was enhanced because they were almost entirely a male workforce. The female relatives on whom many smaller farmers relied for labour could not vote. This meant that about 70 per cent of all males in agriculture were labourers.[54] Moreover, as labourers tended to have a low rate of residential mobility they were unlikely to be disfranchised under the residence requirements of the Third Reform Act.[55] It is, therefore, reasonable to suppose that a large part of the Liberals' success in rural England can be ascribed to the votes of the newly-enfranchised agricultural labourers, even if 'Three acres and a cow' was not a very significant issue at local level. There was a modest factual basis in the contemporary analysis of the English county results in 1885.

But however the results were interpreted, Chamberlain had not made the

---

however, was 10,160 (figures calculated from F. Craig, *British parliamentary election results, 1885–1918*, London 1974).

[50] *Instructions to boundary commissioners*, PP 1884–5, lxii. 255.

[51] A. Jones, *The politics of reform, 1884*, Cambridge 1972, 206–7.

[52] See appendix for this calculation.

[53] M. Reed, 'The peasantry of nineteenth-century England: a neglected class?', *HWJ* xviii (1984), 53–76.

[54] See the able interpretation of census figures in A. Howkins, *Reshaping rural England: a social history, 1850–1925*, London 1991, 11.

[55] P. Clarke and K. Langford, 'Hodge's politics: the agricultural labourers and the Third Reform Act in Suffolk', in N. Harte and R. Quinault (eds), *Land and society in Britain, 1700–1914: essays in honour of F. M. L. Thompson*, Manchester 1996, 119–36.

provision of allotments official Liberal policy in 1885. The Whig leadership was sceptical about the whole idea – which Gladstone had never officially endorsed. Lord Spencer declared cautiously 'I do not at all like the idea of pledging myself to his [Chamberlain's] methods for increasing allotments & small owners: but I do not want to pledge myself against his views without hearing out all his arguments.'[56] Lord Kimberley claimed

> It is very easy to declaim on this subject – very hard to discover practical reme-
> dies . . . allotments to labourers, of which I have had a good many always on
> my Estate, are useful things in their way, but will do but little to solve the prob-
> lem of giving the rural population a more direct interest in the land.[57]

But when Collings put down a motion embodying his allotments policy in January 1886, Gladstone selected it as the issue on which to defeat the minority Tory government and so form a Liberal administration. Gladstone was probably moved by the need to rally radical support for his Irish policy, rather than any enthusiasm for rural reform, but his action provided a post-humous endorsement of the significance of the land issue at the 1885 election and in subsequent politics.[58] Most Liberals, however Whiggish, followed Gladstone's lead and only eighteen voted against the Collings amendment. This was a clear sign, as W. C. Lubenow has pointed out, that land reform was becoming a clear dividing line between Tories and Liberals.[59] This was partly because of the Liberals' Irish land policy, reinforced in 1886 by the applica-tion of similar principles to the Scottish crofters. But it also reflected the enhanced importance of radical MPs in the Liberal parliamentary party after 1885. These men felt few qualms about voting for anti-landlord policies when such issues arose.

From Liberalism to Radicalism

These developments were reinforced by the various catastrophes that over-came Liberalism in 1886. The first and most damaging in the long term was the defection of the Liberal Unionists over Gladstone's espousal of Irish Home Rule. Although this was not a straightforward division of opinion between moderates and radicals, most radicals remained with Gladstone while a significant percentage of cautious Liberals defected.[60] This opened

---

56 Lord Spencer to W. Gladstone, 5 Oct. 1885, W. Gladstone papers, MS Add. 44312, fos 190–5.
57 Lord Kimberley to W. Gladstone, 13 Sept. 1885, ibid. MS Add. 44228, fos 205–11.
58 See Barker, *Gladstone and Radicalism*, 44–5, and *Hansard*, 3rd ser., 1886, cccii. 443–6, for Collings's amendment.
59 W. C. Lubenow, *Parliamentary politics and the Home Rule crisis: the British House of Commons in 1886*, Oxford 1988, 146–8.
60 Ibid. 283–5.

the way after 1886 for radical policies on everything from licensing to Welsh Church disestablishment to become Liberal policy – a trend summarised in the famous Newcastle Programme adopted by the National Liberal Federation in 1891. Land reform was one of those radical nostrums that could now jostle for a place in the priorities of a future Liberal government.

The loss of the Liberal Unionists helped increase the significance of land reform in another way. While a majority of landed Liberal MPs and the Liberal front bench in the Lords remained loyal to Gladstone, the great majority of Liberal landowners became Unionists, unable to stomach the thought of abandoning their fellow-landowners in Ireland to the mercies of a Nationalist parliament in Dublin. In 1880, 41 per cent of the House of Lords were Liberals. In 1887 the figure was only 7 per cent.[61] Local studies of counties like Northamptonshire have confirmed the dearth of Gladstonian landowners after 1886.[62] Quite correctly, Liberals believed that the landed elite had abandoned them and, almost to a man, were actively opposing them. This allowed and encouraged Liberals to support anti-landlord policies, including land reform, and to construct an entirely negative picture of the role of landowners in society and politics, which in turn justified the need for land reform.

This tendency was further reinforced by the 1886 election. The Liberals performed disastrously. While they won only 122 of the 456 English seats, just 16 of the 111 constituencies with a substantial agricultural population returned a Liberal. The labourers obviously did not care for Home Rule, but there had to be some other explanation for a result that was so much worse than in the rest of England. Many Liberals felt the obvious solution was that the Unionist landlords had coerced the rural population into voting against the Liberals by a sharp turn of the 'feudal screw'. As Herbert Gardner, Liberal MP for Saffron Walden and future president of the board of agriculture, wrote to Rosebery in 1888, 'The local Tory [a landowner] . . . has so bullied the labourer for voting Liberal that I have a great fear he may choose the broad and easy path of remaining indifferent or voting with those who control his wages and his charities.'[63] In other words, the landowners were exercising a consistent policy of political and economic pressure in the countryside to enforce Tory dominance. This was not mere fantasy. Rural electorates were still fairly small even after 1885, often with fewer than 10,000 voters. Concerns about the secrecy of the ballot were regularly voiced and an election was overturned on the grounds of undue influence by a local landowner (ironically a Liberal) as late as May 1910.[64]

Liberals made numerous efforts over the next few years to try to prove the

---

61 Adonis, *Making aristocracy work*, 20, table 2.2.
62 J. Howarth, 'Politics and society in late-Victorian Northamptonshire', *Northamptonshire Past and Present* iv (1970–1), 271.
63 H. Gardner to Lord Rosebery, 1 Mar. 1888, in Barker, *Gladstone and Radicalism*, 219.
64 H. Pelling, *Social geography of British elections, 1885–1910*, London 1967, 12–13, 136.

baleful influence of landowners and to counteract intimidation. A number of prominent rural Liberals set up a society in 1889, under Lord Ripon's presidency, to expose and report 'the intimidation which in rural districts was terrorising or penalising Radical voters'.[65] The *Daily News* ran a series of graphic articles in August and September 1891 under the title 'Life in our villages' and the reminiscences of doughty rural Liberals like Joseph Arch received widespread publicity.[66] Thoughtful young men in the Liberal camp, like Herbert Samuel, made their own studies of rural life – in his case the nearby Oxfordshire village of Great Milton when he was a student at Balliol in 1889–93. These investigations painted a relentlessly bleak portrait of rural society. Not only was political intimidation rife, but labourers were paid starvation wages and lived in miserable hovels. Samuel, in his investigations at Great Milton, found that the average wage was 9s.–10s. per week. The last entry in his notebook is 'Martha W.: 3s. parish relief; 1s. rent; almost starving.'[67]

Thus in the late 1880s Liberals constructed and reinforced a particular vision of rural England in which landlords were labelled as tyrants and labourers portrayed as oppressed serfs. This picture was an essential background for all future Liberal approaches to land reform. But it was not a scene that Gladstone, the guardian of his wife's Hawarden estate, was likely to recognise and for the four years after 1886 the Liberal leadership paid little attention to rural England. They focused on winning the argument over Irish Home Rule, something that did not seem impossible in the aftermath of Parnell's acquittal over the Pigott forgeries. But some Liberals from rural areas were not content to stick to the leadership's line. Like many other Liberals they believed that the party needed to construct a policy that would appeal to English concerns and English voters. The 1885 election had shown that a radical policy could win the countryside for the Liberals and in the next few years they did everything they could to push the leadership in this direction.

Only a small band of stalwarts survived the decimation of the Liberal party in English rural seats in 1886, but they made up in activity for what they lacked in numbers. The core of the group included Frances Channing, Walter Foster, Herbert Gardner, H. P. Cobb and C. H. Seale-Hayne. Their actions were co-ordinated through an 'organisation of the Liberal members representing county Divisions' and chaired by the venerable Sir Bernhard Samuelson, MP for Banbury.[68] A good part of their energies went into internecine feuding with the Liberal Unionists, who had the advantage of the

---

65 Revd W. Tuckwell, *Reminiscences of a radical parson*, London 1905, 202.
66 *Joseph Arch: the story of his life, told by himself*, ed. Frances ['Daisy'] Greville, countess of Warwick, London 1898.
67 Notebook, H. Samuel papers, HLRO, MS A/4.
68 F. Channing to W. Gladstone, 10 Sept. 1887, W. Gladstone papers, MS Add. 44501, fos 272–4.

services of Jesse Collings, still a passionate advocate of land reform.[69] After a bitter struggle in 1887 the Liberal Unionists were expelled from the county Liberal MPs' committee and in 1888 Collings was removed from the leadership of the Allotments Extension Association he had founded.[70] Rather more constructively, the rural Liberals developed an approach that they argued would win the countryside.

One of the most controversial issues of the 1886–92 parliament was how to reform local government in the counties. Once country-dwellers had been granted the household franchise for general elections in 1885, it seemed anomalous to leave local government in the hands of unelected magistrates. The Liberals had often promised to tackle the matter in 1880–5 and had failed. Salisbury responded with the 1888 Local Government Act, setting up county councils. However, the rural Liberal MPs consistently criticised the new councils for their lack of power and distance from the labourers. They argued that only parish councils could be controlled by, and be directly accountable to, the ordinary population in the countryside.[71] Moreover, they suggested that the crucial power that parish councils should be given was the authority to acquire land for allotments.[72] The combination of direct local democracy and land reform would emancipate the labourers from landed tyranny and improve labourers' living conditions.

This policy did not remain the demand solely of a small but noisy group of MPs and it was gradually adopted by the Liberal leadership. Gladstone was initially fairly happy with the idea of county councils, though the Liberals' front bench spokesman on the bill, James Stansfeld, expressed a preference for district councils. Neither liked the idea of parish councils, Stansfeld regarding the parishes as 'very numerous, very various in size and population, and many of them too small to be local government areas at all'.[73] But the expectations of many Liberals that the new county councils would merely be the old quarter sessions in disguise were largely confirmed and Gladstone finally admitted the case for parish councils in December 1889.[74] This policy commitment was soon being linked to an entirely new interest of the Liberal leadership – allotments. On 1 July 1887 the Unionists had lost their first by-election of the new parliament in the rural Lincolnshire seat of Spalding.

---

[69] See, for instance, the quarrel between Chamberlain and Channing over who should receive the credit for amendments to the 1887 allotments bill: *Hansard*, 3rd ser., 1887, cccxx. 185–90.

[70] Collings and Green, *Life of Collings*, 196–205.

[71] See F. S. Stevenson, H. Gardner and H. Stewart on the second reading of the local government bill in 1888: *Hansard*, 3rd ser., 1888, cccxxiv. 1804–9; cccxxv. 44–51, 59–61.

[72] The argument was encapsulated in H. P. Cobb's bill for parish allotments committees: ibid. 1887, cccxv. 227–32.

[73] J. Stansfeld to W. Gladstone, 26 Oct. 1888, W. Gladstone papers, MS Add. 44505, fos 57–60.

[74] J. Dunbabin, 'Expectations of the new county councils, and their realisation', *HJ* viii (1965), 353–79. Only three out of forty-seven councils had a clear Liberal majority: *Times*, 3 Dec. 1889.

The Liberal victor, Halley Stewart, was an enthusiast for land reform and put the allotments policy at the heart of his campaign.[75] The defeat at Spalding produced some unease in the Tory ranks and two weeks later the government responded with its own allotments bill, giving rural boards of guardians powers to acquire land for allotments.[76] Another motive behind the timing of this move may have been the wish to provide the remaining radicals among the Liberal Unionists with some tangible rewards after they had, with some reluctance, supported the government's Irish Coercion Act.[77] But the bill was not an entirely cynical policy as Tories were not totally hostile to allotments. Many landlords voluntarily supplied some land to labourers to supplement their wages. Lord Onslow had founded a Land and Glebe Owners Association for the Voluntary Extension of Allotments in 1886 and Henry Chaplin had introduced a bill on the matter the same year. As Balfour explained, legislation to provide allotments would only 'oblige the minority of bad landlords to do that which all good landlords did voluntarily'.[78] The Liberal leadership could scarcely allow themselves to be outflanked by the Tories on this issue. By re-stating their own enthusiasm to provide allotments and combining this policy with the promotion of parish councils the Liberal leaders acquired an effective method of attacking the Tory Party's new-found collectivism on the grounds that it lacked a proper democratic basis.[79]

The combined policy of allotments and parish councils gradually forced its way up the agenda of the Liberal leadership, especially once the Parnell divorce scandal of 1890 finally convinced them that Home Rule was unlikely to win over the English electorate on its own. A 'forward' policy in the rural areas might repair some of the damage. In April–May 1891 there were five by-elections in rural England, with the Liberals holding one seat (Buckingham) and gaining two (Stowmarket and Harborough) from the Unionists. The Liberal leadership began to believe that rural England might swing decisively against the government. As Arnold Morley, the chief whip, wrote to Gladstone, rural by-elections showed 'that the agricultural vote is with us'.[80] On 3 August 1891 John Morley made a set-piece speech to a huge audience at Stoneleigh Park in which he outlined in some detail the Liberals' plans for parish councils with the power to provide allotments.[81] At the NLF conference on 2 October 1891 Lord Ripon moved a motion on behalf of the

---

[75] R. Winfrey, *Leaves from my life*, privately printed, King's Lynn 1936, 67–9, 82.

[76] A sequence of events highlighted by Sir W. Harcourt on the bill's second reading: *Hansard*, 3rd ser., 1887, cccxix. 139.

[77] Jay, *Chamberlain*, 155.

[78] M. Fforde, *Conservatism and collectivism, 1886–1914*, Edinburgh 1990, 76–7; Lubenow, *Parliamentary politics*, 76–7; A. Balfour, memorandum, 29 Dec. 1891, Balfour papers, BL, MS Add. 49689, fos 170–87.

[79] See speech made by Gladstone at Lowestoft reported in *Times*, 19 May 1890.

[80] A. Morley to W. Gladstone, W. Gladstone papers, 25 July 1891, MS Add. 44254, fos 130–1.

[81] Barker, *Gladstone and Radicalism*, 228.

leadership covering the same ground and the NLF then went on to organise a rural reform conference on 10–11 December, which was addressed by Gladstone.[82] A total of 50,000 copies of its proceedings were distributed in January and February 1892.

The government's response showed that they, as much as the Liberals, continued to believe that land reform was the key to success in rural England. They amended their Allotments Act in 1890 and supplemented it with an Allotments Compensation Act in 1887, a Glebe Lands Act in 1888 and an Allotments Rating Act in 1891. Finally, as a sop to Jesse Collings, the Commons appointed a select committee in 1888 to look into the feasibility of promoting small farms (smallholdings as they were usually known) for agricultural labourers.[83] While allotments would merely supplement labourers' wages, smallholdings would transform them into fully-independent cultivators.[84] The Conservative response to the committee's report in 1890 was less than enthusiastic. But in 1892 Henry Chaplin, the president of the board of agriculture, resuscitated the issue. He was particularly worried about the Tories' popularity in the eastern agricultural counties, a concern he shared with Middleton, the chief agent. Chaplin believed it was essential to show the agricultural labourers 'that we really are sympathetic to their legitimate aspirations'[85] and land reform was the way to make this point. He pushed the government into producing a Smallholdings Act, empowering county councils to acquire land for small farms and sell it to prospective peasant proprietors. The Tories were already promoting the creation of such figures in Ireland so it was not a great step to make a gesture (which is all the act remained) in the same direction in England. The Liberals were able to pour scorn on this measure because county councils would have no power to acquire land compulsorily, and lacked any real accountability to rural workers.[86] But the act confirmed that land reform would be a crucial component of the coming electoral struggle.

The most prominent issue in the 1892 election was undoubtedly Irish Home Rule. But it was far from the only issue and in rural England Liberal candidates followed their leaders' initiative in 1891 by giving virtually unanimous support and a high priority to parish councils with powers to acquire land for allotments. Of the 102 Liberal candidates in seats with a significant agricultural population 94 mentioned this policy in their election addresses

---

[82] E. Hamilton diary, entries for 10–11 Dec. 1891, E. Hamilton papers, BL, MS Add. 48656, fos 167–70.

[83] *Hansard*, 3rd ser., 1888, cccxxix. 304–5.

[84] See A. Balfour, memorandum, 29 Dec. 1891, Balfour papers, MS Add. 49689, fos 170–87, which sets out this distinction.

[85] H. Chaplin to A. Balfour, 25 Dec. 1891, ibid. MS Add. 49772, fos 70–4.

[86] See *Hansard*, 4th ser., 1892, ii. 1342–9, for H. Gardner's criticism of a 'mere electioneering programme'.

and 64 had it among the first three items they tackled.[87] The result was a modest revival. From a mere sixteen seats in rural England in 1886, the Liberals recovered to thirty-seven in 1892. This did not match the performance of 1885, but neither did the Liberal Party's results in the rest of England. In 1892 the Liberals won just 191, or 42 per cent of English seats. Although they had won only 34 per cent of the rural constituencies, this represented, with London, one of the few discernible areas outside their strongholds in the industrial areas of the north-east, Yorkshire and the east Midlands where the Liberals seemed to make much progress.

The election, therefore, confirmed the status of rural England as a 'swing' area that might be won by either party if it could produce an appealing programme. Moreover, the universal over-estimation of the significance of agriculture in determining results in the county seats greatly reinforced the urgency of producing a rural programme. As Edward Hamilton declared, 'It is the boroughs in Great Britain which have been the stronghold of Conservatism and the counties which have voted radical. It is Hodge on whom the Radicals have had to depend.'[88] The message was reinforced by the enrolment of fifty or so Liberal MPs in the new parliament in the county members' committee concerned with agriculture – a considerable force to a government whose majority, with Irish Nationalist support, was less than forty.[89] There were only thirty-one Welsh Liberal MPs and they managed to hold the government to its promise to produce a bill for Welsh Church disestablishment. So it was with some confidence that rural Liberals looked to Gladstone's last administration to produce the programme they had campaigned for in 1886–92.

The 1892–5 Liberal governments and rural land reform

Gladstone's towering presence and the Liberals' dependence on the Irish Nationalists for a majority ensured that the issue of Irish Home Rule could not be avoided and it dominated the first year of the government's life. But the controversies surrounding land reform, the role of the aristocracy and the state of agriculture that made up the 'land issue' came to occupy second place in the government's concerns. This was partly, but only partly, because of the cabinet's vulnerability to pressure from its supporters in Ireland, Wales and Scotland. After the failure of Home Rule the Irish had to be appeased with an evicted tenants bill, which the Lords blocked. The Welsh received a royal commission to look into the state of their land system to compensate them for

---

87 These figures are calculated from candidates' election addresses, general election, 1892, ii, National Liberal Club papers, University of Bristol Library, Bristol.
88 E. Hamilton diary, entry for 24 July 1892, E. Hamilton papers, MS Add. 48658, fos 66–9.
89 Gardner to W. Gladstone, 14 Dec. 1892, W. Gladstone papers, MS Add. 44516, fos 316–17.

the delay in producing Welsh disestablishment. In 1895 the Scottish secretary, George Trevelyan, produced a bill to amend and extend the 1886 Crofters Act, though this had got no further than its second reading by the time the government fell.[90]

But rural England was not neglected. On 21 March 1893 H. H. Fowler introduced the first reading of a major local government bill. Among its many proposals it planned the introduction of parish councils with powers over allotments and the creation of new rural distict councils to rationalise the second tier of local government in the counties.[91] Gradually, as other measures on electoral registration, Welsh Church disestablishment and temperance were dropped or foundered in the Commons, the significance of the bill in the government's programme grew.[92] In the autumn session of 1893 it was selected along with the employers' liability bill to form one of the two major 'English' proposals the Liberals hoped to carry. This prominence was partly due to the bill's wide appeal to all sections of the Liberal Party. All Liberals favoured the spread of democracy in local government. Nonconformists liked the bill's proposal that parish councils would take over non-ecclesiastical Anglican parish charities. Social reformers applauded the concept that the poor law should no longer be in the hands of ex officio guardians and a propertied electorate. Temperance advocates saw the parish as a potential site for operating a local veto on licensed premises.[93] But the bill's primary purpose was to emancipate the agricultural labourer from being 'at worst a serf, at best a cipher'.[94] A central part of this aim was to place allotment schemes in the hands of the labourers themselves acting through the parish councils. Many Liberals hoped that this would prove the agency for the transformation of rural landholding and the downfall of the great estates. All hoped that it would eventually break the grip of the landlords and the Tories on the countryside.

The Unionists were well aware of the high hopes the Liberals had for the bill and carried out a long campaign of obstruction in the Commons. But eventually they reached a compromise with Harcourt that allowed the bill to go through to the Lords.[95] There Salisbury attempted further resistance, but his followers, particularly the Liberal Unionists led by the duke of Devonshire, refused to support him and the bill survived to reach the statute

---

[90] *The destruction of Lord Rosebery: from the diary of Sir Edward Hamilton, 1894–5*, ed. D. Brooks, London 1986, 38–40; J. G. Jones, 'Select committee or royal commission? Wales and "The land question", 1892', *WHR* xvii (1994), 205–29; *Hansard*, 4th ser., 1895, xxxiv. 881–95.

[91] See ibid. 1893, x. 679–702, for Fowler's outline of the bill's provisions.

[92] Brooks, 'Gladstone's fourth ministry', 141–61.

[93] *Hansard*, 4th ser., 1893, xviii. 89–95 (G. R. Benson on charities), 103–6 (H. L. W. Lawson on the poor law), 389–97 (R. L. Everett on temperance).

[94] Ibid. xviii. 128 (G. W. E. Russell).

[95] Ibid. xx. 1035–6.

books largely intact.[96] Quite simply the Unionists feared the bill's popularity and were unwilling to face popular anger by rejecting it outright or amending it beyond recognition. The government and their followers in rural England were jubilant. They had delivered their promises to the rural constituencies and could hope for an appropriate reward.

At first, these hopes seemed justified. Surveys of the first parish council elections showed that in some areas, like Norfolk, labourers could be elected to the new bodies in considerable numbers.[97] Once the councils took over existing allotments schemes previously run by the boards of guardians the numbers renting land grew steadily. By 1902 local authorities had 45,393 tenants on their allotments, compared to the 5,500 provided for in 1887–94 under the Tories' Allotments Act.[98] The rural population seemed to appreciate the government's efforts. There was a spate of seven by-elections in March–April 1894 and, despite the fact that the Liberals' majority was reduced in most of them, they held the highly marginal rural seat of Wisbech despite having a majority of only 122 in 1892.

Unfortunately for the Liberals, this success proved short-lived. In December 1894 they lost the Lincolnshire seat of Brigg and this was followed the next year by a run of bad results in rural seats at Evesham, Mid-Norfolk and West Dorset. This was bitterly disappointing, but in some ways not surprising. The parish councils could hardly live up to all the expectations that had been heaped upon them. For instance, they produced more publicly-controlled allotments, but hardly a revolution in landholding. Over 90 per cent of small agricultural holdings remained privately-owned, and the number provided by landowners in the late 1880s seems to have increased substantially in a largely successful attempt to pre-empt the need for publicly-supplied land.[99] Just as important, the Liberals had the misfortune to be in power at the nadir of Victorian agriculture's fortunes. A combination of bumper harvests abroad together with exceptionally poor weather at home made the mid-1890s a traumatic time for some areas of British farming. In late 1894 wheat prices reached a record low. Farmers responded by cutting labourers' wages and reducing the weeks for which they were paid, especially in the severe winter of 1894–5. More and more labourers faced the prospect of applying for poor relief. But, despite the universal recognition of the significance of poor law reform in agricultural areas, the government was unwilling to undertake directly so contentious and expensive a task.[100] The Liberals contented themselves with democratising elections to the boards of

96   See ibid. 1894, xxi. 10–12, 93–7, for the Salisbury–Devonshire quarrel.
97   R. Heath, 'The rural revolution', *Contemporary Review* lxvii (1895), 183.
98   N. Smith, *Land for the small man: English and Welsh experiments with publicly supported smallholdings, 1860–1937*, New York 1946, 58.
99   *Returns as to the number and size of agricultural holdings in Great Britain*, 1895, 1896 (C. 8243) lxvii.
100 Gardner to Sir W. Harcourt, 15 Nov. 1892, Harcourt papers, Bod. Lib., MS AI/83, fos 1–2; E. Hamilton diary, entry for 11 Feb. 1895, in *The destruction of Lord Rosebery*, 216.

guardians in the 1894 Local Government Act and appointing a royal commission on the aged poor in 1893. Useful as this was, it hardly matched the Liberals' promises to make the fields of England 'wave with golden corn' again and the phrase returned to haunt them in the gleeful speeches of their Unionist opponents.[101]

The government was well aware of its difficulties. As early as January 1893 Herbert Gardner, the new president of the board of agriculture, had warned Gladstone that 'unless some steps are taken towards alleviating the present agricultural distress very considerable Parliamentary embarrassment may evince in the coming session'.[102] The cabinet's decision to appoint a royal commission on agriculture in 1893 was no more than a holding measure, though it was hoped it would occupy the 'superfluous energies' of troublesome Liberal MPs.[103] The Queen's Speech of 1895 promised a light railways bill to make it easier to build new lines to take agricultural produce to market, but in a crowded programme it failed to receive its second reading. The rural Liberals had their own solution. Ever since the government had taken office, they had been pressing for a new agricultural holdings bill to give farmers fuller compensation at the end of their leases for improvements they made to the land.[104] This would, it was hoped, show the farmers that the Liberals were not neglecting them and might allow Liberals to claim that they had a policy to revive agriculture by encouraging farmers to invest more in improvements. As J. W. Logan, MP for Harborough, declaimed, 'Why does the small proprietor of other countries beat our men? Because he has security for his outlay, the necessary incentive, the magic of property which turns sand into gold.'[105] More cynically, Herbert Gardner pointed out that while 'The farmers are generally considered a *quantité négligible* by our party . . . that is not so', if only because hostile farmers could make life difficult for 'stalwart' Liberals among the labourers.[106] George Lambert, a backbench Devon farmer, duly produced a land tenure bill in 1895 to reform the Agricultural Holdings Act. Lambert's bill was taken over by the government in May of that year and trumpeted as a further instalment of land reform to revive agriculture, though the administration fell before it could proceed further than a second reading.[107]

These rather desperate manoeuvres did not lead rural Liberals to face the election of 1895 with any confidence and 41 out of 111 English agricultural

---

101 *Times*, 22 Sept. 1891.
102 Gardner to W. Gladstone, 25 Jan. 1893, W. Gladstone papers, MS Add. 44517, fos 28–9.
103 Gardner to Sir W. Harcourt, 26 Jan. 1893, Harcourt papers, MS AI/83, fos 31–2.
104 Gardner to W. Gladstone, 14 Dec. 1892, W. Gladstone papers, MS Add. 44516, fos 316–17. A few MPs wanted to go further and proposed land courts to determine rents: C. H. Seale-Hayne, *Agricultural distress: its causes and remedies*, Exeter 1895.
105 *Hansard*, 4th ser., 1893, xiii. 699.
106 Gardner to Sir W. Harcourt, 25 Jan. 1893, Harcourt papers, MS AI/83, fos 27–30.
107 See *Hansard*, 4th ser., 1895, xxxiii. 1281–5, for Gardner's speech agreeing to give the bill government support.

seats went uncontested. The Liberal leaders gave no clear lead to their followers and the election manifestos of candidates in rural seats lacked the sense of purpose that had characterised the campaign of 1892. Most mentioned the Local Government Act, but often with suggestions that it should be amended to increase the councils' powers, and only twenty-six candidates put the act among the first three items in their manifesto. Most also mentioned Lambert's bill, with varying degrees of enthusiasm.[108] In contrast to this hesitant display, Tory candidates focused on the deepening of the agricultural depression under the Liberals and forty-three of the seventy Conservatives in contested seats emphasised Lord Salisbury's hint that he would reduce the amount of rates payed by agricultural land.[109] This was portrayed as a policy that could revive agriculture and increase wages and employment.

The 1895 election proved a major setback for the Liberal Party as a whole. It won only 112 English seats, ten fewer than in 1886. As in 1886, performance in agricultural seats was weaker than the average Liberal vote. The Liberals won only eighteen rural seats, some 16 per cent of the total, compared to 25 per cent of the total English seats. In 1886 the agricultural voters had been faced with an unpalatable diet of Home Rule. In 1895, on the other hand, the Liberals could argue that the rural areas had, if anything, been given preferential treatment. The Liberals had provided the labourers with parish councils empowered to provide allotments, something that everyone in politics regarded as a major reform, and they had still lost badly.

Thus 1895 was not only a defeat for the Liberal Party, but for the idea that land reform would deliver rural England into the Liberals' hands. The state's relationship with the land remained intensely controversial. Most notably in 1896 the Liberals denounced the Tories for halving land's liability for local rates in the Agricultural Land Rating Act. They claimed it would be a direct subsidy to landowners and showed the Unionists 'going back to the bad principles of class legislation which have always characterised the Tory and the landed party when they had the means of laying their hands on the public purse'.[110] The issue confirmed Liberal hostility to landowners but it did not lead Liberals to turn back to their own positive proposals for land reform, which had failed to help them in 1895. It was noticeable that in the next general election, that of 1900, 'the land' was not prominent in the manifestos of rural Liberal candidates, who fought an almost entirely negative campaign aimed at the Tory government's record and the decision to call the election on a stale register.[111] The party seemed to have given up on rural England and

---

[108] These figures are calculated from candidates' election addresses, general election, 1895, National Liberal Club papers.

[109] *Hansard*, 4th ser., 1894, xxxv. 262–71; candidates' election addresses, general election, 1895, National Liberal Club papers.

[110] *Hansard*, 4th ser., 1896, xlii. 490 (Sir W. Harcourt in inimitable style).

[111] Only thirty out of fifty-six candidates in rural seats mentioned any sort of land reform

only 56 of 111 agricultural seats were contested though, ironically, the Liberals marginally improved their showing to twenty-four seats. The leadership, too, lost interest in what seemed to be the fruitless cause of land reform and turned to their personal rivalries and increasingly bitter disputes over Home Rule and imperialism. Far from being an obsession of late Victorian radicals, rural land reform was a cause that was abandoned with remarkable ease once it seemed to have lost its usefulness.

'demoralised & disheartened': the Liberal Party and the aristocracy, 1892–5

The land issue was not, though, just about the countryside. Liberals were interested in it because it was a means of attacking the role of landowners in politics and society; if Liberals could have made this subject a central political issue then land reform could have become a matter of vital concern to the whole party, rather than just its rural supporters. The most obvious method whereby landowners came into collision with the whole Liberal Party was when the House of Lords obstructed a Liberal government's legislation, but this tended to be a short-lived phenomenon. When, in the summer of 1884, the Lords blocked the Third Reform Bill there was a huge wave of protests, with more than 1,500 meetings across the country condemning the Lords.[112] But once a compromise was reached later in the year these protests died away. The experiences of Gladstone's fourth government, however, seemed to reassert the idea that the landowners in the Lords represented the Liberal Party's most important enemy.[113] The Lords rejected Irish Home Rule in 1893, so deleting the major item in the Liberals' programme and precipitating Gladstone's resignation the following year. Gladstone made the need to reform the Lords the subject of his final speech and his anger was clearly shared on the Liberal backbenches, who carried an amendment to the address calling for the abolition of the Lords' veto. The NLF endorsed this view later in the year.[114]

But though many Liberals were more convinced than ever that the 'House of landlords' was their bitterest foe, they failed to launch a successful campaign against the Lords. This was partly because of Salisbury's skill. He accepted, sometimes reluctantly, that the Lords should not obstruct legislation, like the Local Government Act, that might be genuinely popular and

anywhere in their address: candidates' election addresses, general election, 1900, National Liberal Club papers.

112 Cannadine, *Decline and fall*, 41.

113 For the best treatment of this issue see Adonis, *Making aristocracy work*, 121–5.

114 H. C. G. Matthew, *Gladstone, 1875–98*, Oxford, 1995, 354–5; *Hansard*, 4th ser., 1894, xxii. 194–202, for Labouchere's amendment, carried 147:145 against the cabinet's wishes; *Times*, 21 June 1894.

which might leave the Lords open to the charge of acting in their own interests as landlords. Instead, the Lords only blocked legislation to which most of the electorate was hostile or indifferent, like Irish Home Rule, or where the Tories possessed a popular alternative policy, as with the employers liability bill in 1894.

The best chance the Liberals had of making the role of landowners a major issue was Harcourt's budget of 1894.[115] In order to meet a potential deficit of over £4 million Harcourt suspended some schemes of debt repayment, increased duties on beer and spirits, raised income tax by 1d. and consolidated and graduated the system of death duties. This latter proposal was unwelcome to all holders of large fortunes, but particularly to landowners, as land was deprived of its more lenient treatment under the old succession duty and dealt with on the same footing as all other property by the new death duties. The Unionist backbenchers were furious at a budget that 'knocked a nail into the coffin of the dying landed interest', while Harcourt made a number of robust speeches hailing his budget for ending the 'intolerable injustice' of privileged treatment for landowners.[116] But the issue never caught fire. The Unionist leaders feared that the budget would prove popular and felt it divided their ranks. They did not make it a major issue in the country and Salisbury ensured it passed the Lords, without a division.[117] The Liberals, too, failed to make much of the issue. Rosebery was on poor terms with Harcourt and scarcely mentioned the budget in his speeches, while Liberal MPs were pleased just to get the budget through the Commons, given the government's narrow majority.

Rosebery fared no better in making landownership a central political question when he raised the matter of how to reform the Lords in public in October 1894. His colleagues were not in agreement on the subject and the Liberals were at a loss to point out how the Lords had obstructed any really popular measure of the previous two years. Lewis Harcourt lamented that 'The battle with the House of Lords has been declared at the wrong time and in the wrong way; the party is thoroughly demoralised & disheartened and disorganised.'[118] The Lords issue failed to prevent the Liberal disaster in 1895 and while the upper house retained an important place in Liberal demonology, the experience of 1894–5 hardly encouraged Liberal leaders to make the aristocracy the focus of their political campaigning.

---

[115] See M. Daunton, 'The political economy of death duties: Harcourt's budget of 1894', in Harte and Quinault, *Land and society in Britain*, 137–71.

[116] *Hansard*, 4th ser., 1894, xxiii. 1291 (Sir R. Temple), 484 (Sir W. Harcourt).

[117] See ibid. 1894, xxvii. 1222–9, for Salisbury's speech, allowing the budget's passage but denouncing its 'violent and revolutionary departure from former principles of finance' and asserting the Lords' right to amend future budgets.

[118] L. Harcourt journal, entry for 19 Feb. 1895, Harcourt papers, MS 415, fo. 40.

The emergence of the urban land issue

However, by the 1890s another aspect of the land issue – what was sometimes known as the 'urban land question' – had started to emerge. Urban land-ownership raised a whole host of questions, many of baffling complexity, that divided and confused Liberals as much as they united them against land-owners. Partly as a result of these difficulties, the urban land question was much less prominent in the late Victorian era than its rural counterpart. But it also had the potential to make the land issue relevant to far more of the electorate.

Most of the momentum behind the early hostility to the urban holdings of great landowners originated in London. Much of the capital was built on the short leasehold system, whereby the owners of large blocs of land leased their property, usually for ninety-nine years, to developers and contracted them to construct suitable buildings on the site. The developers would then sell or lease the housing. But at the end of ninety-nine years the land and buildings would revert to the original (or ground) landlord – a species which included some very prominent aristocratic families like the dukes of Bedford and West-minster. This system had many advantages and resulted in the construction of some harmonious and elegant estates. But it also produced tensions between the differing interests of ground-owners and leaseholders and encouraged Liberals to talk about 'the monopoly of London by three or four Dukes'.[119]

One obvious difficulty was local government. Most councils relied on rates to fund their expenditure, but rates were paid by occupiers, not owners. Thus in London in the nineteenth century the owners of great estates saw the value of their land soaring as a result of the buildings constructed on their sites, but they did not have to contribute to local taxation.[120] This was particularly galling as increased expenditure and debt by councils was sending the rate burden in London steadily upward in the late nineteenth century. Many London radicals were keen on council projects of all kinds, but were well aware of the unpopularity of rate rises, as rates were paid by all occupiers, however humble. One possible solution was to tax the ground landlords. As the radical paper *The Sun* declared

> It is time that the Duke of Westminster and scores of others in his position were legally requested to disgorge a small percentage of the wealth they did not earn. Land has been made valuable in London, not by ground landlords, but by the public who pay rent to those landlords, and who afterwards pay the taxes that ought to be born by the capital values wholly created by them-selves.[121]

[119] J. Morley to J. Chamberlain, 7 Jan. 1883, J. Chamberlain papers, MS 5/54/474.
[120] See J. F. Moulton, *The taxation of ground values*, London 1889, for a succinct and outraged account of the situation.
[121] *The Sun*, 17 Jan. 1894.

After 1886 the increased significance of radicals in the party was nowhere more apparent than in London.[122] The small band of Liberal MPs who survived the 1886 election began to work together to press the leadership to support a 'London Programme' of radical reforms, including attacks on the urban landlords of London. They gained some authority after the Progressive party's victory in the first LCC elections in 1889 made them the spokesmen of the most prestigious local authority in the country. The taxation of ground rents was endorsed by the NLF in 1888 and the London MPs started to raise the matter in Commons debates.

These discussions revealed that matters were far from simple, though. The London radicals were divided and unsure about how exactly landlords should be taxed and the impact of different schemes on ratepayers and occupiers. When James Stuart, MP for Hoxton, moved a motion on land taxation on behalf of the London Liberals on 12 March 1891 he proposed separate rates for land and houses, a tax on the reversion of leases and a municipal death duty all in the same speech, concluding lamely, 'the fact that none of these proposals are complete is no argument against some portion of them or some combination of them being adopted'.[123]

When a Liberal government took office in 1892 the matter became pressing as the London MPs were a difficult group to ignore. London had been one of the few areas where the Liberals had made an unqualified break-through in 1892, winning thirteen seats not held in 1886. Officially, the London Liberals were committed to a separate rate on land values but, as the chairman of the LCC confided to Harcourt, 'it has every merit, except that of being easy', especially as it would 'necessitate an entirely new valuation on a duplex system', which was 'neither easy, cheap nor acceptable'.[124] However much the LCC disliked landowners, it needed rapid action to soften the impact of rising rates on poorer voters and land taxation would take far too long to implement. It was, therefore, shelved in favour of the LCC's minimum immediate programme for the 'equalisation' of rates, whereby richer areas would subsidise poorer (Liberal) areas.[125] The government was willing to accept a solution that did not demand money from the exchequer or the devising of a new system of taxation and Shaw-Lefevre, who had succeeded Fowler at the local government board in March 1894, promoted an Equalisation of Rates Act, which levied a uniform 6d. rate over the whole city.[126] Unfortunately this was far too little too late to make any practical difference to hard-pressed London vestries in the East End. Nor did it prevent

122 Barker, *Gladstone and Radicalism*, 138–40.
123 *Hansard*, 3rd ser., 1891, cccli. 943.
124 *Daily News*, 17 Jan. 1894; B. F. C. Costelloe to Sir W. Harcourt, 24 Oct. 1892, Harcourt papers, MS AIII/187, fos 85–92.
125 J. Renwick Seagar to Sir W. Harcourt, 11 May 1893, enclosing resolutions of the London Liberal and Radical Union, ibid. fos 133–5.
126 See *Hansard*, 4th ser., 1894, xxvii. 813–25, for Shaw-Lefevre's second reading speech, explaining the bill in detail.

a Liberal disaster in London in 1895, which reduced the party to eight seats. As a result, land taxation retained its attractions for London Liberals as a long-term solution to the problem of rising rates. In the 1895 election 65 per cent of London Liberal candidates included the issue in their election addresses, compared to 22 per cent of all Liberal candidates.[127]

As should be clear, this London-based agitation originated independently of the notorious Henry George and his doctrine of the single tax.[128] George was an American whose book, *Progress and poverty*, was a best-seller in Britain in the 1880s, effectively publicised by three visits to Britain by the 'Sage of San Francisco'. George's message that all poverty and inequality was the fault of landowners was not a new one to British radicals, but the vigour of his denunciations won him many admirers. His specific remedy was less well understood. Basically, George advocated the replacement of all taxation by a tax on the capital value of land (the single tax). This tax would be equivalent to the rental value of the land, thus rendering landownership literally worthless. The doctrine acquired a small but very vocal band of followers, organised in the English and Scottish Land Restoration Leagues.[129] They pursued a relentless propaganda campaign and practised the tactics of entryism within the Liberal Party, gaining a significant presence in local government in London and Glasgow, in particular. But the Georgeites were essentially adjuncts to the cause of land taxation, which was becoming popular within Liberalism for quite other reasons than the doctrine of the single tax. If anything they probably harmed their own cause by associating it with political extremism. In the 1890s the movement had no influence on the Liberal leadership and the only committed single taxer in parliament was the eccentric William Saunders.[130]

Just as important in the late Victorian era was the issue of leasehold enfranchisement.[131] This was, as with land taxation, largely a London issue. It sought to compel ground-owners to sell their land and buildings to the leaseholders when the ninety-nine years of the lease was up. This idea had come to the fore when the leases of a number of prominent London estates came up for renewal in the 1870s and 1880s. A Leasehold Enfranchisement Association was founded in 1884 to promote the cause and a select committee was set up in 1886 to examine the issues involved. However, leasehold enfranchisement embodied many of the limitations of the urban land question. As less than a third of English towns were built on the short leasehold system, it was necessarily a minority concern, though it did gain a good deal of support in

---

127 P. Readman, 'The 1895 general election and political change in late Victorian Britain', *HJ* xlii (1999), 492, table 11.

128 This is most sensibly discussed in Offer, *Property and politics*, 184–200.

129 S. Ward, 'Land reform in England, 1880–1914', unpubl. PhD diss. Reading 1976, chs vi–vii.

130 For Saunders see J. A. Spender, *Life, journalism and politics*, London 1927, i. 26–34.

131 D. Reeder, 'The politics of urban leaseholds in late Victorian England', *IRSH* vi (1961), 413–30.

some areas like north Wales and the West Country where local forms of lease-hold created grievances against landowners.[132] Moreover, as a policy it directly conflicted with ideas like land taxation and there were some acrimonious disputes about leasehold enfranchisement among Liberal MPs in the early 1890s.[133] Perhaps its most positive feature for the Liberals was that it divided the Tories even more. Some London Conservatives, like Blundell Maple, MP for Dulwich, wished to capture leasehold enfranchisement as a locally popular measure that would build up the ramparts of property, but Salisbury was horrified, claiming that this 'would excite very angry passions on the part of owners of property' and would merely be running 'the risk of alienating old friends without conciliating any new adherents'.[134]

But the urban land issue was not merely a patchwork of local concerns and sectional issues. There were beginning to be signs by the end of the nineteenth century that it might provide a means for Liberals to tackle some of the most pressing urban problems of the day. Again, London was the focus of many of these concerns. In the mid-1880s there had started to be real concerns about a perceived housing crisis in the metropolis and Dilke had appointed a royal commission to look into the matter in 1884.[135] Local authorities, particularly the new LCC, were gradually becoming more active in slum clearance and under part III of the 1890 Housing Act the LCC was allowed to buy land to build housing for its local population. These developments had the potential to turn concerns about housing into an attack on landlords, because they could be blamed for charging local authorities extortionate prices for land and for allowing slums to develop on their property (the advocates of leasehold enfranchisement sometimes used the latter argument to support their cause). In 1890 and 1892 the young Liberal MP, R. B. Haldane, inspired bills to make land purchase by councils easier – something that did not endear him to the leasehold enfranchisers.[136] But this was very much an issue for the future, especially as concern over a London housing crisis slackened off in the 1890s.

Similarly significant for the future was the interest shown in the 1890s in land reform as a solution for unemployment. This was a very old nostrum of working-class radicalism, promoted by the Chartists and the old Land and Labour League in the late 1860s. In the depression of the 1880s radical heroes like Bradlaugh, Arch, Labouchere and Thomas Burt all showed some commitment to settling the urban poor on the land. What was new was the interest that economists like Alfred Marshall and social investigators like

---

132 Land enquiry committee, *The land*, ii, London 1914, 342–52.
133 See *Hansard*, 4th ser., 1892, iv. 105, for Asquith's attack on leasehold enfranchisement. See also R. B. Haldane, *The unearned increment*, London 1892, 8.
134 Lord Salisbury to Blundell Maple, 14 Mar. 1892, Balfour papers, MS Add. 49690, fos 6–8.
135 A. S. Wohl, *The eternal slum*, London 1977, 200–20.
136 *Hansard*, 3rd ser., 1890, cccxliv. 307–52; 4th ser., 1892, iv. 66–136.

Charles Booth started to show in the issue.[137] Both believed that the economic downturn had revealed a 'surplus' urban population that would have to be removed from the towns – an idea linked to notions of racial degeneration in great cities. Thus land colonies served a variety of different ends for their proponents, from radical alternative to capitalism to a species of penal colony. Particularly high unemployment in the early 1890s prompted interest in land colonies from both the Salvation Army and the radical Poplar board of guardians. Keir Hardie proclaimed the need for 'home colonies on the idle lands about which we have heard so much discussion'[138] and the board of trade looked into foreign farm and labour colonies in 1893.[139] But the government did not have the energy, confidence or money to take such ideas too seriously. They remained in circulation, though, into the next decade, surfacing whenever unemployment was high.

The urban land issue was still in embryonic form in 1895. It was mainly a London affair and its impact on government was intermittent and diffuse. To most people, 'the land' still meant rural reform, particularly allotments and smallholdings. By 1895, however, this phase of the land issue seemed to be over. Publicly-provided allotments were freely available after the legislation of 1887 and 1894. But all their efforts to promote the issue had not saved the Liberals from disaster in the election of 1895 and the Tories had managed a crushing victory without promising land reform. Thus, while the land issue was of some significance to Liberals by the 1890s they could scarcely claim to have profited greatly by their association with the cause. In 1895 it looked like another radical fad of limited appeal outside the ranks of the Liberal faithful, like Scottish Church disestablishment or local option. It was far from inevitable that 'the land' would return to the forefront of the party's concerns.

[137] Biagini, *Liberty, retrenchment and reform*, 184–91; J. Harris, *Unemployment and politics: a study in English social policy, 1886–1914*, Oxford 1972, 118–19, 124–40.
[138] *Hansard*, 4th ser., 1893, viii. 730.
[139] *Board of trade report on agencies and methods for dealing with unemployment*, 1893 (C. 7182).

2

The Failure of Rural Reform, 1906–1910

The 1900 election probably represented the nadir of interest in land reform in the period 1885–1914. But, in the years between the end of the Boer war and the Liberal landslide of 1906, 'the land' gradually re-emerged as a live political issue. The revival of rural land reform owed something to Tory as well as Liberal politicians. In 1895–1900 the Conservatives had rewarded their allies among the landowners and farmers as richly as they dared. The halving of the liability of agricultural land for local rates in 1896 was only the most controversial 'dole' the government produced. The same year, for instance, they finally banned the importation of all live cattle from abroad, thinly disguising this quasi-protectionist move as a public health measure.[1] These kinds of policy allowed the Unionists to pose as the representatives of all who made their living from agriculture and removed the need to dabble any further in land reform, especially as rural Liberalism was so weak in England after 1895. After 1903, though, this situation started to change.

New directions in rural land reform

This was partly because of the arrival of the earl of Onslow at the board of agriculture that year. Onslow's varied career had included spells as governor of New Zealand and leader of the Moderate group on the LCC, but he also had a long record of interest in land reform. The acts of 1887 and 1894 had secured a satisfactory supply of publicly-owned allotments, but Onslow wished to reform the Tories' 1892 Smallholdings Act, which had proved a dead letter. He failed to interest Balfour in his schemes, but he was successful in raising the public profile of the issue. As compensation for his removal from office in March 1905 he was able to secure the chairmanship of a departmental committee on smallholdings, packed with sympathetic figures.[2] It gathered evidence from a wide range of experts and managed to stimulate a good deal of informed debate among those concerned with agriculture and its reform. Rural Liberals showed some real eagerness to enter this field of controversy for the first time in nearly a decade. The launch of Chamberlain's

---

[1] J. R. Fisher, 'Public opinion and agriculture, 1875–1900', unpubl. PhD diss. Hull 1973, 294–5.
[2] *Report of the departmental committee appointed by the board of agriculture on smallholdings in Great Britain* (Cd. 3277) 1906.

tariff reform campaign in 1903 led many to believe that they had to produce an alternative to protectionist propaganda in the countryside and to show how they would revive agriculture without tariffs. Moreover, the real possibility of a Liberal return to power stimulated discussion about what a Liberal agricultural policy should be.

Almost all Liberals could agree that providing smallholdings for agricultural labourers was a laudable policy. The allotments acts had shown that there was some demand for publicly-supplied land. But the modest success of this policy had not made the labourers throw off the landlord and Tory yoke in the counties. One solution to this conundrum was to suggest that the labourers needed to be offered the chance to become independent cultivators, rather than just to supplement their wages with work on allotments. This line of thought was promoted by a number of prominent rural Liberals, but attempts to draw up definite plans revealed differences of approach about how smallholdings should be promoted and the priority that should be accorded to this policy. The more traditional line was championed by Frances Channing, the Liberal MP for Northamptonshire East. Channing's interest in agriculture had been aroused in the 1880s by the Irish land issue and the Farmers Alliance and since then he had been a prominent Liberal spokesman on rural issues, serving on the 1893–7 royal commission on agriculture and Onslow's smallholdings committee in 1905–6.[3] Channing found a public platform for his views by assuming the chairmanship of a committee of the Land Law Reform Association (LLRA) that was producing agricultural proposals for the expected Liberal government. The LLRA had been founded in 1897 by the amalgamation of the Free Land League and the Leasehold Enfranchisement Association.[4] It functioned as a forum for Liberals interested in all moderate forms of land reform and was reasonably well-regarded by the party's leadership – Campbell-Bannerman addressed its annual conference on 11 May 1904.[5] It at least provided a sort of collective authority for Channing's pamphlet, An agricultural policy, that outlined his conclusions in 1905.

The most obvious feature of Channing's approach was that he was as much concerned to appeal to the farmers as to the labourers. Farmers' grievances took up most of his pamphlet, relegating smallholdings to the final two pages. This attitude did not merely reflect the concerns of the 1880s and the days of the Farmers Alliance. In 1895–1905 agricultural Liberalism was reduced to its areas of greatest strength and about half of the small band of English rural Liberal MPs was usually drawn from those parts of the periphery where the smaller, Nonconformist farmers continued to vote Liberal. In particular, the Devon MPs Lambert, Soares, Luttrell and Seale-Hayne provided a solid phalanx pressing for action on farmers' grievances. Their central policy

3 Channing, Memories, 1–3, 144.
4 Free Land League, 12th annual report, 1897, London 1897.
5 LLRA, 17th annual meeting, 1904, London 1904.

remained Lambert's land tenure bill of 1895 which had fallen with the last Liberal government. Thus, an emphasis on farmers' grievances partly reflected the existing balance of interests inside the Liberal Party at Westminster.

Even on smallholdings themselves, Channing was cautious. In particular, he was prepared to support schemes for cultivators to buy smallholdings, rather than become council tenants on the lines the 1894 Local Government Act had laid down for allotment holders.[6] The former policy had increasingly become identified with Unionist strategy, as outlined in the virtually inoperative 1892 Smallholdings Act. But in the 1880s, before Gladstone's Irish land purchase bill of 1886 had crystallised the party's hostility to state loans as 'outdoor relief' for landlords, moderate Liberals had not been averse to this policy. Even in 1892 the Liberals' fire had been mainly aimed at the lack of compulsory powers and democratic local authorities in the Tory act, rather than its failure to provide for council tenancy. So it was not unnatural for older rural reformers like Channing to support ownership. If the only impetus for rural land reform had come from Channing, smallholdings need not have become the central element in the Liberal approach to the countryside. Moreover, any action taken could have been along the lines pioneered by the Unionists in 1892.

However, Channing was not the only person interested in mapping out a future Liberal government's agricultural policy. The group of writers and politicians centred around *The Speaker* (soon to become the *Nation*) and the *Daily News* were also deeply interested in rural issues.[7] C. F. G. Masterman had been stimulated to study smallholdings when he took over the editorship of a book on the subject commissioned by the *Daily News* in 1905–7.[8] But others of the group, like J. A. Hobson, had an even longer-standing interest in rural land reform.[9] However they had come to the subject, though, when they were attempting to outline policies for the next Liberal government they did not regard smallholdings as an obsolete or irrelevant issue. Instead they attempted to elevate land reform to a new significance in Liberal politics. As *The Speaker* declared on 5 May 1906, 'The reconstruction of the English village is the chief task that faces a party that exists to make society the master rather than the victim of its circumstances.'

Smallholdings were a particularly attractive policy for New Liberals because they offered a way, not only to attack landlord privilege and hegemony in the countryside, but to improve the social conditions of the down-

---

6 See Channing's letters to *The Speaker*, 26 Mar., 3 Dec. 1904.
7 Emy, *Social politics*, 132–4. In the early 1900s L. T. Hobhouse, J. A. Hobson, C. F. G. Masterman, Roden Buxton, Noel Buxton, Percy Alden and Harold Spender, among others, were all writing for J. L. Hammond at *The Speaker* and Massingham at the *Daily News*.
8 C. F. G. Masterman, W. Hodgson and others, *To colonise England: a plea for a policy*, London 1907.
9 J. A. Hobson (ed.), *Co-operative labour on the land*, London 1895.

trodden labourers. 'Feudal' dependence would be broken and the labourers would benefit materially as well. Liberals could believe that 'The whole purpose of this policy is to build up a new type of village, a village that will be co-operative and self-governing' but also that 'The agrarian movement . . . is the counterpart of the Labour movement in the towns.'[10] Increased material prosperity and increased personal liberty could fit neatly together. Furthermore, the decades of criticism of English agriculture since the 1870s allowed the smallholdings policy to be presented as an attempt to revive a decaying industry. The necessity was for a 'system of collective effort based on the application of science and modern invention to the industry of agriculture' and for this 'the smallholder, independent, secure, must precede the co-operative system through which agriculture can be restored'.[11] In this case, at least, social reform could not interfere with wealth production.

These were all good reasons for starting any programme of social reform in the countryside, especially as smallholdings did not evoke any hostility amongst the vast majority of Liberals. But the group around *The Speaker* was anxious that if a future Liberal government did take up land reform it should do so from a suitably progressive perspective. This meant that they had to develop their own strategy and interest the Liberal leadership in their ideas, rather than leaving the field to more senior politicians like Channing. The leading role in this endeavour was taken by Roden Buxton, a Liberal journalist, lecturer and parliamentary candidate for Hertford.[12] He was a member of a body called the English Land Colonisation Society, founded in 1893, which, under the leadership of the Congregationalist minister, J. B. Paton, had become devoted to the cause of resettling the urban poor on the land.[13] In 1904 Buxton led a breakaway of like-minded members to form the Co-operative Smallholdings Society. This society was interested in improving the conditions of agricultural labourers, rather than urban migration to the countryside. Active members included Buxton's friends, C. F. G. Masterman, G. P. Gooch and Percy Alden, all shortly to become Liberal MPs.[14] Its main ideas for promoting state-sponsored smallholdings centred around the need for compulsory powers to acquire land, a central body to stimulate inactive local authorities and the primacy of tenancy over individual ownership.[15] The latter policy reflected the society's deep distrust of Unionist schemes for peasant proprietors to act as 'bulwarks of property' and allies of the landlords and farmers. The society recognised that their

[10] *The Speaker*, 16 Dec. 1905; Frank Rogers, MP for Devizes, in Masterman and others, *To colonise England*, 117–18.
[11] A. G. Gardiner, 'Introduction', ibid. pp. xiv, xx.
[12] V. de Bunsen, *Charles Roden Buxton: a memoir*, London 1948, 34–41, 51–4.
[13] J. Marchant, *J. B. Paton*, London 1909, 167–8.
[14] Minute book of executive committee of the Co-operative Smallholdings Society, 26 Oct. 1904, BLPES, Coll. Misc. 64.
[15] Ibid. 4 Aug. 1905.

programme might well alienate the farmers. 'We shall not have the sympathy of the majority of farmers' as Roden Buxton bluntly stated.[16]

However, if these plans were to be implemented, the Co-operative Smallholdings Society needed to attract the support of those Liberal leaders likely to be given responsibility for agriculture in a future government. Their main hopes rested on the man they persuaded to become the society's president, Lord Carrington. Carrington had only held junior office in the 1892–5 administrations, but by the early 1900s his status had risen – if only because he was one of the few Liberal peers who had remained active during the long years of opposition.[17] He was also an important landowner in Buckinghamshire and Lincolnshire and had chaired the royal commission on Welsh land in 1893–7. Most significantly for the society, however, he had become interested in smallholdings under the influence of Richard Winfrey, a county councillor in the Holland division of Lincolnshire, Liberal candidate and newspaper owner.[18] Winfrey's attempts to implement the Unionists' 1892 Smallholdings Act in Lincolnshire had been frustrated by the cumbrous nature of the legislation and the Unionists' victory in the 1894 Holland county council elections. He responded by organising labourers into smallholdings associations and asking sympathetic landowners to rent them land. Carrington had agreed to help and by 1902 he had rented 650 acres to one of Winfrey's associations. The experiment proved a success and Carrington became a convinced advocate of smallholdings.[19] His experience of them on his Lincolnshire estates meant that he was receptive to the ideas of the Co-operative Smallholdings Society. He believed that local councils, like Holland county council, were not always the best judges of demand for smallholdings and might, on occasions, have to be over-ruled by a central authority. Moreover, renting land to a smallholdings association convinced him of the merits of tenancy.[20]

The Co-operative Smallholdings Society pursued a vigorous campaign to publicise its views, both in *The Speaker* and the *Daily News*, and endeavoured to support its case by assembling facts and figures, many of them collected by Buxton's sister-in-law, Louisa Jebb, and turned into her authoritative tome *The smallholdings of England* (London 1907). But their hopes of seeing their ideas turned into action rested with Carrington. In fact the smallholdings strategy represented an area where New Liberals did not propose a new departure. Rather, they provided intellectual and propaganda support for an

16 *The Speaker*, 19 Nov. 1904.
17 A. Adonis, 'Aristocracy, agriculture and Liberalism: the politics, finances and estates of the third Lord Carrington', *HJ* xxxi (1988), 871–97.
18 Winfrey, *Leaves*, 104–11.
19 J. H. Diggle, *The creation of smallholdings in Lincolnshire and Norfolk*, King's Lynn 1903, 7–9.
20 Lord Carrington, 'The land and the labourers', *The Nineteenth Century* xlv (1899), 368–77.

existing strand of thought within Liberalism, exemplified by Carrington, which itself was a development of the party's approach to rural issues in the 1890s.

'A peaceful agricultural revolution'? Rural reform, 1906–7

Thus, when Balfour's government resigned in December 1905, Carrington and Channing were associated with two rather different approaches to rural policy. Either could, plausibly, be expected to be appointed president of the board of agriculture. But Carrington had two factors working against him in the new prime minister's eyes: he was a supporter of the Liberal League (Rosebery was his cousin); and Edward VII had expressed a strong wish to have his old friend as Lord Chamberlain.[21] However, Campbell-Bannerman chose Carrington, while Channing received a baronetcy as compensation. This decision is most easily explicable in terms of the prime minister's own preference for a wide-ranging policy of land reform. Carrington had certainly let Campbell-Bannerman know of his plan for an agricultural policy based on smallholdings in a letter of 5 November 1905.[22] Moreover, as far as his leisurely nature allowed, the prime minister was consistently supportive of his new minister's approach. Unlike Herbert Gardner, his only Liberal predecessor as president of the board of agriculture, Carrington was given a seat in the cabinet. Smallholdings also received a favourable mention in Campbell-Bannerman's great pre-election oration at the Albert Hall on 21 December 1905.[23] His knowledge of crofting communities in the Scottish Highlands made him favourably disposed to the general idea of increasing the number of small cultivators.[24] But Campbell-Bannerman was probably also influenced in this direction by his closest political ally, and ex-private secretary, Jack Sinclair, whom he made secretary for Scotland in December 1905. Sinclair was a devotee of Scottish land reform – a subject which dominated his term of office. His own researches into the workings of the crofters acts had convinced him of the superiority of tenancy over ownership for smallholders and the need to bypass conservative county councils in providing them.[25]

Prime ministerial approval was certainly crucial to Carrington's hopes of giving land reform any priority in the crowded government programme.

[21] H. C. G. Matthew, *The Liberal imperialists: the ideas and politics of a post-Gladstonian elite*, Oxford 1973, 119; CD, entry for 6 Dec. 1905, Lincolnshire papers, Bod. Lib., MS Film 1105.
[22] Ibid. entry for 5 Nov. 1905.
[23] *Times*, 22 Dec. 1905.
[24] J. Wilson, *CB: a life of Sir Henry Campbell-Bannerman*, London 1973, 596.
[25] Marjorie Sinclair, Lady Pentland, *Memoir of Lord Pentland*, London 1928, 69–72, 85–92. Sinclair's legislation is dealt with in J. Brown, 'Scottish and English land legislation, 1905–11', *SHR* xlvii (1968), 72–85.

Though he had come to office on a wave of approval from Liberals interested in rural reform – *The Speaker* urged him to 'do for England what Lord Carrington, the landowner has done for Lincolnshire' – he faced a number of handicaps.[26] He was new to senior political office in 1905 and throughout his term of office he suffered long bouts of ill-health. His department dated only from 1889 and was not highly regarded in Whitehall – Edwin Montagu described it as 'by no means popular and by no means respectable'.[27] Before 1905 its main functions were the production of statistics and the control of infectious animal diseases.[28] Carrington was also faced with a powerful and conservative permanent secretary, Sir Thomas Elliott – known to his staff as 'the ogre'.[29] Campbell-Bannerman's support meant that Carrington's aim of 'a peaceful agricultural revolution' did not stall at the start.[30] This was most explicitly demonstrated when Carrington sent the prime minister his proposal for legislation on smallholdings for the 1907 session on 7 February 1906. Campbell-Bannerman raised the matter at the cabinet the next day and secured its agreement.[31]

The new president of the board of agriculture decided on a cautious first year in office in order to allow the existing Unionist-appointed committee on smallholdings time to report and to prepare the way for smallholdings legislation with speeches and articles, many of them to be provided by his new private secretary, Richard Winfrey, who had been elected as MP for Norfolk South-West in 1906.[32] Carrington's most important policy in his first year was to attempt to concentrate control of all government land in his own department and demonstrate that smallholdings could work by introducing them on this land. To this end, he gained the king's approval to bring the crown lands under board of agriculture control, and replaced the existing land agents with the firm of Carter Jonas, who handled Carrington's Lincolnshire smallholdings.[33] They were instructed to place smallholders on farms as they became vacant. Carrington also made unsuccessful attempts to gain control of the ecclesiastical commissioners' land.[34] His aim was to turn the board of agriculture into a 'Land Ministry' rather than a policing and technical advice office. Ultimately, though, his attempts to hive off some of

26 *The Speaker*, 16 Dec. 1905.
27 E. Montagu, 'Memorandum on the development commission', Apr. 1909, Runciman papers, University of Newcastle Library, Newcastle, MS 30/2.
28 Fisher, 'Public opinion and agriculture', 270–94.
29 CD, entry for 1 Feb. 1906. For Elliott see Viscount Long, *Memories*, London 1923, 117.
30 CD, entry for 31 Dec. 1907.
31 Lord Carrington to H. Campbell-Bannerman, 7 Feb. 1906, Campbell-Bannerman papers, BL, MS Add. 41212, fos 302–9; CD, 8 Feb. 1906.
32 Carrington to Campbell-Bannerman, 7 Feb. 1906, Campbell-Bannerman papers, MS Add. 41212, fos 302–9.
33 CD, entries for 12 Feb., 5 Sept. 1906.
34 Carrington to A. Ponsonby, 26 Oct. 1906, Campbell-Bannerman papers, MS Add. 41242, fos 182–3.

the board's non-landed functions, like fisheries, were thwarted.[35] Liberals anxious for legislative action on smallholdings had to wait for 1907.

However, it was not just action on smallholdings that Carrington had suggested to the prime minister on 7 February 1906. He had also asserted the need for some movement on farmers' grievances over compensation for disturbance and improvements, freedom of cropping, shooting rights and a variety of other problems. Roden Buxton might be able write off the farmers' support, but Carrington could not. He was forced into action earlier than he had planned, though, by Channing and his allies in the LLRA. As soon as parliament assembled, Channing organised a meeting of about a hundred MPs sympathetic to the association. The meeting decided to try to promote two bills that session, one on rural housing and another on land tenure.[36] The latter was taken up by Thomas Agar-Robartes, MP for Bodmin, who had secured one of the top places in the ballot for private members' bills. The bill he introduced was similar both to Lambert's bill of 1895 and the proposals Carrington had made to the prime minister in February 1906. Carrington clearly could not repudiate this section of his own strategy, nor ignore the feeling among some Liberal MPs in favour of a gesture towards farmers' interests. When the bill was given its second reading on 9 March 1906 Carrington was able to persuade his colleagues to adopt it as an official measure in return for its sponsors accepting government amendments.[37] Thereafter, the land tenure bill dominated agricultural politics for the rest of 1906. The tribulations Carrington endured to ensure the bill's passage were an ominous warning of the problems awaiting his smallholdings legislation, or, indeed, any attempt to tackle the land question. First, the bill provoked a storm of opposition and obstruction from landowners, Unionists and a small group of conservative Liberals. Landed society was so opposed to the measure that Carrington was forced to write to Edward VII to assure him that reports he had heard that revolutionary changes were afoot were greatly exaggerated.[38] The Unionists fought the bill to a standstill in committee in the Commons and six extra days of government time had to be allocated to save it.[39] Finally, the bill was too harsh on the landlords for some of the more Whiggish Liberal MPs. Eleven voted for Balfour's motion on 6 November 1906 to suspend indefinitely further consideration of the measure and there were further revolts over the bill's details.[40] Nine of the eleven rebels were Liberal Leaguers, including Rosebery's son, Lord Dalmeny, and other close allies of

---

[35] Carrington to Lord Crewe, 31 Aug. 1906, Crewe papers, Cambridge University Library, MS C/31.

[36] LLRA, *19th annual meeting, 1906*, London 1906.

[37] CD, entries for 9, 29 Mar. 1906.

[38] Ibid. entry for 17 Nov. 1906.

[39] LM xiv (1906–7), 676–81.

[40] *Hansard*, 4th ser., 1906, clxiv. 389–90.

the ex-leader like Ronald Munro-Ferguson and J. M. Paulton.[41] Their objections to the bill were probably a warning to the government of their dislike of forthcoming Scottish land legislation, to which Rosebery and his friends offered prolonged resistance in 1907–8.[42]

However, in the face of resolutions from farmers' clubs and chambers of agriculture favouring the bill, the Unionists were willing to allow an amended version through the Commons.[43] Carrington was willing to accept compromise, too. The cabinet was not greatly exercised by the bill's fate and was unwilling to insist on retaining it intact.[44] If the bill was to pass the Commons and Lords by the end of the session, Carrington had to have Unionist agreement. After lengthy negotiations this was arranged and the land tenure bill passed its third reading on 23 November with the opposition of only twenty-seven diehard Unionists.[45] But many Liberal backbenchers were outraged at this collusion with the opposition and the landed enemy and expressed their disapproval in forceful terms. For instance, no fewer than 151 MPs voted against the government when it accepted a Unionist-inspired amendment to exclude strawberry plants from the list of improvements to a property for which a landlord would be required to compensate a tenant at the end of a lease, even if the landlord had not been notified of the improvement.[46] One backbencher noted in his diary that the 'rank and file of [the] party are v. indignant' over the whole episode.[47] Even after these compromises, the House of Lords insisted on further changes. The bill finally passed in December 1906, but its operation was delayed for two years, the procedure for compensation for crop damage by winged game was drastically modified and only buildings were added to the list of improvements for which compensation to tenants was compulsory at the end of a lease, even without notice to the landlord.[48]

Carrington was delighted to have steered even an emasculated bill through the Commons and Lords, though he must have been apprehensive about the effect of Unionist hostility and Liberal divisions on his forthcoming smallholdings bill. This experience may have contributed to Carrington's decision to produce a relatively moderate smallholdings bill for the cabinet's consideration in March 1907.[49] Another conservative influence may have

41 The other rebels were F. W. Chance, C. Cory, A. L. Renton, Sir E. Tennant, H. J. Tennant, S. H. Whitbread, together with the non-Leaguers T. W. Nussey and Sir R. Hobart.
42 A. Sykes, *Tariff reform in British politics, 1903–13*, Oxford 1979, 153–4.
43 CD, entries for 3 Apr., 28 May 1906; Munro-Ferguson in *Hansard*, 4th ser., 1906, clxiv. 373–4, for the bill's popularity with farmers.
44 CD, entry for 12 Nov. 1906.
45 *Hansard*, 4th ser., 1906, clxv. 1175–6.
46 Ibid. clxiv. 1595–1600.
47 E. W. Davies journal, entry for 14 Nov. 1906, E. W. Davies papers, NLW, Aberystwyth, MS A1984/105/6.
48 *LM* xiv (1906–7), 676–81.
49 'Various bills etc', Harcourt papers, MSS 1986 Add. 161–9, contains successive drafts of the smallholdings bill.

been Lord Ripon, whom Carrington had initially consulted over the wisdom of combining his legislation with that proposed for Scotland.[50] Carrington suggested that responsibilty for promoting smallholdings be given to county councils, with commissioners of the board of agriculture acting only in case of default; councils should be given power to acquire land compulsorily, and cultivators could become owners or tenants. But the cabinet took a very different attitude to that it had adopted over the land tenure bill. As John Burns confided to his diary, that bill was 'hardly worth the trouble except as an olive for the next meal off [the] same fare'.[51] In other words, the real battle for the countryside would occur over smallholdings, rather than any reforms to land tenure, and on the former the cabinet was determined to pass far-reaching legislation.

This was partly because the prime minister, once again, showed his commitment to smallholdings, urging Carrington to give central authorities more powers to force recalcitrant county councils to act.[52] But the cabinet was also 'entirely against' schemes of land purchase, and these proposals were made continuously more uninviting when compared to those for council tenancy in successive drafts of the bill.[53] Treasury pressure may have been an element here, as loans to potential owners would have to be subsidised to be attractive. But it could also be argued that tenancy would be more effective in promoting smallholdings because it did not require a deposit.[54] This motive would correspond with the widespread enthusiasm for the bill noted in the cabinet.[55] In turn, this may have reflected a desire to attack the landlords after the Lords' destruction of the education bill in 1906 and evidence that rural Liberal MPs had responded to the smallholdings policy with enthusiasm.[56] But electoral calculations were not absent. The smallholdings bill was the government's one opportunity to restructure rural society in a way more favourable to the Liberals and permanently remove the party's disadvantage in agricultural areas by breaking the dominance of the landowners. Though the party had won 74 of the 111 English rural seats in 1906, twenty had been won for the first time and ten for the first time since 1885. To keep these gains once the Unionists started to recover from their disaster in 1906 it was plausible to argue that rural society itself would have to be changed. The fragility of the Liberals' hold on rural England had already been forcefully demonstrated on 26 February 1907 when they lost the Lincolnshire, Brigg,

---

[50] Carrington to Lord Ripon, 8 Jan. 1907, Ripon papers, BL, MS Add. 43544, fos 111–14; Ripon to Carrington, 20 Mar. 1907, ibid. fos 121–2.
[51] J. Burns diary, entry for 14 Nov, 1906, J. Burns papers, BL, MS Add. 46324.
[52] CD, entry for 18 Mar. 1907.
[53] Carrington to Ripon, 2 Apr. 1907, Ripon papers, MS Add. 43544, fos 125–6.
[54] Sir T. Elliott, 'Memorandum on occupancy versus ownership', 1 June 1907, Harcourt papers, MSS 1986 Add. 161–9.
[55] Burns diary, entry for 15 Mar. 1907, MS Add. 46325; CD, entry for 18 Mar. 1907.
[56] Ibid. entries for 5 Nov., 22 Dec. 1906, 12 Mar. 1907.

by-election on a 9.3 per cent swing – their first loss in a straight fight with the Unionists since the general election.

The centre-piece of Carrington's legislative strategy was introduced into the Commons on 27 May by Lewis Harcourt, himself a prominent landowner in Oxfordshire. Despite a moderate and conciliatory opening speech by Harcourt, the bill immediately ran into a barrage of criticism from Walter Long (a substantial Wiltshire landowner) which ably summed up the Unionists' dislike of virtually every feature of the smallholdings legislation.[57] Long claimed that landowners had supplied smallholdings wherever they were economically viable and that the government knew little of agricultural conditions. If there was any outstanding demand it should be met by providing land to be sold to owner-occupiers. Long's bitterest criticisms, however, were reserved for the proposals to acquire land compulsorily. All of these strictures were repeated again and again, with differing emphases depending on the speaker, as the bill wound its tortuous way through the Commons. While Balfour was sceptical of the demand or need for smallholdings, for instance, Jesse Collings was still anxious to push his own nostrum of owner-occupancy.[58] All Unionists could agree, though, in damning the smallholdings bill's encroachment on the powers of county councils and the rights of landowners to enjoy their land in peace. When the bill finally reached the Lords it was encrusted with a battery of amendments, particularly focusing on the method of calculating compensation to landowners whose land was compulsorily acquired.[59]

But, in contrast to the land tenure bill, the cabinet insisted on retaining the substance of the bill. In particular, Harcourt rejected out of hand the House of Lords' plan for arbitration when calculating compensation for landowners. The cabinet's determination to carry the smallholdings bill was heightened by the demise of the two other major bills of the year – the Irish councils bill and the licensing bill. As Carrington remarked, this left his measure as 'the big Bill of the Session'.[60] But it also held intrinsic importance for the Liberal government and they were unwilling to compromise. Walter Long had hoped that the bill would be crowded out of the legislative timetable by continued obstruction, but, faced with a determined cabinet, the Unionists allowed the bill through the House of Lords.[61] The deciding factor in this capitulation was probably the Unionists' attitude to Sinclair's Scottish small landholders bill, which was also before the Commons. This bill was even more obnoxious to Unionists than Carrington's measure because it proposed to give the smaller Scottish tenants security of tenure and 'fair rents' on the lines of the crofters acts. Balfour (a Scottish landowner) was utterly

---

57 *Hansard*, 4th ser., 1907, clxxiv. 1377–88 (Harcourt), 1388–95 (Long).
58 Ibid. clxxv. 1640–55 (Balfour); clxxiv. 1421–8 (Collings).
59 Ibid. clxxxii. 419–23.
60 CD, entry for 25 May 1907.
61 W. Long to Balfour, 29 June 1907, Balfour papers, MS Add. 49776, fos 203–5.

opposed to this bill, but unwilling to expose the House of Lords to acrimony north of the border by urging its outright rejection.[62] In response to this dilemma, he persuaded the Lords to suspend discussion of Sinclair's bill and demand that the government apply Carrington's bill to the Scottish Lowlands instead, on the grounds that its agriculture was similar to that of England. This ingenious strategy could only look plausible if the Lords were willing to pass the English smallholdings bill.

The Unionists were not Carrington's only problem. In many ways his own backbenchers gave him just as much trouble. On the one hand a small group of conservative Liberal MPs agreed with some Unionists that ownership was preferable to tenancy for smallholders. Their leader was Sir John Dickson-Poynder, a Wiltshire landowner and recent convert from the Unionists, who feared the bill's supporters 'desired gradually to extinguish ownership throughout the country'.[63] However, only eighteen Liberals voted for his amendment on 13 August 1907 – some motivated by a general dislike of state ownership, others worried by possible charges on the county rate.[64] Carrington's bill retained the option of ownership (albeit on unfavourable terms) and this was sufficient to head off any more widespread revolt, either from senior rural reformers like Channing, or the occasional MP from the Celtic fringe, like Llewellyn Williams, who wished to promote peasant proprietorship. Channing did not press his ideas beyond voting for some of Jesse Collings's amendments in standing committee. Williams confined himself to one speech in the Commons.[65]

More troublesome to Carrington was the much larger group of Liberal MPs who felt that his bill did not go far enough in promoting smallholdings. The most prominent rebel was C. F. G. Masterman, who peppered the bill with amendments in standing committee. In a lengthy letter to Lewis Harcourt he explained that his aims were to eliminate county councils from the administration of smallholdings, as they were 'in the hands of the very class against which we are fighting the battle of the rural labourer', gain security of tenure for the smallholder and prevent landlords benefiting from rises in land values due to the creation of smallholdings.[66] On some of his amendments, Masterman was able to gather impressive support. Seventy-three MPs voted for his clause to allow the board of agriculture to overturn land sales to county councils when the price paid was excessive.[67] Carrington was deeply annoyed by Masterman's activities, describing them as 'our chief difficulty', but, in the

[62] Balfour to the duke of Portland, 6 Aug. 1907, ibid. MS Add. 49859, fos 167–8.

[63] *Hansard*, 4th ser., 1907, clxxx. 1082.

[64] Ibid. clxxx. 1116; F. Verney to L. Harcourt, 10 July 1907, Harcourt papers, MSS 1986 Add. 161–9.

[65] Report from the standing committee on smallholdings and allotments bill, ibid; *Hansard*, 4th ser., 1907, clxxiv. 1419–21.

[66] C. F. G. Masterman to L. Harcourt, 18 June 1907, Harcourt papers, MSS 1986 Add. 161–9.

[67] *Hansard*, 4th ser., 1907, clxxx. 1145–6.

end, the bill was sufficiently radical to prevent major discontent on the Liberal benches.[68] The Co-operative Smallholdings Society, for instance, thought Masterman was unduly critical.[69] The significance of Masterman's opposition was that it revealed some unease on the backbenches about whether Carrington's bill would be effective.

If the bill did not produce smallholdings though, it would not be for lack of support from the Liberal Party. No fewer than eighteen regional conferences were organised by the NLF between October 1907 and February 1908.[70] At these local MPs addressed county councillors and other prominent Liberals on how to implement the new Smallholdings Act. In addition, Corrie Grant, Liberal MP for Rugby, produced a handbook to guide local authorities on how to use the act.[71] The party was convinced that its hopes of continued success in the English rural seats were intimately bound up with the fate of Carrington's act, which was intended to do nothing less than transform the structure of English agriculture.

The failure of the 1907 Smallholdings Act

However, the act was a gamble. There was no clear evidence that smallholdings would be popular with agricultural labourers. As with allotments in the 1890s it was a policy that Liberals thought labourers should want but they could not be sure of its appeal. The Liberals had certainly won an overwhelming victory in rural England in 1906, and smallholdings and allotments had been more prominent in the Liberal campaign than in 1900. But while 68 of the 111 candidates in rural seats mentioned the issue in their manifestos, only eighteen had put it among their first three points.[72] Even enthusiasts like Richard Winfrey admitted that they regarded the 1902 Education Act and Free Trade as far more important than smallholdings in the Liberal victory.[73] This was probably correct. Most observers of rural politics emphasised the continued significance of the Anglican–Nonconformist divide. R. W. Perks, for instance, claimed that in his seat of Louth, the 300 Methodist preachers were, in effect, Liberal Party agents, while seventy-two of the seventy-four Anglican priests were Unionists.[74] In these circumstances the 1902 Education Act was sufficient to galvanise rural Nonconformists into action on behalf of the Liberals. Perhaps even more significantly, enthusiastic protectionists admitted that Tariff Reform had made 'very little headway, so

---

68 CD, entry for 18 June 1907.
69 W. Moore to L. Harcourt, 28 June 1907, Harcourt papers, MSS 1986 Add. 161–9.
70 Liberal Publication Department, *Pamphlets and leaflets, 1908*, London 1908, 16–21.
71 C. Grant, *Allotments and smallholdings handbook*, London 1908.
72 These figures are calculated from candidates' election addresses, general election, 1906, National Liberal Club papers.
73 Winfrey, *Leaves*, 150, 155.
74 Sir R. W. Perks, *Autobiography*, London 1936, 111, 115.

far, in the agricultural counties'.[75] Ailwyn Fellowes, ex-president of the board of agriculture, insisted that 'the labourers . . . will not have their bread taxed. If this is insisted upon, then the county seats will go worse in the future than even at the last general election.'[76] Tariff Reform not only alienated the labourers, farmers were divided on its merits and many members of the rural middle class, like their urban counterparts, were unconvinced.[77]

The Liberal triumph in rural England in 1906 was based on a revulsion against the Unionists among virtually all groups in rural society. Smallholdings were a minor factor at best. Other evidence for the popularity of a state-sponsored smallholdings policy was difficult to assess. The agricultural labourers' trade union that had been re-founded in 1906 included smallholdings and allotments among its aims. But it was heavily dependent on Liberal politicians and their funds for survival – Winfrey was its treasurer and George Nicholls, another Liberal MP, was its president.[78] Land reform was more their policy than the labourers'. Similarly, Winfrey could boast of some success with his smallholdings associations in the Holland division of Lincolnshire, but it was scarcely possible to argue from this that they would be popular throughout England.[79] The fact remained that until 1907 there had never been any effective legislation to test whether there really was a demand for state-provided smallholdings in the countryside. Only the response to the 1907 Smallholdings Act could prove whether such demand existed.

However, it soon became clear that the act was going to be a great disappointment to the Liberals. The 1911 report of the smallholdings commissioners revealed that, up to 31 December 1910, only 65,953 acres had been let to 4,846 smallholders.[80] This was a great advance on the Unionists' 1892 act, but scarcely a revolution in rural society. Throughout England between 1908 and 1914 only 2 per cent of agricultural labourers applied for smallholdings.[81] By 1910 it was clear that the high hopes of 1907 had been dashed. The response of rural Liberals, though, was to question, not the policy, but how it was being carried out. In particular, Masterman's criticisms about the role of the county councils provided a ready-made explanation for the failure of the Smallholdings Act. As early as July 1908 Lord Carrington received three 'stormy' deputations of Liberal MPs complaining about the

[75] Long to A. Bonar Law, 1 Dec. 1907, Bonar Law papers, HLRO, MS 18/3/49.

[76] A. Fellowes to Balfour, 24 Oct. 1907, Balfour papers, MS Add. 49859, fos 183–5.

[77] H. Matthews, memorandum, 'The dairy farmer and tariff reform', n.d., Bonar Law papers, MS 27/1/17; A. K. Russell, *Liberal landslide: the general election of 1906*, Newton Abbot 1973, 175–7.

[78] A. Howkins, 'Edwardian Liberalism and industrial unrest: a class view of the decline of Liberalism', *HWJ* iv (1977), 143–7.

[79] Winfrey, *Leaves*, 29–32, 37–9, 114–27.

[80] *Annual report of proceedings under the Smallholdings and Allotments Act 1908 part 1, smallholdings for 1911* (Cd 5615), 3.

[81] Smith, *Land for the small man*, 216.

inertia and conservatism of the county councils.[82] Rural MPs like Philip Morrell seized on the 'incessant delays, the frequent demand for extortionate rents, the refusal of local authorities to act in case of any show of opposition from landlords or persons having sporting rights'[83] to explain the act's failure. Most demanded that county councils be bypassed, probably by a thoroughly reformed board of agriculture. These criticisms effectively allowed Liberals to avoid any major rethinking of their rural strategy or consideration of whether there really was a demand for state-sponsored smallholdings.

In fact, the reasons for the failure of the 1907 Smallholdings Act were implicit in the nature of rural society. The experiments of Winfrey and Carrington in Lincolnshire had revealed that there was a demand for more smallholdings to be organised for at least some agricultural labourers. But the workings of the act showed that this demand was limited to areas where market gardening was already well-established. Although only 2 per cent of labourers applied for smallholdings in 1908–14, 22.8 per cent of those in the Isle of Ely did so. Six of the seven counties that provided the most small-holdings under the 1907 act contained substantial market gardening areas.[84] In areas like the Fenland, the Vale of Evesham and Biggleswade in Bedford-shire exceptionally good soil, moderate rainfall and good communications allowed high-yield and high-profit crops like strawberries, asparagus and bulbs to be intensively cultivated on a small plot. This situation allowed smallholders to make a decent living and in these areas there was keen competition for land among men, or their families, who worked allotments and smallholdings and the 1907 act proved useful in meeting an unsatisfied demand.[85]

But these areas were not typical. Most labourers lacked the incentive to transform their economic role. To become a smallholder, a labourer needed the requisite technical knowledge, good business sense, the willingness to work himself and his family ruthlessly hard and, most importantly, capital. Outside established market gardening areas, migration to the towns or abroad always seemed a more attractive and realistic option to ambitious labourers.[86] To the surprise of most Liberals, labourers were never a majority of those applying for land under the Smallholdings Act. It had more appeal to inter-mediate rural groups, like village tradesmen, who often needed land for raising fodder or grazing horses.[87] Outside areas like the Isle of Ely, the labourers who were most likely to find smallholdings attractive were either the remnants of marginal groups like the foresters of Winterslow and the

82 CD, entries for 22, 23, 29 July 1908.
83 Land Club League, *Land Club convention, 1909*, London 1909.
84 Smith, *Land for the small man*, ch. vi.
85 F. Beavington, 'The development of market gardening in Bedfordshire, 1799–1939', *AgHR* xxiii(1975), 23–47.
86 G. Mingay, *Rural life in Victorian England*, Stroud 1990, 103–5.
87 C. Harmsworth to W. Runciman, 19 Oct. 1913, Runciman papers, MS 82.

nailmakers of Catskill, who used them to eke out seasonal or irregular work, or labourers who lived close to major population centres, especially in the south-east.[88] It was in these latter areas that nurserying and market gardening were beginning to expand before 1914, in order to meet the demand from nearby towns for a more varied diet. The only way the Smallholdings Act could have succeeded widely would have been if it had appealed to agricultural workers in this expanding sector. It is unlikely that the inertia of the county councils was the only factor involved in its failure to do so. It may be that those labourers who had the inclination and capital to become smallholders in these areas had little trouble acquiring land without recourse to the county council. Certainly the work of Mick Reed has drawn attention to the widespread persistence into the early twentieth century of small plots of agricultural land.[89] In addition, the procedure under the Smallholdings Act was slow and cumbersome, particularly if land had to be compulsorily acquired, and rents charged tended to be fairly high to cover the costs of adaptation and equipment and the sinking fund on the land.[90]

'debacle': the Liberals and the 1910 elections in rural England

Disappointed in their hopes of the Smallholdings Act, Liberal candidates did not give it first place in their campaign in January 1910. Only 14 of 110 candidates in English agricultural seats put it among the first three issues in their manifestos.[91] But Liberals did not go into the election without hope in rural England. There was no reason to believe that food taxes were any less unpopular with the agricultural labourers than in 1906. When Balfour reflected on the January 1910 result, he wrote that 'so far as the wage earning population is concerned, any proposal to tax food hampered the rural candidate even more than the urban candidate'.[92] This opinion was confirmed by a survey undertaken of the opinions of agricultural labourers in Eye, Suffolk, in 1913 by the local Unionist organisation. Those who expressed an opinion declared 76:4 against any food tax.[93] The Unionist programme for 1910 contained little in the way of positive proposals to overcome the labourers' dislike of this aspect of tariff reform. Their main idea to win the labourers' votes was a repackaging of the terms of the virtually inoperative 1892 Smallholdings Act, which had provided loans for labourers to buy, rather than rent, smallholdings. However, Balfour was sceptical of this policy and it

---

[88] For the former see Jebb, *Smallholdings*, 180–93, 350–63; for the latter see Howkins, *Reshaping rural England*, 210–15.

[89] Reed, 'Peasantry of nineteenth-century England'.

[90] Land enquiry committee, *The land*, i, London 1913, 212–16.

[91] These figures are calculated from candidates' election addresses, general election January 1910, ii, National Liberal Club papers.

[92] Balfour to C. Bathurst, 11 Nov. 1910, Balfour papers, MS Add. 49861, fos 63–5.

[93] Memorandum, n.d. [1913], Bonar Law papers, MS 41/M/14.

was promoted in a distinctly confused and half-hearted manner. If state-sponsored smallholdings had little appeal to labourers anyway, as the Liberals' 1907 act seemed to show, this policy had little real chance of improving Unionist fortunes in the countryside.

The Liberals had also provided the labourers with one great benefit in 1908 – old age pensions. The Unionist agricultural adviser, Trustram Eve, declared that

> The rural worker is grateful for old age pensions, which is the best tangible result of politics they have ever known. They are reminded of this each week, when their old relatives actually fetch the five shillings and thus saves the pocket of the young relative who formerly helped his aged relative.

Walter Long agreed. He thought 'old age pensions hold the field and are doing our cause immense harm' in rural areas.[94]

The Liberals could, therefore, look to the rural areas with at least some hope in 1910. However, there were indications long before the election that all was not well. The swing against the government in English rural seats in 1907–8 was consistently high. In the two rural by-elections in 1907 (Brigg and Rutland) it averaged 7.3 per cent, against a national average of 2.8 per cent. In the four agricultural constituencies contested in 1908 (Ashburton, Ross, Newport and Chelmsford) it averaged 8.1 per cent, compared to the national average of 4.3 per cent.[95] After the Liberals lost Ashburton, with C. R. Buxton as their standard-bearer, Carrington wrote 'It is all very well to say Buxton was a bad candidate, but I have got the Land Tenure Bill and the Smallholdings Bill through Parliament and this is the answer of the farmers and villagers.'[96]

These fears were amply confirmed in January 1910 when the Liberals suffered a 'debacle' in the English rural seats.[97] They managed to hold only thirty of the 111 rural seats, compared to seventy-four in 1906. Twelve of these MPs came from Lincolnshire, Cambridgeshire and Norfolk – the most solid geographical block of Liberals from an English agricultural area. Blewett calculates a pro-Unionist swing of 6 per cent in rural seats in January 1910, similar to the 6.2 per cent swing in middle-class seats and much higher than the 3.8 per cent average in working-class seats.[98]

---

94 T. Eve, memorandum, 8 Aug. 1912, ibid. MS 27/1/28; Long to Balfour, 8 Apr. 1907, Balfour papers, MS Add. 49776, fos 199–200.

95 The national averages are from P. Clarke, 'The electoral position of the Liberal and Labour parties, 1910–14', *EHR* lxxxx (1975), 834. The one English rural by-election in 1909, at Stratford, saw a pro-Unionist swing of 19%, but the sitting Liberal MP had resigned to fight on a conscriptionist platform, so perhaps a bad result could be excused.

96 CD, entry for 17 Jan. 1908.

97 H. Samuel to H. Gladstone, 22 Jan. 1910, H. Gladstone papers, BL, MS Add. 45922, fos 235–6.

98 N. Blewett, *The peers, the parties and the people: the general elections of 1910*, London 1972, 400.

Most Liberals favoured a simple explanation for this result. They claimed that the landlords had once again applied the feudal 'screw' to force the labourers to vote Unionist. R. L. Outhwaite, who fought the Horsham division of Sussex in January 1910, provided a typical reaction. He wrote

> Polling day was a revelation to me. So enthusiastic had been the labourers at my village meetings that I thought I had stirred them to revolt. The last two nights the labourers did not attend and on polling day I saw them driven to the booths by their lords and masters who polled them like Tammany bosses. . . . The agricultural labourers are in the balance, their instincts are all against the Protectionists but fear makes them a prey.[99]

The moral drawn by Outhwaite was that further efforts were needed to make the labourer independent, and this meant more vigorous attempts to provide smallholdings. The Liberals' success in the eastern counties reinforced this view. As Edwin Montagu wrote, 'South West Norfolk and West Cambridgeshire were conspicuous for the success of the Smallholdings Act and *therefore* remained true to Liberalism.'[100] Thus the rural disasters of 1910 did not weaken the Liberal commitment to smallholdings. If the counties had been lost because of 'feudal' dominance, the only solution seemed to be to change the nature of the economic and social relationships in the countryside and turn the labourer into an independent producer, rather than a dependant of the farmer and the landlord.

However, the assumptions behind this response were open to serious challenge. It is difficult to accept that intimidation was the only, or even the main, reason for the Liberal defeats in rural areas in 1910. It may have been one factor. Lord Salisbury, for one, pointed to the exceptional efforts made by landlords to return Unionist candidates in 1910.[101] But the Unionist advantage in the counties lay not only in the direct power of landlords and farmers to coerce labourers, but also in the fact that because most wealthy men in rural areas were Unionists, their organisation was far better and they had much more money to spend. Philip Morrell emphasised this factor in his defeat at Oxfordshire South, observing

> Tariff Reform suppers and concerts had been given in almost every public house through the division, with paid speakers and entertainers everywhere.

[99]   R. L. Outhwaite to C. P. Trevelyan, 1 Feb. 1910, C. P. Trevelyan papers, University of Newcastle Library, Newcastle, MS 27. See also Yorkshire Liberal Federation, executive committee minutes, 9 Feb. 1910, Yorkshire Liberal Federation papers, WYAS, Leeds, for calls for action against intimidation in 'rural constituencies of Yorkshire'.
[100]   E. Montagu to W. Churchill, 14 Mar. 1910, in R. Churchill, *W. S. Churchill: young statesman, 1901–14*, London 1967, companion vol. ii. 994–5.
[101]   Lord Salisbury, memorandum, 2 Feb. 1910, Bonar Law papers, MS 41/M/1.

Every cricket club, football club and slate club has been subsidised . . . there has been an enormous distribution of clothes, blankets and meat.[102]

If the Unionists' greater efforts in the intensely partisan atmosphere of 1910 contributed to their victory, their money and organisation probably persuaded more voters than the use of fear.

It is also highly likely that Liberal policies reduced the enthusiasm of some labourers for the party. The smallholdings strategy probably attracted little support. In fact, the Unionists may have had some success in convincing labourers that they would lose their jobs if the farm they worked on was taken over for use as smallholdings.[103] On the other hand, Nonconformity was an important element in rural voting patterns and the Liberals had notably failed to satisfy Nonconformist grievances over the 1902 Education Act. Home Rule was also more of an issue in 1910 than 1906 and D. W. Bebbington has emphasised that this policy was not popular with many Nonconformists, especially Methodists, who were probably the strongest group among rural Dissenters.[104] This point also emerges very clearly from the autobiography of R. W. Perks, MP for Louth.[105] Many labourers may also have been indifferent or hostile to the land taxes in the 1909 budget. J. A. Spender claimed that 'the landlords and the farmers have taken the labourers with them to the polls on the grounds that the Government is "taxing land" and hitting the countryside'.[106] Certainly, many rural Liberals doubted the popularity of the land taxes in the countryside. Lloyd George's initial budget proposals for a tax on the capital value of all land were modified to exclude agricultural land as far as possible after Asquith circulated the cabinet with the protests of three MPs from agricultural areas.[107]

Even if agricultural land was exempted the labourers had nothing to gain from the taxes. On the other hand they might well have something to lose, if the land on which their cottages were built was subjected to taxation. Most labourers paid low rates because their cottages were under-rented as part of their wages. A tax or rate on the capital value, rather than the use value, of the site would be bound to increase the labourer's rates. In a sample based on the effect of a 1d./£ capital value land tax on the Essex village of Manuden in 1913, the Liberals' land tax expert, Edgar Harper, found 'the extraordinary result of all other classes of property in the parish being relieved at the expense of cottages of a rateable value of £12 p.a. and under'.[108] The undevel-

---

102 P. Morrell to Samuel, 2 Feb. 1910, H. Samuel papers, MS A155(iv), fos 25–6.

103 LM xv (1907), 385–8.

104 D. W. Bebbington, 'Nonconformity and electoral sociology, 1867–1918', HJ xxvii (1984), 633–56.

105 Perks, Autobiography, 136–7.

106 J. A. Spender to J. Bryce, 3 Feb. 1910, J. Bryce papers, Bod. Lib., MS 139.

107 B. Murray, The people's budget, 1909/10: Lloyd George and Liberal politics, Oxford 1980, 131–2.

108 E. Harper to Samuel, 27 Mar. 1914, Treasury papers, PRO, Kew, MS 171/73.

oped land duty did, in fact, cause a number of anomalies, particularly by hitting those allotment-holders whose land had a relatively high capital value if sold for building.[109]

If some labourers at least were alienated in 1910, it is difficult to resist the conclusion that the Liberals lost support among the farmers, despite the land tenure legislation of 1906. Not only were Nonconformist grievances much less in the Liberals' favour than in 1906 but farmers could scarcely be expected to favour any proposals to tax or rate land, whatever the Liberals promised about exempting agricultural land. On most farms the value of buildings would only be a small fraction of the value of the land, so any proposal to shift the tax burden to land would leave farmers worse off. Many farmers were enraged by what they saw as Liberal legislation to favour the labourers at their expense, particularly the 1907 Smallholdings Act. When addressing a meeting in December 1907, even Lord Carrington had to admit of the act that 'the farmers hate it and one corner of the room was very hostile'.[110] Farmers feared that 'the result would be to evict them from their homes and take the eyes out of the farm they were farming'.[111] Philip Morrell confirmed the deep loathing felt by many farmers towards smallholdings legislation.[112]

In addition to the farmers, the Liberals faced a loss of rural middle-class votes, in line with the general middle-class swing against the Liberals in 1910, especially in southern England, noted by Blewett.[113] This was particularly important because the middle-class commuter and residential population of the southern counties was growing rapidly.[114] Middle-class voting strength in the counties was also boosted by the votes of the borough freeholders, who could make a considerable impact in some constituencies.[115] This reaction, when added to disillusion among farmers and labourers, meant that the Liberals faced a falling-back of support among all sections of rural society in 1910.

There is, therefore, no need to see the coercion of the labourers as the central reason for the Liberal losses in English rural areas in 1910. The probability is that their support declined on a broad front and that they were faced with a more united and committed Unionist opposition. The smallholdings policy that the Liberals put their faith in was actually an electoral handicap, rather than a recipe for success. It is, therefore, difficult to judge the Liberals' rural policy of 1906–10 as other than a failure. In fact, they had repeated the

---

[109] A. Black to Lloyd George, Apr. 1912, ibid. MS 172/84.
[110] CD, entry for 10 Dec. 1907.
[111] Ibid. entry for 23 Sept. 1908.
[112] Morrell to Samuel, 2 Feb. 1910, H. Samuel papers, MS A155(iv), fos 25–6.
[113] Blewett, Peers, 400.
[114] Howkins, Reshaping rural England, 210, 217–18, 231–2.
[115] N. Blewett, 'The franchise in the United Kingdom, 1885–1918', P&P xxxii (1965), 43–51.

experience of 1892–5, when a policy of land reform had been vigorously pursued, only to result in electoral disaster in the English countryside. If the Liberals were to repeat their rural successes of 1906 a drastic reassessment was needed.

3

The Transformation of the Urban Land Issue, 1906–1910

The growth in support for land taxation

The revival of interest in rural land reform after 1900 was matched by the increasing prominence of the urban land question. In the 1890s land taxation had seemed a fairly minor matter to most Liberals – something that owed its place in the Newcastle programme mainly to the enthusiasm of Liberals from London. But by 1906 this situation had changed. In the general election of that year, 52 per cent of all Liberal candidates endorsed land taxation – more than even mentioned unemployment or housing.[1] Following the election, Campbell-Bannerman received a deputation that (allegedly) represented the views of more than 400 MPs, demanding some progress towards land taxation.[2] This remarkable transformation occurred largely because the proponents of land taxation were able to present it as a remedy for immediate and pressing problems. This process had two aspects – housing and the growing crisis in local government finance – but both centred around the reform of the rating system.

First, land taxation could be seen as an easy and simple remedy for housing shortages. Such a policy was particularly appealing just before the Liberals returned to power, in 1898–1904, when builders were failing to keep up with increasing demand for more housing and local authorities were under pressure to take some action to deal with the problem.[3] It could be argued that the replacement of the existing form of rates with a system based on the rating of site values would increase the supply of houses and lower their price, without the need for extensive state intervention. Under the existing system, rates were levied on a percentage of the theoretical annual rental value of each hereditament i.e. plot of land plus any buildings and other improvements on that land. However, this rental value was calculated on what the hereditament could command if it was used for its present purpose. Thus, a plot of land with a large capital value if sold for building, but used for farming, would pay rates only on its much lower agricultural rental value. If rates were levied on the actual selling value of the land, 'it will bring into the market, by taxing

---

1   Russell, *Landslide*, 65.
2   P. W. Raffan, *The policy of the land values group in the House of Commons*, London 1912, 9.
3   Offer, *Property and politics*, 239–41; M. Swenarton, *Homes fit for heroes*, London 1981, 30.

vacant land which is ripe for building, large quantities of land on the holding back of which there is now a premium'.[4] This would, in turn, lead to the provision of more and cheaper houses. Moreover, as existing rates were levied on the value of land and buildings together, when vacant land was developed this increased the rates bill. Enthusiasts for land taxation claimed this discouraged house-building and therefore rates should be levied on the value of land alone. 'There is no encouragement to spend money on building when it alone, amongst all the sundry wants of life, is taxed so heavily' claimed no less an authority than Charles Booth.[5]

What became known as site value rating offered a similarly appealing solution to the crisis in local government finance that was becoming acute in the early 1900s. Financial pressures had driven Liberals on the LCC to press for land taxation in the 1890s, but by 1906 most local authorities were under pressure as the duties of borough and county councils expanded relentlessly, debts accumulated and central grants failed to keep pace with rising expenditure. The unavoidable consequence was an overall increase in rates, which rose on average by 141 per cent in the period 1875 to 1900.[6]

This inexorable rise was a particular difficulty for the Liberals as they were identified as the party of municipal expansion and enterprise on many councils, not just the LCC. 'It is not a sufficient answer to say you must either cut down or at any rate arrest your expenditure', Asquith told a deputation of local authorities, 'we have adopted, and we are constantly adopting a higher and more exacting standard of municipal life.'[7] But Liberals could not look with equanimity on rising rates. Because they had the greatest needs but the lowest property values, rate rises were highest in the poorest local authorities. For instance, West Ham's rates rose from 5s.8d./£ to 10s.8d./£ between 1888 and 1905.[8] Rates were the only direct tax which most working- and lower middle-class people paid (though they were often compounded in with the rent). They were also a regressive tax as rent made up a higher percentage of the expenditure of the poor than the rich. This was also true of business rates. It was estimated, for example, that while retailers paid, on average, 13 per cent of their income in rates, stockbrokers paid only 1.9 per cent.[9] Thus rate rises were a source of worry to many of Liberalism's poorer supporters and there were signs that the Unionists were having some success in working the anti-rates issue. This trend was most spectacularly illustrated when they won control of the LCC for the first time in 1907.[10]

---

4   C. P. Trevelyan, quoted in anon. (probably UCTLV), *Land values in parliament*, London 1903, 4.
5   C. Booth, *Rates and the housing question in London*, London 1904, 4.
6   P. Waller, *Town, city and nation: England, 1850–1914*, Oxford 1983, 257.
7   *LV*, Mar. 1906, 200.
8   E. Howarth and M. Wilson, *West Ham: a study in social and industrial problems*, London 1907, 61–2.
9   G. Howell Thomas, 'Local taxation', 5 Apr. 1914, Treasury papers, MS 171/70.
10 Offer, *Property and politics*, 301–8.

But Liberals were unwilling to extend central grants because, as rates were paid by occupiers, it was assumed that if they were reduced by state subsidies, landlords would be able to reap the benefits by raising rents. As Josiah Wedgwood put it, 'At the present, if you relieve rates at the expense of the Exchequer, the landlord gets the benefit.'[11] Liberal suspicions of state subsidies had been confirmed in the 1890s, when Unionist governments had used central grants to reduce the rates paid by their supporters.[12] In these circumstances, Liberals preferred to look to another source of income for local authorities. The advocates of site value rating pointed out that a rate on the capital value of vacant and undeveloped land would bring in much more than the existing rate on its use value. C. P. Trevelyan, for instance, claimed that a modest 1d./£ levy on the capital value, rather than the use value, of land would produce £15.6 million a year.[13]

The strength of these arguments on housing and revenue soon began to produce pressure from Liberals on local authorities for the introduction of site value rating, as enthusiasm for the scheme spread outwards from London and Glasgow. In 1898 the Association of Municipal Corporations endorsed the idea.[14] There were conferences of rating authorities to draw up appropriate bills in 1899, 1902 and 1903.[15] Site value rating bills even managed to pass the Commons in 1904 and 1905 because of the reluctance of urban Unionists to oppose them.[16] In 1906 Campbell-Bannerman received a deputation representing 518 local authorities calling for the rating of site values.[17] This pressure was marshalled and reinforced by the activities of the single taxers, who could claim six or seven MPs after the 1906 election landslide, most notably Josiah Wedgwood.[18]

But the widespread support and the reasonable nature of the arguments behind site value rating ensured that it did not remain the sole property of the single taxers. In fact most of the forward-looking groups in the Liberal Party supported the idea. The Liberal Imperialist leaders Haldane, Asquith and Grey maintained their interest in land issues from the 1890s and voted solidly for the 1904 site value rating bill.[19] Prominent single taxers like C. P. Trevelyan and Alexander Ure were to be found among the sympathisers of the 'Limps'.[20] The Liberal newspaper most closely allied to them, the *Westminster Gazette*, was strongly pro-land taxation, probably because of the influ-

---

[11] J. Wedgwood, 'Memorandum on the taxation of land values', n.d. [1909], Inland Revenue papers, PRO, Kew, MS 73/2.

[12] Offer, *Property and politics*, 207–17.

[13] C. P. Trevelyan, *Land taxation and the use of land*, London 1905, 9.

[14] AMC, annual meeting, 28 Mar. 1898, AMC papers, PRO, Kew, MS 30/72/27.

[15] LV, Dec. 1902, 99; Feb. 1904, 139; Mar. 1907, 191.

[16] *Hansard*, 4th ser., 1904, cxxxi. 912; 1905, cxlv. 264.

[17] Raffan, *Land values group*, 7–8.

[18] J. Wedgwood, *Memoirs of a fighting life*, London 1940, 67.

[19] *Hansard*, 4th ser., 1904, cxxxi. 912.

[20] Wedgwood, *Memoirs*, 67.

ence of its editor, J. A. Spender, who had been introduced to journalism by his uncle, William Saunders, the early single taxer.[21]

The group of writers around the *Daily News* and *The Speaker* were even more enthusiastic. *The Speaker* referred to site value rating as 'an indispensable and capital part of any scheme of urban reconstruction'.[22] To this group, land taxation was a paradigm of how they hoped taxation would develop in the future. It was central to the thought of men like Hobson and Hobhouse that each factor of production – land, labour and capital – had a 'necessary' return from any enterprise, but could also extract an unproductive 'surplus' above this, through use of an unfairly favourable bargaining position.[23] This surplus was really the property of the community and could be taxed without interfering with the process of production. This argument could be applied to the surplus accumulated by both land and capital, but a tax on the increment in land values was an easily identifiable starting point. It already had widespread support in the Liberal Party and the analogy could be extended to capital once a land tax was in place. As the *Nation* (as *The Speaker* had become in March 1907) put it

> The true nature of 'unearned' income is . . . most plainly recognised when we turn to the movement for reform of local taxation. . . . But it is not only in the creation of land values and rent that public activities enter. Other forms of property and incomes carry the impress of public energy and public needs, bearing values often far in excess of what is needed to evoke the ability and industry of the business and professional men who own this property and receive these incomes.[24]

The Liberals and land taxation, 1905–8

Support for some form of land taxation was thus vociferous and widespread within the Liberal Party when it took office in 1905. This support was reflected by the party's leaders, particularly Campbell-Bannerman, who assured C. P. Trevelyan that land taxation was one of those issues that should be 'kept well to the front'.[25] Indeed, it often made an appearance in his speeches, as for instance at Partick on 28 November 1905, when he called for 'a moderate application of the principles of site value taxation'.[26] Land taxers

---

21 Spender, *Life, journalism and politics*, i. 34.
22 *The Speaker*, 14 May 1904.
23 This argument is summarised in P. Clarke, *Liberals and social democrats*, Cambridge 1978, 51–2, and S. Collini, *Liberalism and sociology: L. T. Hobhouse and political argument in England, 1890–1914*, Cambridge 1979, 61–5.
24 *Nation*, 27 Apr. 1907.
25 Campbell-Bannerman to C. P. Trevelyan, 6 Oct. 1903, C. P. Trevelyan papers, MS 13.
26 *Times*, 29 Nov. 1905.

could, therefore, look forward with a good deal of hope to the new Liberal government which took office in 1905.

That the government failed to take any action to fulfil those hopes was not due to any diminution of enthusiasm once the Liberals took office. As early as February 1906 Asquith, the new chancellor of the exchequer, investigated the possibilities of introducing some form of land taxation.[27] But no immediate action could be taken. As Asquith told a deputation of land taxers on 26 February 1906, the first step would have to be a reform of the valuation system.[28] This was an essential preliminary, not a delaying tactic. Britain had no separate valuation of land, as distinct from the valuations of the combined worth of land and improvements carried out by local rating authorities. The separate value of the land alone would have to be obtained before any measure of land taxation could be introduced. Even the most committed land taxers accepted this situation and their parliamentary group set about drafting a valuation bill.[29] In the government, this task fell on the local government board, headed by John Burns, as it was responsible for all matters concerning the local rating authorities.

This prospect did not initially dismay the land taxers. Burns had been one of the sponsors of a bill on the subject in 1903.[30] In 1905 he insisted on the appointment of a parliamentary secretary to the local government board with detailed knowledge of site value rating, as the subject would probably have to be handled by his department.[31] In fact Burns's three deputies in 1905–8 – Runciman, Macnamara and Masterman – were all keen advocates of site value rating.[32] But no valuation bill appeared in 1907 or 1908. This was not because the government had lost interest in the matter. Both Campbell-Bannerman and Asquith put pressure on Burns to produce the necessary valuation bill.[33] Nor was the task impossible, as equivalent legislative proposals for Scotland showed. Enthusiasts for land taxation were particularly numerous among Scottish Liberal MPs and in March 1906 two of them, John Sutherland and Robert Laidlaw, introduced a bill to value Scottish land separately and impose a 2s. rate on site values.[34] The two Scottish law officers,

27 E. Hamilton diary, 28 Feb. 1906, E. Hamilton papers, MS Add. 48683.

28 Raffan, *Land values group*, 7–8.

29 *LV*, Apr. 1906, 214–15.

30 *LM* xi (1903), 114.

31 C. P. Trevelyan to M. K. Trevelyan, 13 Dec. 1905, C. P. Trevelyan papers, MS Ex. 20.

32 For Runciman see C. P. Trevelyan to M. K. Trevelyan, 18 Dec. 1906, ibid. MS Ex. 21. For Macnamara see G. Whiteley to J. Pease, 15 Jan. 1907, Gainford papers, Nuffield College Library, Oxford, MS 85. For Masterman see Masterman to H. H. Asquith, 13 Apr. 1908, Asquith papers, Bod. Lib., MS 11, fos 95–6.

33 C. P. Trevelyan to M. K. Trevelyan, 18 Dec. 1906, C. P. Trevelyan papers, MS Ex. 21; Asquith to J. Burns, 16 Apr. 1908, Burns papers, MS Add. 46282.

34 See *Hansard*, 4th ser., 1906, cliv. 741–804, for the second reading debate.

Tom Shaw and Alexander Ure, shared the backbenchers' views and the bill was referred to a select committee dominated by friendly Liberals.[35] It emerged as the land values (Scotland) bill, a government proposal to determine the capital value of all Scottish land. Introduced in 1907 and 1908, it was rejected, then amended out of all recognition, by the House of Lords.[36]

The situation in England was more complicated, but the difficulties were scarcely insurmountable. The first stumbling block was the chaotic nature of the existing arrangements for valuing land and improvements. The basic unit of valuation outside London was the poor law union, of which there were no fewer than 648. Each parish was valued by its overseer of the poor, who reported to an assessment committee of the parish's union. The committee then prepared a valuation list. These lists were usually out of date, both because new properties were not always added and because the lists rarely took account of fluctuations in property values. An additional source of confusion was that the boundaries of boroughs and counties which had to set their rates on the basis of the valuation, did not coincide with those of the poor law unions.[37]

Both Unionists and Liberals agreed that this system was inaccurate, time-consuming and open to widespread favouritism and abuse.[38] It is not surprising that Burns thought it incapable of producing a quick and reliable separation of land and improvement values.[39] The rest of the cabinet foresaw no great difficulties in remedying the situation, though, and pressing on towards some form of site value rating. Campbell-Bannerman promised a valuation bill for the 1907 session.[40] But Burns proved incapable of producing a bill both to reform the valuation machinery and to separate land and improvement values. He complained to his diary that any proposed changes 'touched vested interests land officials . . . authorities at every point' and work in his department proceeded at a snail's pace.[41] This was, perhaps, not surprising, given the conservatism and inefficiency of many local government board officials and Burns's inability to prod them into action.[42] It was not until 28 December 1907 that he was able to put a scheme to the cabinet.[43] Despite the proposal's lengthy gestation period, Burns only proposed to reform the valuation machinery. He suggested that local surveyors of taxes should produce a national valuation, with local authorities reduced to

---

35 Ibid. cliv. 771–8; clv. 1013.
36 Offer, *Property and politics*, 321; R. Douglas, *Land, people and politics: a history of the land question in the United Kingdom, 1878–1952*, London 1976, 139–40.
37 The valuation system is described in J. Burns, 'Valuation (England and Wales)', 28 Dec. 1907, cabinet papers, PRO, Kew, MS 37/90/114.
38 W. Long, 'Valuation', 24 Dec. 1901, ibid. MS 37/59/140.
39 Burns diary, entry for 31 May 1907, Burns papers, MS Add. 46325.
40 *Times*, 19 Dec. 1907.
41 Burns diary, entry for 30 Oct. 1907, Burns papers, MS Add. 46325.
42 K. Brown, *John Burns*, London 1977, 110–15, 124–6.
43 Burns, 'Valuation', cabinet papers, MS 37/90/114.

hearing appeals against the surveyors' decisions. Though Burns cheerfully stated that 'such a valuation would, in my opinion, best lend itself to any alteration which may subsequently be proposed in the basis of assessment and rating'[44] he produced no such scheme. No draft bill based on even the limited proposals of December 1907 was forthcoming for the cabinet to discuss until June 1908.[45] By then matters were being further confused by the attorney-general, Sir William Robson, who had been brought in by the cabinet to spur Burns into action. Robson and Burns could not agree on how to separate land and improvement values and how this should be related to the reform of the method of valuation.[46] With the cabinet mired in the details of their controversies, Asquith had no option but to announce, once again, in October 1908, that there would be no valuation bill that session.[47]

These delays produced irritation among Liberal backbenchers and local councillors and apoplexy among the committed single taxers.[48] Most of their wrath descended on Burns, who was, C. P. Trevelyan declared, 'simply a Tory on the question'.[49] In fact, an impasse had been reached. The government remained committed to the idea of site value rating which had widespread support across the party. But, by the autumn of 1908, the complexity of the subject, combined with the inefficiency of Burns, meant there was still no prospect of any early action on the subject. The cabinet had tried to make him act, but the subject was not so pressing that Burns was removed or over-ridden – as he was over unemployment in 1908.[50] Site value rating was popular with many Liberals, but the mechanics of local government finance was far too abstruse an issue to constitute a pressing matter of public debate. Moreover, if Burns had produced a bill, it would certainly have been rejected by the Lords, as Scottish land valuation legislation was in 1907 and 1908. This would have enraged committed Liberals, but judging by the public's indifference to the fate of the Scottish valuation bills it would not have transformed the significance of land taxation. In 1908 the outlook for the issue seemed bleak.

The 1909 budget and the land issue

This situation was only transformed when the taxation of land values was taken up by Lloyd George, the new chancellor of the exchequer. During 1908 he had become aware that there would have to be increases in taxation in the

44 Ibid. p. 12.
45 Burns to Asquith, 20 June 1908, Burns papers, MS Add. 46282.
46 Compare W. Robson, 'Valuation bill', Sept. 1908, Harcourt papers, MS 576, with J. Burns, 'Valuation bill', 10 Oct. 1908, cabinet papers, MS 37/95/122.
47 *Hansard*, 4th ser., 1908, cxciv. 320.
48 Ibid. clxxxiv. 764–6.
49 C. P. Trevelyan to M. K. Trevelyan, 18 Dec. 1906, C. P. Trevelyan papers, MS Ex. 21.
50 Brown, *Burns*, 141–4.

1909 budget.[51] Typically, Lloyd George made the decision to use this situa-tion as an opportunity, rather than see it as a problem. He determined to produce a budget that would revive the government's fortunes by its boldness and radicalism. This meant developing a strategy whereby he would not only raise general taxes like income tax but also devise taxes to assail the Liberals' enemies. The brewers were prime candidates for this role, but so were the landowners. In 1906–8 the Lords had repeated their tactics of 1892–5 in rejecting bills of concern to Liberal activists but not to the public. Measures on education, licensing, plural voting and Scottish land had all met their end at their lordships' hands. As in 1892–5 the party was united in its anger at the aristocracy. But the government's poor record in by-elections seemed to indi-cate that Balfour and the Lords had chosen their ground well. Lloyd George was not prepared to accept this situation and determined to carry the attack to the Lords.

As early as 5 September 1908 Lloyd George wrote to Sir Robert Chalmers, head of the Inland Revenue, that he was considering a land tax for his budget and by December 1908 he had fixed on a $1d./£$ tax on all land, to be paid by the occupier, but deducted from the rent.[52] Though this was a modest begin-ning, it would necessitate a new national land valuation, which Lloyd George proposed should be carried out by the Inland Revenue. This might, in turn, prove the starting point for future attacks on landlordism. During cabinet discussions in February and March 1909, however, this relatively simple scheme was transformed into three complex and cumbersome duties. Most of the cabinet were worried by the practical effect of the chancellor's radicalism and would not allow land taxation to affect agricultural land or small property owners, or allow occupiers to deduct the tax from rent where this would break existing contracts to pay all rates and taxes. As the budget wound its way through the Commons the taxes became even more involved, as Lloyd George attempted to exclude owner-occupiers, builders, smallholders and market gardeners from their scope.[53]

Despite his difficulties Lloyd George was determined to press on and there could soon be little doubt that he had managed to revolutionise the role of land taxation in British politics. First, by proposing a national land tax and valuation he cut the whole subject free from the toils of the local government board and the complexities of reforming the finance of local authorities. Second, by placing his proposals in the budget, Lloyd George guaranteed land taxation's place in the government programme and he and his colleagues assumed that they had placed the taxes beyond the reach of interference by

---

51 This situation is outlined in Murray, *Budget*, 117–47.
52 Lloyd George to Sir R. Chalmers, 5 Sept. 1908, and Chalmers to Lloyd George, 3 Dec. 1908, Inland Revenue papers, MS 73/2.
53 Murray, *Budget*, 149–71, 183–6.

the House of Lords.[54] The log-jam that had held up the implementation of land taxation was broken. But, even more importantly, Lloyd George transformed the significance of land taxation. By putting the land taxes at the forefront of his hugely ambitious budget, which carried all the hopes of the Liberal government, Lloyd George put the land issue at the heart of political controversy. To confirm this, he carried out a number of oratorical assaults on British landowners during the course of the budget's progress through the Commons. The violence of his language, at Limehouse and Newcastle in particular, was unprecedented from a cabinet minister, but it was carefully calculated. It meant that the House of Lords would be faced with humiliation when it passed the budget. Its authority as a bulwark against radicalism would be destroyed and Liberalism would have scored a great victory.

The Unionists certainly found the land taxes the most hateful part of the budget and held them up in the House of Commons for twenty-two days.[55] So distasteful was the budget to most Tories that it became increasingly clear that the Lords would take the risk that Salisbury had declined in 1894 and reject the finance bill. This action, unprecedented in two hundred years, provoked a constitutional crisis. But it also had the effect of swallowing up the issue of land taxation inside the question of the role of the House of Lords. After a brief heyday in the summer of 1909, the land issue was demoted to make way for the constitution at the centre of politics. The Liberals had no option, if they wanted to remain a party of government, but to dissolve parliament and fight an election on the House of Lords and its power to veto legislation. The centrality of this question in the ensuing election of January 1910 was obvious to all, with at least 96 per cent of candidates referring to the Lords in their election addresses.[56]

But, despite this outcome, the budget did still transform the significance of the land issue in politics. First, the Liberal performance in by-elections picked up markedly once the budget was introduced and the land taxes received much of the credit for this improvement.[57] As Lloyd George said, 'We wanted something to rouse the fighting spirit of our own forces. This the land proposals have undoubtedly succeeded in doing.'[58] Increasingly, many Liberals came to believe that the land issue might be a vote-winner among significant sections of the electorate. This analysis was confirmed by the experience of many leading politicians from all sides in the 1910 elections. Prominent Unionists like Lord Salisbury, Acland Hood, Jack Sandars, Lord Balcarres and Austen Chamberlain all warned that land taxes had been

---

[54] The older view, that Lloyd George set a trap for the Lords, 'now finds little favour': G. Searle, *The Liberal Party: triumph and disintegration, 1886–1929*, London 1992, 86.

[55] Murray, *Budget*, 209–35.

[56] Blewett, *Peers*, 317, table 15.4.

[57] Murray, *Budget*, 188.

[58] Lloyd George to J. A. Spender, 16 July 1909, J. A. Spender papers, BL, MS Add. 46388, fos 201–4.

popular in the big conurbations, particularly in London, the West Riding and Lancashire.[59] In December 1910 Unionist candidates were urged not to campaign for the repeal of the taxes and generally to say as little as possible on the matter.[60]

In addition, Unionists found it difficult to justify the actions of the land-owners in the Lords. In rejecting the budget, they laid themselves open to the charge of acting selfishly by refusing to contribute to expenditure on social reform and naval expenditure. They also appeared to be acting in contraven-tion of the constitution of which they were allegedly the guardians. Peers who campaigned in January 1910 on the defence of the Lords' powers and the role of their class generally had a poor reception.[61] In December 1910 the Union-ists were driven to portray the Lords in the unlikely guise of defenders of the referendum in an effort to offset their unpopularity.[62] The result was not just that the role of landowners in the Lords became of central importance but that both Unionists and Liberals believed that the assault on the landlords had helped the Liberals remain in power.[63] The Liberals had won by making 'The Peers versus the People' seem more significant than Tariff Reform.

It is difficult to emphasise how important these developments were for the land issue. Before 1909 'the land' had been a matter of concern for certain sections of the Liberal Party, mainly those from rural England and those inter-ested in reforming the rating system. In neither role had it been very successful. The events of 1909–10 put the land issue at the centre of politics for the first time, and though it was soon overtaken by the constitutional question, demonstrated that land reform could be popular on a broad elec-toral front. Moreover, the success of the Liberal assault on the House of Lords showed, again for the first time, that an anti-landlord policy could unite and enthuse Liberals and disconcert their enemies, if it was presented with suffi-cient skill.

However, the legacy of the 1909 budget for the narrower issue of land taxa-tion was less clearcut. By 1913–14 only £612,787 had been collected from the three land duties, while it was estimated the valuation would cost over £2 million.[64] Moreover, court cases had, by July 1914, totally suspended the collection of undeveloped land duty and partially suspended increment and

---

[59] Salisbury to Lord Selborne, 11 Jan. 1910, Selborne papers, Bod. Lib., MS 6, fos 33–9; Acland Hood to J. Sandars, 2 Nov. 1910, Balfour papers, MS Add. 49767, fos 21–2; Sandars to Balfour, 2 Oct. 1910, ibid. fos 1–4; *The Crawford papers: the journals of David Lindsay, 27th earl of Crawford and 10th earl of Balcarres, 1871–1940, during the years 1892 to 1940*, ed. J. Vincent, Manchester, 1984, 166–7, entry for 14 Nov. 1910; A. Chamberlain to Balfour, 29 Jan. 1910, Balfour papers, MS Add. 49736, fos 63–5.

[60] Sandars to Short, 24 Oct. 1910, ibid. MS Add. 49767, fos 13–17.

[61] Blewett, *Peers*, 114–16.

[62] Ibid. 171–5.

[63] Adonis, *Making aristocracy work*, 266–7.

[64] Murray, *Budget*, 296.

reversion duty.[65] In other words, land taxation did not seem to represent a significant new source of revenue. In addition, the land taxes did not seem to have stimulated the building industry. The Liberals' own land enquiry committee later admitted that the budget had, in fact, probably retarded house-building by making some property owners feel insecure, alerting mort-gagees to the slump in property values and making builders fear that their profits would be taxed.[66] Unionists were not backward in blaming local housing shortages on the budget.[67]

The high hopes of the single taxers had proved unfounded. On the other hand, the rating of site values had not been tackled in 1909 and for Liberals it remained an obviously appealing solution to the continuing financial prob-lems of local authorities. The national land valuation, started in 1910, also made site value rating much easier to introduce in the future and land taxa-tion generally seemed to have been popular in 1910. It remained a real possi-bility for a future Liberal government and the events of 1909–10 seemed to have assured land taxation of first place in the Liberal approach to the land question. A major shift in policy would be required to overturn this priority.

Town planning and land reform

Ironically, the seeds of just such a shift were being sown at the same time as land taxation was reaching the peak of its importance. By 1909 it was begin-ning to become clear how the urban land issue could be linked to the devel-oping concept of town planning. The connection between housing and 'the land' had been slow to develop. But this was because housing did not become an important political issue until the Edwardian era. Although concern at the state of British housing had reached a climax in the mid-1880s, this should not disguise the fact that the building industry, lightly regulated by local authorities, had been remarkably successful in providing housing for the growing urban population. Between 1851 and 1911 town-dwellers increased from 51 per cent to 79 per cent of the population, yet the building industry met the demand by providing nineteen million new homes.[68] From the 1870s onwards, as real wages rose and the price of building materials fell, the stan-dard of housing improved, though there were naturally great regional and local variations. Nevertheless, over most of England the single-family terraced house or cottage was established as the norm. Density per dwelling fell from 5.46 to 5.05 between 1881 and 1911 and dwellings designated as

---

[65] Anon., 'Finance bill 1920', n.d., Inland Revenue papers, MS 63/95.
[66] *The land*, ii. 82–3.
[67] *Budget taxes and the building industry* (Land Union pamphlet no. 117), London 1913.
[68] This and the following statisics are from J. Burnett, *A social history of housing, 1815–1985*, 2nd edn, London 1986, 140–5.

'overcrowded' were a small and declining minority of the housing stock – reduced from 11.2 per cent to 7.8 per cent between 1891 and 1911.

Local authorities had two roles. They issued by-laws, mainly under the 1875 Public Health Act, to regulate the minimum quality of housing, and they undertook a limited amount of slum clearance. However, they built very few units themselves, even to rehouse those displaced by slum clearance. In 1914 less than half of one per cent of the housing stock had been built by local councils.[69] Houses require land, sometimes from major landowners, but the success of the building industry in providing new homes seemed to show that there was no land 'shortage' and that landowners were not holding up urban development. The centre of towns, where slums were concentrated, usually had a wide variety of small land- and house-owners and this directed attention away from big landowners.[70] In the late nineteenth century, housing and the land issue were only really connected in London, which exhibited the unique combination of high-profile great landowners, the short leasehold system, high rates and particular concern about over-crowding.

Despite this general picture of success, though, problems remained and these became increasingly difficult for both people and politicians to tolerate at a time of rising expectations and improving living standards. Obvious blackspots of insanitary overcrowding remained in most towns and it was widely accepted, even by cautious groups like the Moderates on the LCC, that local authorities should continue their work of slum clearance and limited resettlement.[71] But, by the 1890s, criticism was also being voiced of the minimum standard of housing laid down by local authorities. The by-law housing regime produced a high density of houses per acre, built on a rigid, grid-like plan, without regard to aspect. Houses were usually narrow and dark and the norm still varied widely, from Tyneside's 'up and down' flat to Northampton's six-room house.[72]

If this situation was to be improved, a higher standard of housing had to be made available, but kept at a reasonable cost, to put it within reach of as many people as possible. Fortunately, it seemed that the growth of new working-class suburbs at the end of the nineteenth century offered an opportunity to provide just these conditions. Rising real incomes, a building boom and the development of cheap, mass public transport, particularly the electric and horse-drawn tram, allowed half a million new acres to be opened up for building between 1893 and 1908.[73] Suburban land was cheaper than that in

69 S. Merrett, *State housing in Britain*, London 1979, 26.
70 Burnett, *Housing*, 152–3.
71 Swenarton, *Homes fit for heroes*, 30.
72 The most trenchant contemporary criticisms are contained in R. Unwin, *Nothing gained by overcrowding*, London 1912.
73 A. Sutcliffe, *Towards the planned city*, Oxford 1981, 56; W. Ashworth, *The genesis of modern British town planning*, London 1954, 182.

city centres and thus allowed better quality houses to be built at affordable rents.

However, to allow this opportunity to be seized to the full, two problems had to be solved. First, new rules guaranteeing a better standard of housing had to be developed. Second, a method had to be found of preventing the rise in land values once a new area was opened for building wiping out the advantages of suburbanisation. Solutions to these difficulties were worked out at the turn of the century by an interlocked group of social reformers who coalesced into what became known as the town planning movement.

The best-known demonstrations of how housing in the new suburbs could be built to a higher standard were provided by the manufacturers W. H. Lever, George Cadbury and Joseph Rowntree.[74] All three men were active Liberals and social reformers. Between 1888 and 1902 they were all involved in constructing new housing estates, at Port Sunlight, Bournville and New Earswick, partly to house workers at new factory sites. These estates were intended, in varying ways, to provide examples of the kind of housing that should be built in the future. Most importantly, the estates were laid out according to an overall plan, with ample provision for gardens, parks and allotments. The straight rows and blocks of by-law housing were broken up by a variety of curves and squares to take advantage of the land. The crucial new feature was a low density of housing per acre, allowing houses more street frontage, windows and gardens.

These ideas were obviously capable of wider application and they received their most ambitious form in the plan of Ebenezer Howard to construct an entire 'Garden City'.[75] Though Howard was more a visionary than anything else his idea was taken up by Ralph Neville and Thomas Adams, two enthusiasts for housing reform. They secured the support of Lever and Cadbury and conferences were held at Port Sunlight and Bournville in 1901 and 1902 to formalise plans to construct the new town. The architects chosen for the task, Barry Parker and Raymond Unwin, were the same partnership that had built New Earswick.[76] Despite the grandeur of the scheme, nearly 4,000 acres in Hertfordshire were acquired in 1903 and work began. Letchworth Garden City became a tribute to the spirit of its pioneers and a superb advertisement for new ways of planning housing. But its troubled early history did not encourage further large-scale experiments. The garden city company paid no dividends. All the working capital disappeared in the provision of services and many of the planned features were never created. Financial problems forced the company to sell, not lease, its plots of land, and it lost overall control of architectural development.[77]

---

[74] W. Creese, *The search for environment: the garden city: before and after*, New Haven 1966, 110–203.
[75] E. Howard, *Tomorrow: a peaceful path to real reform*, London 1898.
[76] Sutcliffe, *Planned city*, 64–8.
[77] F. Jackson, *Sir Raymond Unwin*, London 1985, 70–1.

A more modest, but ultimately more influential, experiment was started in 1906 with the development of Hampstead Garden Suburb.[78] It grew out of the passionate determination of Henrietta Barnett, wife of Canon Samuel Barnett, to preserve part of Hampstead Heath from speculative development. Instead, she organised the purchase of the proposed building site and, on part of it, promoted the design of a new residential district, to accommodate all classes, embodying the ideals pioneered on estates like New Earswick. Unwin was again one of the architects and Cadbury and Lever were trustees for the debenture stockholders.[79] The suburb provided a practical demonstration of how new housing developments on the outskirts of cities might be planned in the future to a higher standard. The term 'town planning' to describe this movement was popularised by J. S. Nettlefold, the chairman of Birmingham housing committee, and a devotee of the new ideas.[80] T. C. Horsfall introduced British readers to the ways in which German local authorities were empowered to plan their new suburbs.[81] The obvious development of the town planners' ideas was to campaign to extend similar powers to English local authorities.[82]

However, housing reformers not only had to formulate rules to provide a higher standard of housing, they also had to prevent the rise in land values wiping out the advantages of suburban building. The method adopted was to entrust ownership of the land to the community before any development was started. At Bournville and New Earswick all the land was owned by trusts on behalf of the residents. At Letchworth and Hampstead, garden city companies owned all the land.[83] This simple idea meant that land could initially be offered for development at reasonable prices and later increments in land values could be ploughed back into the community in the form of better amenities and lower rates. Again, the obvious development of this plan was to suggest that local authorities should be empowered to buy up land on their outskirts and then offer it for development.[84] This idea linked town planning to the land issue, for it made the supply of affordable, good-quality houses depend on the ability of local authorities to acquire large tracts of land.

During the early 1900s the nascent town planning movement launched an energetic campaign to translate these ideas into legislation. Its main forum was the National Housing Reform Council (NHRC), set up in 1900 by the housing reformers William Thompson and Henry Aldridge, and soon joined by the most important advocates of town planning like Horsfall and

---

[78] B. Green, *Hampstead Garden Suburb, 1907–77: a history*, London 1977.

[79] Creese, *Garden city*, 227.

[80] Jackson, *Unwin*, 100. For Nettlefold's role in Birmingham see G. Cherry, *Factors in the origins of town planning in Britain: the example of Birmingham, 1905–14*, Birmingham 1975.

[81] T. Horsfall, *The improvement of the dwellings and surroundings of the people: the example of Germany*, Manchester 1904.

[82] See, for instance, W. Thompson in *The Speaker*, 23 July 1904.

[83] Swenarton, *Homes fit for heroes*, 9–11.

[84] *The Speaker*, 23 July 1904.

Nettlefold.[85] The council found its most sympathetic hearers in the Liberal Party, particularly those sections that were trying to develop new policies to deal with urban problems. As early as 1901 C. F. G. Masterman had told the Church Congress of the pressing need for

> placing . . . the environs of all our great cities within a radius of many miles under some central Board with powers to enforce certain conditions of development, such as broad avenues, wide streets, sites reserved for public buildings and churches, garden spaces, parks and playgrounds.[86]

The Speaker endorsed the ideas of the town planners wholesale in 1905 in its series of articles 'Towards a social policy'.[87]

Like all reformers, the lobbyists for town planning looked with some optimism to the new Liberal government of December 1905. Campbell-Bannerman fuelled these hopes in his omnibus election speech of 21 December, when he referred in passing to the need for local authorities to do more to 'promote orderly and healthy development on the outskirts'.[88] The NHRC, spearheaded by Nettlefold, immediately launched into a series of meetings with prominent Liberals.[89] Thompson and Nettlefold also used their appearance before a select committee on rural housing to impress their views on Liberal MPs interested in housing reform.[90] The campaign culminated in an NHRC delegation to Burns and Campbell-Bannerman on 6 November 1906.[91] The prime minister was genial but vague. Burns left the door open to possible future action, but generally he was not welcoming. This attitude reflected his dislike of many of the associates of the town planners. On a visit to Letchworth in October 1906 he had referred to its inhabitants as 'A picturesque array of cranks . . . foreman called them "monkey nuts and macaroni" . . . sandals, no hats, Liberty Ties etc'.[92] But his officials were also profoundly sceptical. The brief they drew up for their minister dismissed the need for, or practicality of, town planning.[93]

Fortunately for the advocates of town planning, Burns decided to draft a housing bill for 1907. Originally, it was intended to deal only with rural housing, which had long been a matter of special concern for Liberals. The

---

[85] Sutcliffe, Planned city, 61.

[86] L. Masterman, C. F. G. Masterman: a biography, London 1939, 45.

[87] 'Town development', The Speaker, 7 Jan. 1905.

[88] Times, 22 Dec. 1905.

[89] J. Nettlefold to C. P. Trevelyan, 2 Oct. 1906, C. P. Trevelyan papers, MS 16.

[90] Select committee on the housing of the working classes acts amendment bill, 1906 (H. of C. 376), 58, 129.

[91] The delegation's memorandum and the responses are preserved in H. Aldridge, The case for town planning, London 1915, 161–82.

[92] Burns diary, entry for 11 Oct. 1906, Burns papers, MS Add. 46324.

[93] Anon., 'Memorandum for 6 Nov. 1906 meeting', Housing, Local Government Board papers, PRO, Kew, MS 29/96.

LLRA had organised a conference on the matter as far back as 1897.[94] This concern stemmed not merely from worries over shortages of rural housing and the high percentage of dilapidated and insanitary cottages. It reflected the fact that many labourers lived in cottages tied to their jobs. It was felt that this system gave landowners and farmers an unacceptable degree of control over their labourers and was a crucial part of their state of 'feudal' dependence on their superiors.[95] Increasing the supply of non-tied cottages could be seen by Liberals as promoting the labourers' personal freedom as well as a matter of social reform. Rural Liberals were, therefore, willing to argue for a surprising degree of state intervention in this area of housing.

This was particularly so because little could be expected of private enterprise. The wages of agricultural labourers were so low that no speculative builder was prepared to construct cottages for them. Rural reformers therefore invested their hopes in strengthening the powers of local councils to construct cottages.[96] In 1906 the LLRA brought in a rural housing bill, entrusted to Frederic Mackarness, MP for Newbury, to accompany their land tenure bill.[97] Burns was sympathetic. He had a very low opinion of landowners – a 'coterie whose privileges were maintained by the subjection of the disinherited' as he informed his diary.[98] Moreover, he had circularised rural councils to see how many houses they were building as soon as he came into office.[99] Despite Mackarness's moderate place in the ballot, his bill was referred to a select committee with a majority of sympathetic Liberals. They concluded that the only way to encourage local authorities to build cottages was to transfer responsibility for housing from rural district to county councils and allow the public works loan board to lend them money at rates below those at which the Treasury could borrow – in effect a state subsidy.[100]

Burns may have been sympathetic to rural reform, but he was even more hostile to any form of 'dole'. He saw himself as 'adamantine in my injunction to arrest the flood of pauperism that has been let loose in recent years'.[101] Asquith, the chancellor of the exchequer, agreed with him. He described a policy of subsidies as 'objectionable and dangerous'.[102] The bill Burns prepared in March 1907 therefore only proposed to ease slightly the terms on which councils could borrow money. It did not even transfer rural housing to county councils, instead giving them powers to act in default by rural district councils.[103]

---

94 LLRA, *Proceedings of conference, 25 May 1897*, London 1897.
95 *The Speaker*, 5 Nov. 1904.
96 LLRA, *14th annual meeting*, London 1901.
97 G. P. Gooch, *Frederic Mackarness: a brief memoir*, privately printed, London 1922, 35.
98 Burns diary, entry for 3 Nov. 1906, Burns papers, MS Add. 46324.
99 Brown, *Burns*, 139.
100 *Select committee on the housing of the working classes*, 29, 36.
101 Burns diary, entry for 29 Mar. 1907, Burns papers, MS Add. 46325.
102 Asquith to Burns, 28 Feb. 1907, Housing, Local Government Board papers, MS 29/96.
103 'Draft of Bill 207–1', 16 Mar. 1907, ibid.

This response was seen as rather thin, even within the rarefied atmosphere of the local government board. Burns ordered his officials to comb through the records and see if they could come up with more measures that needed tidying up and might be tacked onto the bill.[104] It was this situation that gave Burns the opportunity and motive to tack on some town planning provisions as a makeweight.

The town planners certainly did their best to keep up the pressure on Burns and convince him that town planning would be a well-received innovation. Successful efforts were made to persuade the Royal Institute of British Architects, the Surveyors Institution and the Association of Municipal and County Engineers to endorse the principle of town planning.[105] On 1 May 1907 P. W. Wilson, MP for St Pancras South and *Daily News* journalist, introduced a Commons resolution on town planning, which received general approval.[106] Burns became convinced that he could strengthen his bill by including some town planning measures. By late March 1907 he had decided in principle in favour of the insertion of a suitable clause.[107] But, crucially, the measure did not provide for local authorities to purchase land on their outskirts, only to issue directives to builders about such matters as housing densities. By limiting the schemes of the town planners in this way, Burns, in effect, transformed their ideas into little more than an optional extension of the existing housing regulations and cut them free from any controversial attachment to the land issue.

His reasons were quite understandable. His officials had heartily disliked the plans for municipal land purchase that they had heard from the town planners on 6 November 1906, seeing them as a Trojan horse for land nationalisation.[108] But, probably more importantly, there was no evidence that the local authorities would welcome such a proposal at a time of increasing financial problems for them. Nettlefold had lobbied hard at the Association of Municipal Corporations to get its endorsement for town planning.[109] But when it sent a delegation to see Burns and Campbell-Bannerman on 7 August 1907, its proposals were noticeably modest. They did not include any plans for wholesale municipal purchase of suburban land.[110] Burns could feel justified in being cautious. After all, he was proposing a concept that was new to Britain and his bill could be seen as an experiment that might be extended later.

Following a lengthy gestation, Burns's bill was finally introduced into the Commons in March 1908. The town planning proposals appeared as part III

---

104 Sir S. Provis to A. Thring, 11 Dec. 1907, ibid.
105 Ashworth, *Genesis*, 180.
106 *Hansard*, 4th ser., 1907, clxxiii. 978–90.
107 Provis to Thring, 27 Mar. 1907, Housing, Local Government Board papers, MS 29/96.
108 'Memorandum', 6 Nov. 1906, ibid.
109 Nettlefold's report to the council from a committee on town planning, AMC minutes, 9 May 1907, 120, AMC papers, MS 30/72/37.
110 AMC minutes, 7 Aug. 1907, ibid. pp. 207–19.

of the bill. Councils were allowed, but not required, to plan new estates (not whole new areas), but only after a marathon exercise in local consultation and approval at two different stages by the local government board. There were no plans for councils to purchase land before it was developed.[111] These provisions were certainly a disappointment to the town planners. But they focused their criticisms on the optional nature of the proposals and the limited areas to which they were to apply.[112] It might be possible to move Burns on these points, although there seemed little hope of achieving municipal land purchase. But, generally, the town planning clauses were non-controversial. They seemed little more than an extension to the by-law regime in the hope of creating more estates like New Earswick or Bournville. The Unionists put up little opposition. Indeed, their main spokesman, Alfred Lyttleton, thought town planning would benefit landowners by allowing them to preserve and enhance the high-class tone of residential districts built on short leasehold land.[113]

However, the bill ran into considerable difficulties over its housing clauses. Burns had jumbled together a huge number of measures, amending and adding to previous legislation. Much of it was incomprehensible and badly drafted and many Liberals were deeply disappointed with its caution. As a result it ran into heavy weather in committee.[114] Burns and his deputy, Masterman, disagreed on how to handle the bill's critics and relations between them deteriorated, further hampering the bill's progress.[115] It was finally withdrawn after twenty-three sittings of the standing committee had failed to plough through the bill's clauses.[116] Reintroduced in 1909 it fared rather better and managed to reach the statute book before parliament was dissolved.

The new act's town planning provisions proved a modest success up to 1914. Seventy-four local authorities drew up 105 schemes, covering 167,571 acres.[117] Unfortunately, the cumbersome procedures laid down meant that only two schemes received final local government board sanction. All these plans covered single estates, not whole areas, and most were areas of middle-class housing. But the operation of the act proved that town planning could actually work. It had moved into the realm of practical politics and further developments could still be presented as a plausible method of achieving higher-quality housing at affordable cost.

111 The bill's provisions and progress are described in *LM* xvi (1908), 263–5.
112 See *Hansard*, 4th ser., 1908, clxxxviii. 988–1000, for Sir John Dickson-Poynders's comments.
113 Ibid. 5th ser., 1909, iii. 742–9.
114 Brown, *Burns*, 141.
115 Masterman, *Biography*, 107–8, 113–14, 121–3.
116 *Hansard*, 4th ser., 1908, cxcviii. 485–6.
117 Ashworth, *Genesis*, 191.

Unemployment and land reform

The return of large-scale unemployment in the early 1900s produced further calls to put men to work on the land as a solution – in the same way as it had in the 1890s. But the period from 1904 to 1908 was to prove crucial to the advocates of land colonies for the unemployed. On the one hand, they came the closest they had ever been to turning their ideas into reality. On the other, the land was decisively, and permanently, rejected as a solution to unemployment.

Two initiatives from the East End of London were instrumental in bringing land colonies to public attention. First, the Poplar board of guardians, under the influence of George Lansbury, and with the help of the radical American soap millionaire, Joseph Fels, acquired two farm colonies in Essex, at Laindon and Hollesley Bay.[118] Second, the warden of Toynbee Hall, Canon Samuel Barnett, with his assistant, William Beveridge, was able to reactivate the Lord Mayor's Mansion House committee and produce a scheme to send unemployed men to Hadleigh and Osea – colonies run by the Salvation Army and the Charrington family.[119] These local initiatives achieved national importance when Walter Long's Unemployed Workmen Act of 1905 set up regional committees to co-ordinate the relief work of local authorities and charities. The committees were empowered to use money from the rates to experiment with measures to relieve unemployment.[120]

In London the co-ordinating committee was the Central Unemployed Body (CUB) of which Lansbury was one of the most forceful members. He persuaded the CUB to set up a colonies committee and take over the management of Hollesley Bay. Lansbury planned to develop a series of self-supporting colonies of smallholders that would provide work and dignity for the unemployed and eventually the nucleus of a future socialist society.[121] However, the hostility of Burns at the local government board blocked these plans. In line with his general dislike of 'doles', Burns believed that Hollesley Bay was a 'costly and foolish experiment . . . a holiday for 250 men from London who degenerate and get soft by a process of coddling'.[122] His suspicions of Lansbury's schemes were confirmed by the outcome of the local government board's investigation of various East End poor law authorities, including Poplar board of guardians, in 1906.[123] The authorities were condemned for wholesale extravagance and incompetence. Burns refused to sanction the development of permanent smallholdings at Hollesley Bay in October 1906

---

118 M. Fels, *Joseph Fels: his life and work*, London 1920, 60–77.
119 J. Harris, *William Beveridge*, Oxford 1977, 109–10.
120 Ibid. 114.
121 G. Lansbury, *My life*, London 1928, 145–7.
122 Burns diary, entry for 13 Apr. 1907, Burns papers, MS Add. 46325.
123 Brown, *Burns*, 117–18, 124.

and Lansbury resigned in disgust from the colonies committee in February 1907.[124]

This decision marked the end of any serious hopes of introducing land colonies. Clearly Burns's personal dislike of Lansbury and hostility to 'pauperising' types of relief were crucial in blocking these schemes. But Burns faced relatively little criticism for his actions, compared to the opprobrium heaped on him over other matters, like land valuation. There was never any serious pressure from his colleagues or party to make him change his mind. This was because his decision reflected more than his own personal prejudices. Lansbury's advocacy had associated land colonies with both an extreme form of socialism and extravagance. Considerable evidence could also be produced to show that land colonies would be hugely expensive and ineffective. When Joseph Fels developed his own land colony at Maryland in Essex, for instance, it cost over £35,000 to convert the bare land into just twenty-one smallholdings.[125] The indefatigable William Beveridge concluded from his study of men sent to Hadleigh and Osea that, for most, it proved just another episode of casual work.[126]

Many impractical schemes have, of course, been pushed a lot further forward than land colonies. But the ease with which Burns brushed them aside showed the relatively weak nature of the support for them. They had no formidable pressure group to back them, like the single taxers or Liberals on local authorities who promoted land taxation. Their electoral appeal was not targeted in the same attractive way as the call for smallholdings. But, above all, land colonies did not have the same emotional appeal to Liberals that land taxation or smallholdings did. They were not a direct attack on landlords. Rather, they were part of the much more confused debate about unemployment. Few Liberals had any clear idea about how to tackle this question, or even whether it was the state's role to do so.[127] They preferred to concentrate on more straightforwardly partisan matters and hope unemployment would pass of its own accord.

By 1908, though, the fortunes of the government were reaching their nadir in terms of by-election results. This coincided with a sharp rise in unemployment.[128] There seemed a real possibility that tariff reform would sweep the country and the government out of office. The more energetic and imaginative members of the cabinet, particularly Lloyd George and Churchill, saw the need for the government to be seen to be doing something, rather than nothing, about unemployment. The schemes they chose to promote were labour exchanges and a limited measure of unemployment insurance.[129]

---

124 Harris, *Unemployment and politics*, 195, 197.
125 Fels, *Joseph Fels*, 77–80.
126 Harris, *Beveridge*, 112.
127 See idem, *Unemployment and politics*, 227, which notes the ignorance of most Liberal MPs about unemployment.
128 Blewett, *Peers*, 45–51.
129 This story is well-known: Harris, *Unemployment and politics*, 278–333.

Neither showed any interest in land colonies. This was partly because they remained under suspicion for extravagance and extremism after the events of 1906–7. But the remedies Churchill and Lloyd George promoted also flowed more naturally from their own departmental interests, while land colonies remained very much the responsibility of the local government board. After all, the labour exchanges administered by the CUB had not been a great success. Unemployment insurance was budgeted to cost £1 million *per annum*.[130] Past failure and cost were obviously not the only factors involved. Possibly, if Churchill had been at the local government board, rather than the board of trade in 1908–9, land colonies would have been tried once more.

However, the new measures worked out in 1908–9 gave the Liberals a new plan to deal with unemployment, in which land colonies had no place. This proved the end, in the pre-war period, of serious attempts to use the land as a solution to unemployment. Labour exchanges and unemployment insurance were not proved to 'work' as depression lifted in 1909–10 and did not return before 1914, but a new apparatus had been set up and the state's interests turned in a new direction. Perhaps most important, in the long run, the government had adopted a more limited, and feasible, approach to down-swings in the trade cycle. Rather than attempting to remove men from an overstocked labour market, it tried to help them through periods of temporary unemployment. This represented a more sophisticated appreciation of the difficulties of skilled and semi-skilled labour in the Edwardian period, and was certainly more realistic than trying to turn them into smallholders. Casual and under-employed labourers had less to gain, though they might have benefited from Lloyd George's development commission and its plans to undertake work like land drainage and afforestation that business would not develop.[131]

Since 1886 the Liberals had been an anti-landlord party. But that had always been only one element in their identity. In 1909–11 it became, for the first time, the party's most important appeal to the electorate, thanks to the House of Lords. The crucial debate in the two elections of 1910 about the role of the aristocracy concentrated on the role of the House of Lords. But any controversy about the place of landowners in politics and society drew attention to land reform. This was particularly the case in this period because it was the land taxation clauses of Lloyd George's budget which had provoked the whole crisis. For both parties attitudes to land taxation became an important symbol of their partisan identity and remained an intensely controversial political issue for the rest of the Edwardian era. Ironically, the land issue had become a central part of politics just as the Liberals' attempts to implement some parts of the traditional agenda of land reform, like smallholdings and

[130] Ibid. 202–5, 311.
[131] Ibid. 334–47.

land colonies, had ended in ignominious failure. Indeed, land taxation itself soon proved to be a futilely complex means of raising money. On the other hand, the new town planning movement was starting to show how land reform could be linked to concerns about housing. Thus the land issue, like much else in politics, was undergoing rapid transformation in 1905–10.

4

New Directions in Rural Strategy:
The Rural Land Report, 1912–1913

In the aftermath of the Liberals' failure in the English agricultural seats in the December 1910 general election, there was little evidence of new thinking about the party's relationship with rural society. Smallholdings remained at the centre of its approach. Liberal backbenchers continued to complain of the inadequacy of the 1907 Smallholdings Act, while Liberal ministers increasingly agreed with them in shifting the blame onto the inactivity of local authorities.[1] Lord Carrington contented himself with increasing the number of smallholdings commissioners and plans to stimulate co-operative societies among smallholders.[2] But in the first major post-1910 reshuffle, Carrington was demoted to the honorary office of Lord Privy Seal, as a preliminary to retirement. This was not a surprising decision. He was sixty-eight years old, in ill health, and had held the same office for nearly six years. The failure of the 1907 Smallholdings Act had destroyed his popularity with the Liberal backbenchers and press.[3] Moreover, his department was being paralysed by an embarrassing feud with his deputy, Sir Edward Strachey.[4]

After failing to lure Samuel to the board of agriculture, Asquith found the 'more vigorous head' he was seeking in Runciman.[5] As the scion of a shipping dynasty, Runciman knew little of agriculture, but he was a competent administrator who became well-respected in the Commons and agricultural press.[6] He was not, though, an innovator. When Lord Carrington visited his old department he was gratified to find all much as he had left it.[7] In particular,

---

1   See, for instance, the House of Commons deputation described in CD, entry for 6 Apr. 1911.
2   Ibid. entries for 5 Sept. 1910, 12 Apr. 1911.
3   Carrington was hurt by the dismissive way the Liberal press treated him on his retirement: ibid. entry for 23 Oct. 1911.
4   The origins of this dispute are obscure, but it was dominating Carrington's thoughts throughout 1911: ibid. entry for 5 May 1911.
5   Asquith to Crewe, 7 Oct. 1911, Asquith papers, MS 46, fos 191–2.
6   Samuel to H. Gladstone, 23 June 1912, H. Gladstone papers, MS Add. 45992, fos 267–72. A Unionist described Runciman as 'the best Minister of Agriculture we have had since the last man who knew nothing about it'.
7   CD, entry for 23 Feb. 1912.

Runciman shared the general Liberal view that obstruction by county councils lay behind the failure of the smallholdings movement.[8]

Providing Liberalism with a 'horizon': the origins of the land enquiry

This pattern was shattered by Lloyd George's first major excursion into rural
politics. In an interview with P. W. Wilson of the *Daily News*, published on
13 May 1912, he announced that 'It is the agricultural labourer on whom we
must concentrate attention' and went on to advocate raising the wages of
farm labourers to £1 per week. This represented an astonishing departure.
Hitherto, no senior Liberal figure had declared in favour of regulating agricultural wages. The whole thrust of Liberal policy had been to try to transform
the labourer into an independent producer. The newspaper interview also
meant an abrupt change of direction for Lloyd George. During most of
1911–12 he had been absorbed in the intricacies of his national insurance
legislation. Despite his village background and great success with anti-landlord propaganda in 1909–10 he had shown little interest in specifically rural
problems. However, the reasons behind Lloyd George's new initiative of May
1912 lay not in the countryside but in the increase in industrial unrest since
1911 and the deteriorating position of the Liberal government following its
great triumph with the Parliament Act.

The decisive incident propelling Lloyd George forward was the national
coal strike of March 1912. Faced with the prospect of widespread industrial
dislocation, the cabinet had reluctantly intervened to try to produce a settlement. The miners demanded a national minimum wage for all their members
– the famous '5 and 2'. Over the period 16–19 March 1912 the cabinet
decided on a compromise.[9] This involved setting up a series of joint boards to
determine minimum wages in different areas of the country, but without
laying down what the minimum figure should be. Eventually, this solution
was accepted and the strike petered out. Although the government insisted
this was an emergency measure to avoid industrial crisis it marked a momen-
tous step forward in state regulation of wages.[10]

Previously, the only wages legislation had been the Trade Boards Act of
1909. This, Churchill's initiative, had followed a campaign by an eclectic
coalition of women's organisations, individual politicians and social investigators, like Dilke and J. J. Mallon, and newspapers, particularly George
Cadbury's *Daily News*.[11] The act of 1909 had first used the method of wages

---

8 W. Runciman to C. P. Trevelyan, 13 Jan. 1912, C. P. Trevelyan papers, MS 28.
9 J. Pease diary, entries for 16–19 Mar. 1912, Gainford papers, MS 39.
10 See *Hansard*, 5th ser., 1912, xxxv. 1723–33, for Asquith's rather apologetic speech introducing the coal mines bill.
11 S. Blackburn, 'Ideology and social policy: the origins of the Trade Boards Act', *HJ* xxxiv
(1991), 43–64.

boards to raise the extremely low wages of largely female workers in trades like millinery and box-making. This legislation was in the tradition of public health laws and factory regulation rather than a conscious step towards intervention in wage bargaining in major industries.[12] The coal strike of March 1912 forced the Liberal government to apply the precedent of the Trade Boards Act in completely unforeseen circumstances. The considerable opposition to this course of action from men like Churchill, Morley and Pease was only overcome by Grey who 'pointed out with "irresistable" logic that there was no other course open, unless chaos, riots, bloodshed . . . and no Government could stand to one side and see such occurrences and ignore their responsibilities'.[13]

Most significantly, it was the settlement of the coal strike that made Lloyd George an enthusiast for the concept of the minimum wage. He had told Riddell as late as 15 February 1912 that he 'did not believe in the practicability' of Parliamentary regulation of wages.[14] But the experience of the coal strike made him into that policy's foremost advocate in the cabinet.[15] His mind was kept focused on this area by the ferment of debate on the minimum wage that the coal strike provoked in the Liberal press.[16] Further industrial disputes, especially the dock strike launched in May 1912, and the cabinet committee that was set up to enquire into the causes of industrial unrest also kept Lloyd George thinking along these lines. He became so convinced of the virtues of the minimum wage that, at the cabinet meeting of 12 June 1912, he argued that when employers' and employees' organisations in a trade agreed on a wage rate this should become a legally binding minimum.[17] This was far too much for more timid souls, like McKinnon Wood and Hobhouse, but Lloyd George did not pursue the matter. He had already embarked on another great scheme to widen the application of the minimum wage, by establishing it in agriculture.

This reflected Lloyd George's belief in the intimate relationship between agricultural and industrial wages. In a Commons debate on industrial unrest of 8 May 1912, Lord Robert Cecil had claimed that conditions for agricultural labourers were better than those for urban workers. Lloyd George had rebutted this statement, declaring that the reverse was the fact and it was worthwhile enquiring into whether the conditions in the agricultural communities did not react upon and tend to depress the wages of the labour

---

[12] See Churchill's memorandum, 'Trade boards bill', 12 Mar. 1909, 1, cabinet papers, MS 37/98/42.

[13] J. Pease diary, entry for 16 Mar. 1912, Gainford papers, MS 39.

[14] Lord Riddell, *More pages from my diary, 1908–1914*, London 1934, 38, entry for 15 Feb. 1912.

[15] Ibid. 47–9, entry for 24 Mar. 1912.

[16] See, for instance, the *Nation*, 20, 27 Apr. 1912.

[17] *Inside Asquith's cabinet: from the diaries of Charles Hobhouse*, ed. E. David, London 1977, 115, entry for 12 June 1912.

market in industrial towns.[18] Low agricultural pay led to migration to the towns, swelling the job market and lowering wages. Employers could fix low wage rates by reference to the prevailing rate for agricultural labourers. Thus a minimum wage in the countryside 'would be much the most effective way of improving the minimum wage in other industries'.[19]

This analysis of the relationship between industrial and agricultural wages was, no doubt, crude. But Lloyd George reflected a widespread and long-standing belief among Liberals that many industrial difficulties were due to the rapaciousness of landlords, who maintained their labourers in menial conditions. It had, after all, been a central point of Joseph Chamberlain's radical campaign in 1885 that an improvement in the lot of the agricultural labourer would redound to the benefit of the town-dweller.[20] It was essential for Liberals that this improvement should occur at the expense of the landlord. In 1885 his land was to be compulsorily acquired for allotments. In 1912 Lloyd George produced an even simpler idea. The required increase in the labourers' wages would come from a reduction in the rent the farmer paid to the landlord, an idea he outlined in conversation with his confidante, Sir George Riddell, on 27 May 1912.[21]

Lloyd George's May initiative was not only a response to the wave of industrial unrest of 1911–12. It was an attempt to focus the Liberal Party's energies on a further assault on the landlords. This tactic had paid off very well in 1909–10 – a point that did not escape hostile commentators. ' "When in doubt play land reform" is a maxim the Chancellor has followed more than once with advantage' as the *Daily Herald* observed.[22] The Liberal government certainly needed a new initiative to restore its spirits. In 1911–12 it faced a trough of unpopularity similar to that which it had experienced in 1907–8. By-elections had started to turn against the Liberals at the end of 1911. On 5 March 1912 South Manchester was lost to the Unionists on a swing of 10.8 per cent – a result that seems to have made a deep impression on Lloyd George.[23] In early 1912 the government did not seem to have any way of fighting the trend, for its next two years were pledged to Irish Home Rule and Welsh Church disestablishment. Though Herbert Samuel remarked, with commendable level-headedness, on the 'flatness' of opposition to Home Rule and the general political 'langour' in the country, few cabinet ministers believed either measure could do anything to improve the government's

---

[18] *Hansard*, 5th ser., 1912, xxxviii. 524.

[19] Lloyd George's interview, *Daily News*, 13 May 1912.

[20] A. Simon, 'Joseph Chamberlain and the unauthorised programme', unpubl. DPhil. diss. Oxford 1970, 240–3.

[21] Riddell, *More pages*, 63–4, entry for 27 May 1912.

[22] *Daily Herald*, 14 May 1912.

[23] Masterman, *Biography*, 234–5.

popularity.[24] As Lord Carrington tersely noted, 'There is little enthusiasm for Home Rule; Welsh Disestablishment is a very tame horse.'[25]

Lloyd George's original view was that both bills would be compensated for by the popularity of his national insurance legislation, completed in 1911.[26] However, it had soon become clear that national insurance was an electoral liability rather than a benefit. Lord Esher noted that 'The Insurance Bill is very unpopular. Like the Education Act of 1870 it will drive its authors from office at the next General Election. I saw Lloyd George in the House of Lords this evening and he fully realises his position.'[27] Masterman doubted whether national insurance would ever be popular.[28] The reasons for this were simple. Unlike old age pensions, national insurance required a direct contribution from those who were eligible for benefits. To the vast majority of the population earning under £160 a year this was the first direct taxation by central government they had ever known, even if it was '9d. for 4d'. This sort of imposition was particularly resented at a time of rising prices when working-class incomes were having difficulty keeping pace.[29]

A strategy based on the minimum wage therefore made sense, for it would both compensate the lower paid for the imposition of national insurance and tackle their concern over rising prices. Minimum wages also avoided the mistake of national insurance in demanding direct contributions from the low paid. They had the advantage of imposing few extra costs on the state, so that middle-class income tax payers need not be scared off by the prospect of rising taxes. As Lloyd George had explained to Riddell, he meant to make the landlord pay for the labourers' wage increases. This process would in turn raise wages in the towns. The increases in pay would be the material under-pinning for the 'horizon' Lloyd George wished to conjure up to inspire the Liberals.[30] This 'horizon' would be a final assault on the political, economic and social power of the landlords – a plea to Liberalism's middle- and working-class supporters of 1910 to rally round and finish the work begun with the destruction of the House of Lords's veto. By recreating the radical coalition against the landlords, Lloyd George hoped to repeat the conditions for the Liberals' electoral victories of 1910.

However, in the *Daily News* article of 13 May 1912 and subsequent conversations, Lloyd George had only presented the barest indications of a programme. Nor had he definitely committed himself to such thoughts as he

---

[24] Samuel to H. Gladstone, 23 June 1912, H. Gladstone papers, MS Add. 45992, fos 267–72.
[25] CD, entry for 29 Jan. 1912.
[26] A. C. Murray diary, entry for 6 Jan. 1912, Elibank papers, NLS, Edinburgh, MS 8814.
[27] Viscount Esher to O. Brett, 11 Dec. 1911, in *Journals and letters of Reginald, Viscount Esher*, ed. M. V. Brett, London 1934–8, iii. 75.
[28] Riddell, *More pages*, 54, entry for 27 Apr. 1912.
[29] T. R. Gourvish, 'The standard of living, 1890–1914', in A. O'Day (ed.), *The Edwardian age: conflict and stability, 1900–14*, London 1979, 13–34.
[30] Riddell, *More pages*, 76, entry for 2 July 1912.

had outlined. Before he could go further he wanted to know the views of Liberal authorities on land issues and then to see if events would prove his instincts correct. Fortunately for Lloyd George, a group of Liberal writers and intellectuals had started to meet to discuss their response to the recent industrial unrest. There were eight members of the group. Four – Joseph, Seebohm and Arnold Rowntree and the solicitor, E. R. Cross, were part of a circle of progressive Liberals based in York. The other four – H. W. Massingham, J. A. Hobson, L T. Hobhouse and Percy Alden – were all connected with the Rowntree-owned Liberal weekly, the *Nation*. On 20 May 1912 the group submitted a memorandum to the government outlining their preliminary ideas.[31] Among these was a general extension of the principle of the minimum wage, with transport and agriculture being covered by wages boards immediately. The memorandum provided confirmation of Lloyd George's views and a nucleus of people he could use to develop his programme further.

Two by-elections provided evidence that Lloyd George's guess that land issues would be an electoral asset was correct. The first of these was at Norfolk North-West on 31 May 1912. The Unionists had high hopes of winning this seat, based on the big pro-Unionist swing at South Manchester, a vigorous campaign against the insurance act and a strong local candidate.[32] Instead of being forced on the defensive, though, the Liberals attacked under the forceful leadership of their candidate, E. G. Hemmerde. He made 'the land' the centre of the Liberal campaign. Moreover, although a committed land taxer, he skilfully tailored his programme to an agricultural constituency by claiming that land taxes meant 'raising wages and solving the village housing problem' and by endorsing the programme of the labourers' trade union, which included extending wages boards to agriculture.[33] Lloyd George sent Hemmerde a carefully worded message of public support, calling for a 'thorough reorganisation of the land system'.[34] Hemmerde retained the seat for the Liberals, reducing the pro-Unionist swing to one quarter of that at South Manchester.

Lord Balcarres commented that the result would be construed 'as a proof that Lloyd George's recent excursion into bucolic problems is the only method of retaining the shires'.[35] The *Nation* claimed that 'The Coming Question of the Land' would sweep the Liberals to victory if the party would only officially espouse the strategy.[36] The prospect of rural gains was crucial to Lloyd George's plans. A 'forward' policy on the land would probably entail

31 Memorandum, 20 May 1912, LG, HLRO, C/21/1/17. See A. S. Rowntree to M. K. Rowntree, 16 Apr. 1912, T. Cadbury papers, Friends House, London, Temp. MS 647, for the origin of these discussions on 'the minimum wage and how to meet the just demands of labour to a fair share of the wealth of the country'.
32 *Times*, 21 May 1912.
33 Ibid. 24 May 1912.
34 Ibid. 30 May 1912.
35 *Crawford papers*, 276, entry for 2 June 1912.
36 *Nation*, 8 June 1912.

giving up any hope of recapturing the suburban support in south and central England that the Liberals had briefly won in 1906. However, it was doubtful that anything but the self-destruction of the Unionists could have won these areas again. But the English rural seats presented a possible area of gain. The Liberals had under-performed badly in these seats in 1910, winning only 30 out of 111, but Liberal victories in the countryside were not impossible.[37] The Liberals had done rather better in agricultural seats in the recent past in both 1892 (thirty-seven seats) and 1885 (fifty-four seats) as well as in the *annus mirabilis* of 1906 (seventy-four seats). Rural England was certainly a more plausible 'swing' area than Unionist bastions like the West Midlands and Merseyside.

The result at Norfolk North-West was reinforced by the Holmfirth by-election of 20 June 1912. In a mixed coalmining and textiles constituency, the Liberal retained the seat, beating off a strong challenge from a Yorkshire miners' union candidate and restricting the Unionist to a 2.1 per cent increase in his vote. The Holmfirth Liberals were committed land taxers and their candidate, Sydney Arnold, featured the land conspicuously among his election issues.[38] Lloyd George encouraged him with a, suitably vague, message urging the need to 'recast our present land system'.[39] P. W. Wilson in the *Daily News* proclaimed Arnold's victory at Holmfirth a triumph for 'land reform and the social policy of Mr Lloyd George'.[40] It was possible to draw the conclusion that land reform would be popular in urban as well as rural seats. More specifically, as H. W. Massingham wrote on 24 June, socialism was 'not a sufficient answer to a bold and definite raising of the standard of land reform'.[41] In other words, an increased Labour challenge in 1915 could be outflanked by convincing potential Labour voters that land reform was the central radical task and that the Liberal government would tackle the matter seriously.

Massingham was writing, as usual, with the benefit of inside information. Lloyd George had decided to develop his initiative of May 1912. Having obtained Asquith's approval, he called a meeting of the eight signatories of the 20 May memorandum, together with fourteen others he thought might prove useful.[42] The latter group included government confidantes, like Elibank, Isaacs and Masterman, rich Liberals willing to finance Lloyd George's projects, including Lever, Mond and Baron de Forest, newspapermen like C. P. Scott and a clutch of land 'experts', notably Richard

---

[37] See appendix.
[38] *Times*, 18 June 1912; T. W. Noble to C. P. Trevelyan, 4 Oct. 1912, C. P. Trevelyan papers, MS 28.
[39] *Times*, 20 June 1912.
[40] *Daily News*, 22 June 1912.
[41] Ibid. 24 June 1912.
[42] Riddell, *More pages*, 70, entry for 19 June 1912; B. S. Rowntree to O. F. Rowntree, 26 June 1912, B. S. Rowntree papers, Joseph Rowntree Foundation, York, MS 1via; A. S. Rowntree to M. K. Rowntree, 18 June 1912, T. Cadbury papers, Temp. MS 647.

Winfrey, Roden Buxton and E. G. Hemmerde. Lloyd George announced that he was going to embark on a great campaign to 'regenerate rural England'.[43] However, he would not proceed along the lines of Chamberlain's radical campaign of 1885. Chamberlain had acted without his colleagues' consent. His campaign had little coherence (most of its contents were abandoned during the course of the 1885 election) and it was based only on a series of articles in the *Fortnightly Review*. Lloyd George intended, on the other hand, to keep in touch with the most influential figures in the cabinet, especially the prime minister, and to launch a consistent programme, backed by extensive research. The obvious precedent was the tariff commission. However, Lloyd George wished the research for his campaign to precede its launch, unlike the tariff reform campaign of 1903. This, he hoped, would give the Liberals a decisive advantage by providing them with a head start in the ensuing debates.

Lloyd George revealed to those present at his breakfast that he wished a group of 'experts' to investigate the whole land question for him.[44] They would provide him with facts and arguments and recommend further policies to 'harmonize' already existing Liberal views on the land.[45] Lloyd George would then be armed with a set of policies to win over his fellow ministers, unite the party and, he hoped, sweep the country. On 27 June news of these developments appeared in the press and Lloyd George's latest initiative was under way, even while his national insurance legislation was struggling to achieve practical form.[46]

The structure of the land enquiry

From its inception it was plain that the land enquiry was Lloyd George's personal creation. It reported directly to him and he intervened at decisive moments to help it formulate policy. Its function was to develop and support the outline strategy he had sketched out in May 1912. Agricultural wages remained central. Technically, the enquiry had no relationship to the government or the Liberal Party. There was never any question of the cabinet giving it formal approval, and its work was discussed only in the most vague and off-hand way at cabinet meetings before October 1913.[47] However, Lloyd George was careful to keep the prime minister and influential colleagues like Grey, Haldane and Churchill informed of the enquiry's work.[48] This allowed

[43] B. S. Rowntree to O. F. Rowntree, 26 June 1912, B. S. Rowntree papers, MS 1via.
[44] Ibid.
[45] *Times*, 29 June 1912.
[46] Ibid. 27 June 1912.
[47] Lord Emmott diary, entry for 30 July 1912, Emmott papers, Nuffield College Library, Oxford, MS 2: J. Pease diary, entry for 23 July 1912, Gainford papers, MS 39.
[48] Riddell, *More pages*, 76, entry for 2 July 1912; Lloyd George to A. H. D. Acland, 8 Oct. 1912, LG, C/2/1/52.

it to work with the government's informal blessing, but not its interference. The arrangement was congenial to Asquith as he was not committed to any of the enquiry's possible conclusions – it remained Lloyd George's private venture.

The enquiry had no official relationship to the Liberal Party either. The NLF welcomed the establishment of the enquiry at its November 1912 conference, but it did not report to any party organisations, only to Lloyd George.[49] It does not even seem to have received funds from the Liberal war-chest. The enquiry had about seventy full-time employees and by 30 June 1913 had spent over £9,000.[50] This money seems to have come entirely from wealthy friends of Lloyd George. The biggest contributor may well have been Baron de Forest; the only other three donors who can be positively identified are William Lever, Joseph Rowntree and Sir George Riddell.[51]

The original plan for the structure of the investigation, as reported in the *Times* for 29 June 1912, was for the group who had met at the 'land breakfast' to constitute a 'larger committee', to whom the enquiry committee would report. This scheme was not followed and the 'breakfasters' were not called together again until they met for a celebratory meal just before the land campaign was launched.[52] Once the enquiry committee was at work, Lloyd George preferred to talk directly to its members and look for advice elsewhere on an *ad hoc* basis, rather than formally convene another committee. Welsh and Scottish matters were considered separately and the main enquiry confined itself to English affairs.[53]

The man chosen to chair the investigating committee was Arthur Acland. He was an old friend of the chancellor's – indeed he had helped Lloyd George run his first election campaign in 1890 and acted as one of the Welshman's sponsors when he took his seat.[54] Moreover, his prestige as an ex-cabinet minister reassured potentially hostile Liberals while his status as heir to a west-country estate gave some credibility to the idea that the enquiry was a fact-finding body, rather than an assault on landlordism.[55] Ill-health permitted Acland to play only an intermittent part in the committee's work

---

[49] Liberal Publication Department, *Proceedings of the annual meeting of the council of the NLF at Nottingham, 21–22 Nov. 1912*, London 1912, 49–50.

[50] 'Expenses', 30 June 1913, LG, C/15/1/8.

[51] B. S. Rowntree to Lloyd George, 26 June 1913, LG, C/2/2/23; J. St G. Heath to Lloyd George, 18 Mar. 1913, LG, C/2/2/5; Joseph Rowntree Social Service Trust, minute book, 8 July 1912, 22 Dec. 1913, Joseph Rowntree Reform Trust, York; G. Riddell to Lloyd George, 19 June 1912, Riddell papers, BL, MS Add. 62970, fo. 149.

[52] Lloyd George did, however, talk to some of them individually in September 1913, just before the land campaign was launched. See, for example, Lloyd George to C. P. Scott, 4 Sept. 1913, LG, C/8/1/9.

[53] *Times*, 29 June 1912.

[54] A. Acland, *A Devon family*, London 1981, 123–5.

[55] Even the rural report's severest Unionist critics had to admit their respect for Acland. See, for example, C. Adeane and E. Savill, *The land retort*, London 1914, p. ix.

and removed him entirely from its operations in the spring of 1913.[56] Though his influence was exerted consistently on the side of caution, not to say timidity, his colleagues were able to bypass him by appealing directly to Lloyd George.[57] Acland's most important contribution was to write a conciliatory and moderate introduction for the rural report – though even this was carefully vetted by J. A. Spender to ensure it conformed with the rest of the report.[58]

There were seven ordinary members of the enquiry committee. Ellis Davies and Ian Macpherson were allotted Welsh and Scottish affairs, respectively, and took little further part in the English rural enquiry.[59] In late July 1912 the committee assigned three of its members – E. R. Cross, E. G. Hemmerde and Baron de Forest – to study urban land problems and they too made little contribution to the rural report.[60] Richard Winfrey played a very small role in the enquiry's work. His only important contribution was to organise its investigations in the eastern counties.[61] Otherwise, he continued to concentrate his energies on politics in the Fens and Norfolk and the smallholdings movement, attending committee meetings infrequently.[62]

This left the final member of the committee, Seebohm Rowntree, as the biggest influence on the rural report. He was the only member of the enquiry with extensive experience of social investigation and he was prepared to devote several days each week to the enquiry's work.[63] Thus, it was not unnatural that he played the central role in deciding how the committee should carry out its work and in recruiting the staff.[64] His principal helper was the committee's honorary secretary, Roden Buxton. Buxton had the reputation of an expert on land reform, mainly because of his leading role in the Co-operative Smallholdings Society and its successor body, the National Land and Home League (NLHL).[65] It was decided as early as 8 August 1912 that Rowntree would write half the rural report – on housing, tenancy and agricultural development – while Buxton wrote the other half on wages, rates and land acquisition.[66] Though their drafts were subject to the approval of the

---

56 *The land*, i. p. lx.
57 R. Buxton to Lloyd George, 11 Aug. 1912, LG, C/2/1/6.
58 Spender, *Life, journalism and politics*, i. 159.
59 Heath to R. Buxton, 17 Aug. 1912, LG, C/2/1/9. Eventually, separate Welsh and Scottish land reports were issued in July 1914: I. Packer, 'The Liberal land campaign and the land issue, *c*. 1906–14', unpubl. DPhil. diss. Oxford 1994, 338–49, and 'The land issue and the future of Scottish Liberalism'.
60 Heath to R. Buxton, 17 Aug. 1912, LG, C/2/1/9.
61 R. Buxton to Lloyd George, 10 Aug. 1912, LG, C/2/1/5.
62 Winfrey, *Leaves*, 173.
63 A. Briggs, *Social thought and social action: a study of the work of Seebohm Rowntree*, London 1961, 65–7. Rowntree had already written *Poverty: a study of town life*, London 1901, and *Land and labour: lessons from Belgium*, London 1911, after extensive investigation.
64 R. Buxton to Lloyd George, 10 Aug. 1912, LG, C/2/1/5.
65 NLHL, *Annual report, 1911*, London 1911, 3.
66 R. Buxton to Lloyd George, 10 Aug. 1912, LG, C/2/1/5.

whole committee, this decision accurately reflected the overwhelming importance of Rowntree and Buxton in determining the contents of the report.

The two most important organisers of the enquiry's work were J. St G. Heath, the paid secretary, and Richard Reiss, head organiser of the rural enquiry. Heath's appointment reflected Rowntree's influence, for he was a previously unknown economics lecturer at Woodbroke, a Quaker college in Birmingham, in which Rowntree took an active interest.[67] Reiss was probably Buxton's choice as head organiser, as the two men had worked together in the NLHL, where Reiss chaired the housing sub-committee.[68] He had fought the Chichester division of Sussex for the Liberals in 1910 and on the basis of the knowledge gained there he was also made head investigator for the home counties.[69]

During July and August 1912, the quadrumvirate of Rowntree, Buxton, Heath and Reiss engaged the enquiry's staff and settled the form of its investigation.[70] A staff of sympathetic economists and social investigators was employed at head office to study official documents and reports. They worked in small groups assigned to different areas of investigation. Each person produced memoranda which were then discussed by their colleagues until agreement was reached.[71] The conclusions from printed sources were then combined with information supplied by local people filling in questionnaires about their own areas. This latter method had been pioneered by Rowntree himself in York and Charles Booth in London.[72] After much revision the questionnaire was divided into two schedules.[73] Schedule A asked for information on wages, housing and smallholdings in the parish of the informant. Schedule B covered land use, tenure and game over a wider area. The staff's work was then embodied in drafts of the report by Rowntree and Buxton, though they worked closely with a number of the head office employees, especially the economists Cleveland Stevens, Gerald Shove, R. B. Henderson and A. K. Ashby.[74] These drafts were then considered by the whole committee and sent to Lloyd George for comment.

Unionists protested vigorously about the enquiry's claim to 'get at the facts impartially stated' and with some justice.[75] There was particular resentment against the questionnaires, the source of all the enquiry's new information.

---

[67] Briggs, *Social thought*, 65.
[68] *Daily News*, 21 June 1912.
[69] R. Buxton to Lloyd George, 16 Aug. 1912, LG, C/2/1/8.
[70] R. Buxton to Lloyd George, 10 Aug. 1912, LG, C/2/1/5.
[71] M. Wilkinson (ed.), *E. R. Cross: a biographical sketch*, London 1917, 26.
[72] See Rowntree, *Poverty*, and C. Booth, *Life and labour of the people in London*, London 1902.
[73] R. Buxton to Lloyd George, 10 Aug. 1912, LG, C/2/1/5.
[74] Heath to Lloyd George, 8 Sept. 1912, LG, C/2/1/17.
[75] *The land*, i. 471, 478. This sentiment was expressed in schedules A and B, which are reprinted here as an appendix.

First, the evidence obtained in the schedules was not published in full, the report merely quoting from selected extracts. There was no way of knowing if these quotations fairly represented the information in the schedules. Moreover, as the names of those who filled in the schedules and the precise areas they were writing about were kept secret (to avoid 'intimidation') even the evidence quoted could neither be confirmed nor challenged.[76] It would seem, though, that almost all the schedules were filled in by Liberal sympathisers. The country had been divided, for the purposes of the enquiry, into twelve districts, each with a head investigator charged with selecting informants to fill in the schedules. Faced with the need to find hundreds of articulate correspondents with a detailed knowledge of agriculture, the head investigators usually turned to Liberal MPs and agents for help.[77] Attempts to entice Unionists to co-operate were met with sharp rebuffs and unwelcome publicity.[78] In other words, the enquiry's claim to present new information was based on quotations from selected extracts of anonymous reports filled out by local Liberals. It is not difficult to see why Unionists refused to accept the claim that the rural report was an impartial investigation of agricultural conditions.

The conclusions of the rural land enquiry

The rural report was substantially written by June 1913 and completed by mid-August 1913.[79] Its structure revealed the priorities laid down by Lloyd George in May 1912. The wages of agricultural labourers was the first subject tackled and the conclusions of this section formed the basis of the report's plans for the English countryside. Essentially, the chapter on wages sought to sustain Lloyd George's view that agricultural wages were unduly low, provide coherent arguments as to why they should be raised and produce a feasible scheme for bringing this about.

The first part of this project was the easiest. Simply by using the figures from the 1901 census and the 1907 board of trade statistics on wages it was possible to calculate that 60 per cent of agricultural labourers earned under 18s. per week for sixty hours work.[80] The careful presentation of this evidence was one of the report's greatest strengths. Even its most severe critics had to

---

[76] *The land,* i, p. xvii.

[77] According to the *Times,* 1 Aug. 1912, Ian Macpherson asked each Scottish Liberal MP to provide between twelve and twenty informants from his constituency. Grey nominated two informants from Berwick at the enquiry's request: Lloyd George to R. Buxton, 7 Oct. 1912, LG, C/2/1/51.

[78] See, for example, the *Times,* 11 Dec. 1912, where the duke of Somerset published the correspondence between himself and C. J. Cawood, head investigator in the West Country.

[79] Heath to Lloyd George, 9 June, 1913, LG, C/2/2/18; W. G. Evans to Lloyd George, 25 Aug. 1913, LG, C/2/2/44.

[80] *The land,* i. 7.

admit that agricultural wages were strikingly low – the best they could do was to claim that real wages were rising, albeit very slowly, and that the report had failed to take into account other forms of income for labourers, especially subsidised rents for their cottages.[81] However, with the fact of low wages accepted by virtually all commentators, it was they who were forced onto the defensive, for unless they produced schemes of their own to raise wages they seemed to be condoning a situation of terrible poverty. [82]

Once the fact of low wages had been established, the report spent little time in explaining why state action was needed to raise wage levels. Smallholdings and trade union organisation would take too long. The Trade Boards Act of 1909 and the Coal Mines Act of 1912 had shown that legislation could increase wages and England surely wished to remove this 'shameful . . . blot on its Religion and its Civilization'.[83] However, the report had to counter the criticism that state regulation of wages would harm the labourer, by leading to a casualisation of agricultural work and more land laid down to grass. To do this, the report could only oppose that it was not in the farmer's best interests to do either. Regular employment would continue because this was the farmer's only way of ensuring an adequate supply of efficient labour. Similarly, 'expert agricultural opinion' was cited as evidence that arable land was more profitable than pasture, though only two 'experts' were quoted – Charles Bathurst and Edward Strutt.[84]

It was clear from the start of the enquiry that it would recommend wages boards as the mechanism to raise agricultural wages. On 6 July 1912, the *Daily Chronicle* reported that 'no special prophetic gift' was required to foresee this conclusion. Wages boards had worked in the 'sweated' industries and the coal mines. Both the agricultural labourers' trade union and the NLHL advocated their extension to agriculture.[85] The only disagreement was over whether the government or some other central authority should set a national minimum wage or whether local wages boards should have discretion to vary wage rates to suit local conditions. Some radical Liberals, like L. T. Hobhouse and the *Daily Chronicle*'s special commissioners on rural matters, felt that a national minimum would be too arbitrary.[86] To catch up with the north, pay rises in the south of England would have to be so large that farmers would be bankrupted. However, if the door was opened to these arguments, the wages boards might not order any substantial wage increases at all. Lloyd George had seemed to favour a national minimum figure in his interview with the *Daily News* on 13 May 1912 and Rowntree supported this opinion in some of his

---

81 See, for instance, Adeane and Savill, *Retort*, 5–11.
82 Land Conference, *The land problem*, London 1914, 17–18.
83 D. Lloyd George, 'preface', 3, in B. S. Rowntree, *The labourer and the land*, London 1914.
84 *The land*, i. 51–4.
85 *LL*, 31 May 1912; NLHL, *Annual report, 1911*, 6.
86 *Manchester Guardian*, 6 Oct. 1913; *Daily Chronicle*, 1 Oct. 1912.

publications.[87] Eventually, a compromise was reached. The report stated that while each board should fix a wage 'at such a sum as will enable the labourer to keep himself and an average family in a state of physical efficiency' it recognised that this might not be achieved immediately in each area.[88] No specific figure was mentioned – probably a wise decision not to give hostages to fortune.

In contrast to the wages question, that of the housing of agricultural labourers had been completely ignored by Lloyd George when he conceived the land enquiry in May 1912. This was, however, a matter of deep and long-standing concern to Liberals involved in rural politics. Following the 1906 select committee's recommendation of a state subsidy for council building in rural areas this policy had become the favoured option of rural radicals. The NLHL adopted it as its policy.[89] It was endorsed by the *Daily News* on 20 September 1912 and the *Daily Chronicle* on 30 September 1912. On 2 July 1912 Lord Strachie, the former Liberal parliamentary secretary to the board of agriculture, told the rural district councils conference at Guild-ford that subsidies represented the only way forward on rural housing.[90]

Not unnaturally, there was a good deal of support for this policy inside the enquiry. Reiss and Buxton had written in support of it to the *Daily News* on 21 June 1912. But state subsidy of rents also aroused considerable opposition inside the Liberal Party. This was clearly revealed when the House of Commons debated the Unionist Social Reform Committee's (USRC) housing of the working class bill on 15 March 1912.[91] Among its provisions was a clause proposing state grants in aid of rural and urban house-building. John Burns set his face firmly against this system of 'doles' and 'charity rents'. His most telling point was to label state grants 'a bonus to employers in aid of low wages', i.e. if the government subsidised rents then farmers could go on paying low wages to their labourers, and high rents to their landlords.[92] This argument persuaded even Liberals who were strong proponents of state action on housing, like Christopher Addison and J. Allen Baker, to vote against the bill.

The minimum wage initiative offered a possible way to avoid this division in the Liberal ranks. If the wages of agricultural labourers were raised by legis-lation, then they would be able to afford a high enough rent for both private builders and councils to construct housing for them at a reasonable return. This neat solution was suggested as early as 4 July 1912 by the Liberal MP, A. W. Black, in a letter to the *British Weekly*. Once the enquiry actually began work, though, it became obvious that matters were a little more complicated.

---

87 Rowntree, *Labourer and the land*, 26–7.
88 *The land*, i. 47.
89 NLHL, *Annual report, 1912*, London 1912, 1.
90 *Daily Chronicle*, 3 July 1912.
91 *Hansard*, 5th ser., 1912, xxxv. 1413–96.
92 Ibid. xxxv. 1488.

The enquiry had little difficulty establishing that rural housing conditions were appalling – they had only to quote the available evidence from medical officers of health, diocesan social service committees and the investigations of the 1906 select committee.[93] Their calculation that 120,000 cottages were needed to make up the shortage of habitable dwellings was more controversial as it was extrapolated purely from the replies to schedule A, but since no other body had carried out a more comprehensive survey, it was difficult to refute definitely.[94] Developing a policy to deal with the situation was more troublesome. The enquiry was forced to conclude that while it was hoped that wages boards would raise wages enough to allow the labourer to pay an 'economic' rent in the future this could not be expected straight away. The enquiry's initial response was to propose giving councils a state subsidy to build cottages. The subsidy would be gradually withdrawn as wages rose. To make this more palatable to Liberals who suspected landlords would ultimately benefit from this 'dole', the subsidy would come from a national tax on land values.[95] This ingenious scheme soon foundered, though. Opinion in the enquiry turned against the idea of a subsidy as too expensive and inimical to the concept of an 'independent' labourer.[96] The taxation of land values was the province of the urban enquiry and it had not decided on a policy before the rural report went to print.[97] On 10 July 1913 the *Times* reported that the enquiry's chapter on rural housing was still in 'embryo' and its policy 'inchoate'.

This situation was resolved by the intervention of Lloyd George. In a conference with the leading figures in the enquiry at Walton Heath he proposed that the wages boards should include a sum sufficient to cover an 'economic' rent in the labourer's wage award.[98] This became the enquiry's policy. Rural district councils would then be cajoled into building cottages by a new central authority and the threatened withdrawal of their state grants if they failed to act. But the enquiry did not make it clear what would happen if agricultural wages could only be raised gradually. In this case they would be unlikely to reach a level at which labourers could pay an 'economic' rent for some time. It was unclear whether there would be no cottage building until wages reached this level, or whether local authorities or the state would subsidise rents. The report effectively avoided rather than solved the problems of rent subsidies and wage levels.

The next main section of the report dealt with smallholdings. This third place ranking reflected how this approach to rural problems had been down-

93 *The land*, i. 92–107.
94 Ibid. i. 131–3.
95 R. Winfrey, memorandum, 27–30 Sept. 1912, in *Great men and others I have met*, Kettering 1943, 25–6.
96 *Times*, 10 Jan. 1913.
97 B. S. Rowntree to Lloyd George, 25 Aug. 1913, LG, C/2/2/48.
98 R. Buxton to Lloyd George, 17 July 1913, LG, C/2/2/31.

graded by Lloyd George's espousal of the minimum wage. The chancellor had become sceptical of the worth of smallholdings, as he revealed in his conversations with C. P. Scott.[99] This was scarcely surprising given the failure of the policy under Lord Carrington. But the rural report was careful to conceal Lloyd George's scepticism. The failure of the 1907 act was once more put down to the hostility of the county councils, even though the report had to admit that very few labourers had applied for smallholdings.[100] High rents for smallholdings were cited as evidence of this demand among labourers, though elsewhere in the report high rents were put down to the cost of equipping smallholdings.[101] This highly dubious analysis was followed by a series of policies to increase the supply of smallholdings, including a land court to fix the price of the land the county council had to acquire and enforce security of tenure and a 'fair' rent for all smallholders.[102]

Continued enthusiasm for the shibboleth of smallholdings in the face of the failure of the 1907 act and the new policies on housing and wages requires some explanation. It partly reflected the continued enthusiasm for smallholdings among many Liberals.[103] The new minimum wage strategy could be presented as a less startling innovation if, as the report claimed, it was the essential step towards the success of the existing smallholdings policy. Higher wages would give labourers more capital and incentive to set up as smallholders.[104] The continued place of smallholdings in the report also reflected a widespread belief among progressive Liberals that the transformation of English agriculture into a system based on smallholdings was still an ultimate ideal.[105] To Rowntree this meant 'the breaking up of what is left of the feudal system and the beginning of a social order based on the co-operation of free men'.[106] The emphasis of the rural report on wages and housing placed this ideal far in the future, though.

After dealing with smallholdings the rural report turned its attention from the labourer to the farmer. The primacy of the minimum wage meant that the Liberals' main appeal would be to the labourer, but the enquiry was determined not to lose what support the Liberals retained among the farmers and, if possible, to increase it. In this the report was merely following the strategy of Lord Carrington in 1905–11 and the Liberal governments of 1892–95. But it was particularly important for the enquiry to develop policies that would appeal to the farmers, as the Unionists were making an assault on the Liberals' residual position with this group through their policy of 'occupying

---

99   C. P. Scott diary, entry for 3 Feb. 1913, C. P. Scott papers, BL, MS Add. 50901, fo. 89.
100   *The land*, i. 193, 218–27.
101   Ibid. i. 212–17.
102   Ibid. i. 229.
103   See Sir J. Jardine to Carrington, 27 Jan. 1906, Lincolnshire papers, MS Film 1137, for Jardine and Molteno's enthusiasm for smallholdings.
104   *The land*, i. 37–38.
105   For example, L. T. Hobhouse in the *Manchester Guardian*, 8 Oct. 1913.
106   Rowntree, *Labourer and the land*, 47.

ownership'. A revival of land prices caused by the modest return to agricultural prosperity after 1900 had allowed some landowners to sell off outlying portions of their estates to clear debts, or invest in more profitable enterprises. This development caused mounting concern among English tenant farmers, as the sale of an estate automatically involved notice to quit for all tenants.[107] Some Unionists were quick enough to respond by promoting schemes to provide state loans with which farmers could purchase the freehold of their farms, should their estate be put up for sale.[108] This policy received an unexpected boost when the Haversham committee, set up by Lord Carrington to examine the matter, reported in favour of a state loans scheme.[109]

The land report revealed the seriousness of the position for the Liberals. Of the tenant farmers questioned 60 per cent admitted to feeling insecure about their tenure and there was 'undoubtedly a considerable body of opinion among tenant farmers in favour' of the Unionist policy.[110] The enquiry's response was to launch an attack on the Unionist plans. It claimed that if the farmer were lent the whole of the price the landlord was asking for the farm he would be saddled with a crippling mortgage and crushed if agricultural prices should fall again. Yet, if the advice of the Haversham committee and some Unionists, like Jesse Collings, was followed, and the state ensured loan repayments did not exceed the previous rent paid, then the state would be subsidising both the farmer and the landowner. No government could or would agree to this.[111]

The other part of the enquiry's response was to provide an alternative policy to reassure farmers. This involved setting up a land court to give tenant farmers complete security of tenure.[112] Justification for this startling change in the English land system was provided by appropriating the arguments of a group of Unionist agriculturists, headed by Christopher Turnor and Charles Bathurst. They had devoted a number of books to claiming that England could profitably produce much more of the agricultural goods it consumed.[113] The enquiry endorsed this conclusion and added its own that 'under-cultivation' was the result of farmers' insecurity of tenure. Once English farmers felt secure they would invest more and agricultural production would

[107] This process is ably outlined in Thompson, *Landed society*, 316–26.

[108] The fullest exposition of this policy is J. Collings, *The colonisation of rural Britain*, London 1914, i. 53–82. The Unionist candidate made much of this in the Norfolk North-West by-election: *Times*, 28 May 1912.

[109] *Report of the departmental committee appointed to inquire into the position of tenant farmers on the occasion of any change in the ownership of their holdings and to consider whether any legislative change is desirable*, 1911–12 (Cd 6030), 12–15.

[110] *The land*, i. 309, 324.

[111] Ibid. i. 326–32.

[112] Ibid. i. 323.

[113] C. Bathurst, *To avoid national starvation*, London 1911; C. Turnor, *Land problems and national welfare*, London 1911.

rise. This speculative argument was only supported by quotations from replies to schedule B.[114] Answers claiming that substantial damage was done to crops by game were also used to support this argument on 'undercultivation'. The report claimed that only the shadow of eviction prevented farmers from dealing with this menace and agricultural yields would rise once they could take effective action.[115]

The next section of the report went on to extend the Liberal appeal to the farmers. It argued that there could be no genuine security of tenure unless land courts subjected rents to judicial review. Otherwise, landowners could force out tenants they disliked by imposing massive rent rises and discourage investment by tenants by raising the rent whenever a farmer's own improvements increased the profitability of the farm. Thus judicial rents were represented as the logical outcome of security of tenure.[116] In fact Lloyd George had included land courts to fix rents in his original conception of a land policy in May 1912, as part of his plans for a minimum wage.[117]

Lloyd George realised that his minimum wage concept was pure loss to English farmers. It would be far better to pass this loss on to the landlord by setting up a land court to reduce the farmer's rent whenever he could show that increased wages would leave him in financial difficulties. As early as July 1912 it was widely predicted that this idea would occur in the rural report.[118] All the enquiry did was to extend this policy. It recommended that all smaller farmers should be able to apply for a rent reduction at any time. Larger farmers could apply when their wage bill rose and whenever their rent was increased or there was a downturn in agricultural prices.[119] This scheme had a major flaw, however. It was widely believed by land experts that most English farms were let at below the rent they could command if the tenancy were auctioned. The Surveyors Institution believed that this applied to between 50 per cent and 75 per cent of English farms.[120] The enquiry had, therefore, to go to extraordinary lengths to produce a formula to allow land courts to reduce rents, rather than being compelled to increase them. The whole idea of a commercial rent had to be rejected, in favour of a 'fair' rent, based on what the land yielded plus a 'reasonable' remuneration for the farmer.[121] Whether this would reassure farmers that their rents would not be raised must remain open to doubt. But this sort of formula did reveal that the whole thrust of this part of the report was to turn the landowner from an active participant in agriculture into a passive receiver of a much reduced rent. By

114 *The land*, i. 313–18.
115 Ibid. i. 277–81.
116 Ibid. i. 365–6.
117 Riddell, *More pages*, 63–5, entry for 27 May 1912.
118 *British Weekly*, 4 July 1912.
119 *The land*, i. 382–3.
120 Adeane and Savill, *Retort*, 129.
121 *The land*, i. 383.

breaking the economic link between farmer and landlord, the report hoped to break the political link and overturn the Tory tradition of English farmers.

The preceding parts of the report contained almost all of its recommendations. Part IV concerned rural rating but it did not outline any policies, merely stated some grievances. This reflected the fact that rating was being dealt with by the urban enquiry which had not reached any conclusions when the rural report went to press.[122] Part V was in many ways the weakest part of the report. Hastily cobbled together by Seebohm Rowntree in June and July 1913,[123] it dealt with largely non-controversial matters involving technical help to agriculture – mainly co-operation, credit, transit and education. The aim of this section was presumably to bolster the impression that the report was a serious examination of how to improve English agricultural productivity. Yet, so hastily had it been thrown together that it failed to make a single recommendation. The reader was merely referred to government reports and existing measures.

The rural land report was contentious in many of its methods, but it represented a formidable elaboration and justification of Lloyd George's sketchy ideas of May 1912. With the rural enquiry behind him he could be far more confident of carrying the cabinet and the party with him. The central idea in the report was the minimum wage. Lloyd George had transferred this idea from an industrial setting, but when applied to rural England it provided a direct and attractive method of appealing to agricultural labourers. It also provided the basis for a wide-ranging attack on every aspect of the economic and political power of the rural landlord. However, Lloyd George was aware that whilst this attack fulfilled the wishes of many urban Liberals, it could be only one component of his attempt to win urban votes. The material interests of the town-dweller would have to be catered for as well. This much more difficult matter was left to the long-delayed urban report.

[122] B. S. Rowntree to Lloyd George, 25 Aug. 1913, LG, C/2/2/48.
[123] Heath to Lloyd George, 4 July 1913, LG, C/2/2/26.

5

New Wine in Old Bottles:
The Urban Land Report, 1912–1914

When Lloyd George had initially formulated his ideas for a new land policy in May–June 1912 he had envisaged that the restructuring of rural society would appeal to the urban population as well. A minimum wage for agricultural labourers would, he argued, gradually raise the wages of town workers too.[1] An attack on the privileges of landlords would unite the whole of society, urban as well as rural, behind the Liberal Party.[2] However, there were good reasons for doubting whether this approach would work. In 1885 Joseph Chamberlain had attempted a similar gambit (with allotments in place of the minimum wage) and had failed to win even a majority of the English boroughs for Liberalism.[3] Moreover, the land issue had acquired a number of urban manifestations that had engaged the attention of the Liberal government between 1906 and 1910. These areas could scarcely be ignored in any wide-ranging enquiry into land problems, but they also offered opportunities to make 'the land' appeal directly to the interests of the urban population.

The organisation of the urban enquiry

In fact, the incorporation of urban land issues within the scope of the enquiry became apparent in a rather haphazard fashion as soon as Lloyd George began to organise it. On 19 June 1912 he mentioned in passing to Riddell that his land courts idea could be extended to deal with urban leaseholds.[4] On 5 July 1912, after the enquiry held its first meeting, the *Daily News* confidently predicted that land acquisition and town planning would come within its field of study. As soon as the members of the enquiry began to organise their work during July 1912 it became clear that a serious investigation of any of these complex issues would require a separate urban enquiry to run parallel with the rural enquiry.[5] To perform this task, three of the five members who

---

1 Lloyd George's speech in the House of Commons, *Hansard*, 5th ser., 1912, xxxviii. 524
2 See the *Daily News*, 22 June 1912, following the Holmfirth by-election.
3 The Conservatives won 116 English borough seats to the Liberals' 109.
4 Riddell, *More pages*, 70, entry for 19 June 1912.
5 *Manchester Guardian*, 25 July 1912; *Daily Chronicle*, 30 July 1912; Heath to Lloyd George, 17 Aug. 1912, LG, C/2/1/9.

dealt with English affairs were designated to form the urban sub-committee: E. G. Hemmerde, Baron de Forest and E. R. Cross.

Hemmerde, who had just won the Norfolk North-West by-election in which 'the land' had figured prominently, was the only representative of the enthusiastic land taxers on the enquiry.[6] Initially, it seemed he might prove an awkward colleague, intent on pressurising the other members of the enquiry into accepting the doctrines of Henry George. With Wedgwood, he played a crucial role in arranging R. L. Outhwaite's candidature in the Hanley by-election of July 1912 and the land taxing campaign that engulfed the constituency.[7] Moreover, in a number of aggressive public speeches, he sought to browbeat any opposition to this policy inside the Liberal Party.[8]

However, Hemmerde was not an incorrigible rebel and oppositionist of the stamp of Wedgwood or Outhwaite. He had accepted the lucrative office of recorder of Liverpool in 1909 and had hopes of becoming solicitor-general.[9] This, indeed, was why he both was asked and agreed to serve on the enquiry. Public campaigning might have some influence on the committee but if the land taxers held out for their full programme and refused all co-operation with the enquiry, they would be isolated and might achieve less than by a judicious balance of compromise and pressure. Hemmerde was at pains, therefore, to prevent a complete break between the enquiry and the land taxers. He stated repeatedly that his policy and that of his associates was not the single tax but the demands enshrined in the memorial to Asquith and Lloyd George presented on 18 May 1911.[10] This called for local authorities to be empowered to levy a rate on site values and for a national land tax to allow the abolition of the food duties and contribute towards rate relief. Hemmerde also made it clear that the land taxers should not rule out other policies from a land campaign, including the minimum wage, which was anathema to more fanatical single taxers.[11]

There were, however, a number of factors that limited Hemmerde's influence on the enquiry. None of his colleagues quite trusted him. Even Heath, the committee's paid secretary, who was fairly sympathetic to the land taxers' case, wrote of Hemmerde 'I do not want him to be responsible by himself without the steadying influence of Mr Cross for the report on rating.'[12] More-

---

[6] *Times*, 29 June 1912. For the by-election see ibid. 21–30 May 1912.

[7] Midland Liberal Federation, minutes of executive committee, 31 July 1912, Midland Liberal Federation papers, University of Birmingham Library, Birmingham, MS 10/1/2, fos 198–204, contains the report of W. Finnemore, the federation's secretary, on this affair.

[8] See *Times*, 19, 20 July 1912, for his speeches to the annual meeting of the English League for the Taxation of Land Values and at a dinner given by the land values group in his honour.

[9] R. Heuston, *Lives of the Lord Chancellors, 1885–1940*, Oxford 1964, 259.

[10] See his letter in *Times*, 23 July 1912. For the memorandum see LG, C/15/1/4.

[11] Compare Wedgwood's letter to the *Westminster Gazette*, 25 June 1912, denouncing the minimum wage, with Hemmerde's conciliatory letter of 28 June 1912.

[12] Heath to Lloyd George, 17 Aug. 1912, LG, C/2/1/9.

over, his attendance at committee meetings was erratic, largely due to the demands of his law practice.[13] This fact was not unconnected with another matter of imponderable importance in Hemmerde's relations with the enquiry – the chaotic state of his personal finances. In 1909 unwise stock exchange speculations had threatened him with bankruptcy. He had to be bailed out by the Liberal whips and by a collection among MPs of several thousand pounds, organised, ironically, by Horatio Bottomley.[14] In return, Hemmerde had to give up his safe seat in December 1910 to fight Portsmouth, at the request of the whips.[15] On his return to parliament in 1912 his finances were still insecure.[16] It must remain a matter of speculation how far these events compromised Hemmerde's willingness to create serious trouble for the enquiry if it failed to adopt a policy acceptable to the land taxers. In fact, his influence on the committee's deliberations seems to have been minimal.[17] Despite the enquiry's very limited endorsement of land taxation he accepted its conclusions without demur and did his best to persuade other land taxers to do the same. Lloyd George was able to congratulate himself on his appointment. 'Hemmerde was specially helpful. That's what comes of meeting troubles in advance', he wrote to his wife.[18]

The other MP on the urban sub-committee, Baron de Forest, proved far more difficult. De Forest was the representative of the land nationalisers, though scarcely a prominent figure in that group.[19] Indeed, when elected to parliament in 1911 he had been classified as an extreme land taxer.[20] The reasons for his appointment probably lay in his vast wealth and his friendship with Lloyd George and Churchill.[21] De Forest made no significant impact on the urban report and he seems rarely to have attended the committee's meetings, possibly through ill-health and commitments abroad.[22] However, when in August 1913 he found drafts of the rural report not to his liking, de Forest

---

[13] Ibid.

[14] Davies journal, 1904–11, E. W. Davies papers, MS 6, fo. 140; W. Churchill to C. S. Churchill, 2 Nov. 1909, in Churchill, *Churchill*, ii, companion vol. ii. 916–17; CD, entry for 23 Feb. 1910.

[15] Davies journal, 1904–11, E. W. Davies papers, MS 6, fo. 140.

[16] See F. Neilson, *My life in two worlds*, Appleton, Wisc. 1952–3, i. 306–7, for Hemmerde's financial status in 1911–12 and their collaboration on the West End play, *A butterfly on the wheel.*

[17] Davies journal, 11 Nov. 1913, E. W. Davies papers, MS 7, fo. 96.

[18] D. Lloyd George to M. Lloyd George, 10 Sept. 1913, Lloyd George papers, NLW, Aberystwyth, MS 20432C.

[19] *Times*, 29 June 1912.

[20] UCTLV, *Annual report, 1911–12*, London 1912, 47. Neilson, *Two worlds*, i. 300–2, claims it was he who converted de Forest to this doctrine. By 1912, though, de Forest was an equally convinced land nationaliser: R. Buxton to Lloyd George, 18 Aug. 1912, LG, C/2/1/10.

[21] For de Forest's unusual background and wealth see A. Allfrey, *Edward VII and his Jewish court*, London 1991, 132–3. For his relationship with Lloyd George and Churchill see Churchill, *Churchill*, ii. 156–8,

[22] De Forest to Lloyd George, 17 Apr. 1913, Lloyd George papers, MS 22525.

was allowed to tack a memorandum onto the end, advocating immediate steps towards land nationalisation.[23] Lloyd George was reluctant to agree to this, but he was finally persuaded by the hope of further financial contributions from de Forest and the fear he would do his best to disrupt the enquiry if he did not get his way.[24] In fact, this concession did not stop de Forest making public attacks on the enquiry while he was still a member of it – he even wrote to the *Daily Citizen* to complain that Labour was not doing enough to attack the land campaign.[25] But he was too isolated and eccentric a figure to mobilise widespread opposition in the Liberal Party. His only ally in his attacks on the rural report seems to have been Josiah Wedgwood, the equally maverick single taxer.[26]

The non-attendance of his two irascible colleagues left the whole burden of the urban enquiry on E. R. Cross.[27] Cross was a Scarborough solicitor and convert to Quakerism, who owed his appointment to his links with the Rowntree family – he had handled a great deal of legal work for Joseph Rowntree, Rowntree and Company and the various Rowntree Trusts and he was the chairman of directors of the Rowntree-owned *Nation* newspaper.[28] He set about collecting information using broadly the same methods as were used on the rural enquiry. In this he was assisted by a group of sympathetic 'experts' who had been recruited to study the already existing evidence on the urban land issue.[29] Some of the more significant were Gerald Shove, a young economist, Adrian Lumley, a rare example of a Liberal land surveyor, and John Orr, a writer and researcher for the land taxation movement.[30] On the latter subject the enquiry relied on the expertise of Edgar Harper, head of the land valuation department at the Inland Revenue.[31] The technical and highly complicated nature of subjects like site value rating, the leasehold system and housing legislation meant that the urban enquiry had to lean more heavily on expert advice and published sources than its rural counterpart, as was acknowledged in the preface to the urban report.[32]

The urban enquiry collected new evidence through schedules sent out to correspondents in various towns across the country, though London was investigated separately by a special committee, headed by Lumley.[33] As with

[23] *The land*, i. 445–70.
[24] B. S. Rowntree to Lloyd George, 4 Oct. 1913, LG, C/2/3/15.
[25] *Daily Citizen*, 7 Nov. 1913.
[26] J. Wedgwood to H. Wedgwood, 10 Nov. 1913, J. Wedgwood papers, University of Keele Library.
[27] Heath to Lloyd George, 17 Aug. 1912, LG, C/2/1/9.
[28] Wilkinson, *E. R. Cross*, 3–12.
[29] Heath to Lloyd George, 8 Sept. 1912, LG, C/2/1/17.
[30] Ibid. Davies journal, entry for 4 Dec. 1912, E. W. Davies papers, MS 7, fos 68–9.
[31] See R. Buxton to Lloyd George, 3 Oct. 1912, LG, C/2/1/49, for the committee's deference to Harper's expertise, and Sir M. Nathan to Heath, 6 Dec. 1913, LG, C/6/6/5 for their reliance on him to interpret statistics.
[32] *The land*, ii, p. xxix.
[33] Ibid. ii, p. xxiv.

the rural enquiry, the vast majority of these informants were committed Liberals.[34] However, the questions in the schedules were so complex that the committee insisted on appointing wherever possible local surveyors, architects or solicitors, who would have a professional grasp of the subjects involved.[35] Once this evidence was returned to the committee's headquarters, it was collated with the findings from published sources and written up, in much the same way as for the rural enquiry. The chapter on land valuation, though, relied very heavily on predictions as to the effects of various different schemes of site value rating. These figures were obtained by the Inland Revenue's valuation department on the instructions of Lloyd George, who, as chancellor of the exchequer, was its departmental head.[36]

The most striking difference between the rural and urban reports was that the urban report took more than five months longer to produce.[37] This was not because Lloyd George regarded the urban enquiry as less significant than the rural enquiry. He was worried by its slow progress and urged the committee to greater efforts on numerous occasions.[38] The problem lay in the brief which the urban enquiry had been given. From the start, those organising the rural enquiry had known the main lines of policy that they had to secure evidence and arguments to support – a minimum wage for agricultural labourers, rent courts for farmers and more smallholdings.[39] But the urban enquiry's only preconceived policy was a form of land court to extend the rights of leaseholders. Cross had no indication from Lloyd George of the direction he might follow on housing and rating.[40] This made it much harder for him to know what sort of information he should be collecting. The initial schedule A had to be followed by a further schedule B 'after some months' and supplemented by *ad hoc* discussions with local officials and 'supplementary enquiries'.[41]

Local informants were also 'difficult to find'.[42] On 18 August 1912 Roden Buxton had to admit that the list was so far 'meagre'.[43] This was because the enquiry needed, not only Liberals, but Liberals who were professionally qualified to handle urban land issues. But professions like surveying and land agency were not noted for their pro-Liberal leanings. Indeed, the Surveyors

---

[34] Heath to Lloyd George, 9 Aug. 1912, LG, C/2/1/4.

[35] *The land*, ii, p. xxiv.

[36] Heath to Lloyd George, 30 Oct. 1913, LG, C/2/3/30.

[37] The rural report was published on 15 Oct. 1913. The urban report finally appeared on 2 Apr. 1914.

[38] For example, R. Buxton to Lloyd George, 18 Aug. 1912, LG, C/2/1/10, where Buxton replies to the chancellor's criticisms.

[39] This was predicted in *Times*, 4 July 1912.

[40] Ibid. The only prediction made as to urban land policy was of land courts for leaseholders.

[41] *The land*, ii, p. xxvi.

[42] De Forest to Lloyd George, 15 Aug. 1912, LG, C/2/1/7.

[43] R. Buxton to Lloyd George, 18 Aug. 1912, LG, C/2/1/10.

Institution spent much of 1912–14 producing anti-land enquiry propaganda.[44] Even enthusiastic Liberal surveyors were put off by the arduous and unpaid work involved in filling in the enquiry's schedules.[45] Moreover, once informants had been found, they took much longer than their rural counterparts to fill out the questionnaires. On 14 September 1912 H. E. Crawfurd, head organiser of the urban enquiry, reported that only five schedules had been filled in and returned.[46] Considerable time was needed to answer questions on levels of housebuilding or the distribution of various forms of housing tenure, and schedules on such matters took months to evaluate. Schedules A and B covered 249 towns, or 58 per cent of urban England. Deducing, for instance, a housing policy from these statistics was a task that overwhelmed Cross. In addition, the entire section on land taxation was halted once it was decided that figures were needed from the Inland Revenue valuation. These did not become available until late November 1913.[47]

However, all the material for the other parts of the urban enquiry had been collected by August 1913.[48] With the rural report substantially written, Rowntree and Heath were able to turn their attention to urban matters. In just over two months, they, together with Cross, formulated the entire urban programme, except for the land taxation section. In late August 1913, Rowntree started sorting through the evidence for the housing chapter.[49] On 17 October he had a 'very scrappy' statement ready for Lloyd George and on 8 November at Middlesbrough the chancellor was able to announce an outline housing programme.[50] Yet the evidence for the housing chapter was not in sufficient order for it actually to be written up until late February 1914.[51] If the housing chapter required a further four months to write, this suggests that when the crucial policy decisions were taken in August–November 1913 much of the evidence that the enquiry had collected could not yet have been analysed. In these circumstances, Rowntree and his colleagues had to rely on their own preconceptions and the advice of 'experts'. As a result, some of the crucial areas of the urban report, particularly the housing chapter, were obviously derived from already existing programmes. The original use of new evidence was confined to the land taxation chapter, which represented a clear break with previous Liberal thinking.

---

[44] For example, memorandum of the Council of the Surveyors Institution, July 1912, quoted extensively by the Unionist committee on land taxation in 1912: Steel-Maitland papers, SRO, Edinburgh, MS GD 80/3/1.

[45] De Forest to Lloyd George, 15 Aug. 1912, LG, C/2/1/7.

[46] H. E. Crawfurd to R. Buxton, 14 Sept. 1912, LG, C/2/1/29.

[47] Sir M. Nathan to Lloyd George, 22 Nov. 1913, LG, C/6/6/3.

[48] B. S. Rowntree to Lloyd George, 25 Aug. 1913, LG, C/2/2/48.

[49] B. S. Rowntree to Evans, 18 Aug. 1913, B. S. Rowntree papers, MS BSR93/XI/1/31.

[50] B. S. Rowntree to Lloyd George, 17 Oct. 1913, LG, C/2/3/19; Times, 10 Nov. 1913.

[51] B. S. Rowntree to J. Rowntree, 30 [sic] Feb. 1914, B. S. Rowntree papers, MS 6(a).

The conclusions of the urban report: housing

The first chapter of the urban report dealt with housing. This was the central element in the report's attempt to provide and justify a programme of urban land reform that would be both practical and popular with the urban working class. If the urban report did not quite promise 'Homes for Heroes' it did attempt to show how better housing could be provided for all the working class. Housing legislation was not, of course, new in Britain.[52] But no political party had previously made housing the central theme of its political appeal. This is what the urban report set out to do in its attempt to prove to the majority of the urban population that land reform could provide them with direct, practical benefits.

The enquiry began by dividing working-class housing into three groups.[53] The first was designated the 'parlour house', occupied by the upper 20 per cent of the working class, typified as a semi-detached house with a garden. Such houses were deemed adequate. Remedies were required for the other two groups. The largest of these consisted of the 70–75 per cent of the working class housed in the 'workman's cottage'. The final 5–10 per cent of the working class lived in 'slums'. These final two groups were treated separately from each other and different solutions were advanced to improve their housing conditions. The vital distinction was a simple one. The enquiry reckoned that those housed in the 'workman's cottage' could afford to pay a sufficient rent to provide an economic return on the dwellings they inhabited. Those in the 'slums' could not.[54] Appropriate adjustment and stimulation of the housing market would provide better housing for the first group. Like the agricultural labourers, the second group required more drastic measures.

The enquiry found two faults with the existing 'workman's cottage' type of housing. The first concerned its quality. Houses were too close together, too small, sanitation was inadequate, they were built in long drab rows without regard to aspect and a high percentage had structural faults. This was scarcely new information, as the enquiry's extensive quotations from the reports of medical officers of health and various social and housing reformers showed.[55] More controversially, the report also claimed that there was a widespread shortage of this class of housing, a shortage which could not be remedied under the existing system of speculative house-building.[56] The report claimed that the 'normal' level of house-building always lagged behind demand, but the Edwardian era had seen the onset of a serious crisis in the housing market. Builders' profits were squeezed by rising interest rates and increases in the cost of building materials. At the same time, rents could not rise to compensate for

---

52 Burnett, *Housing*, 140–5.
53 *The land*, ii. 7–9.
54 Ibid.
55 Ibid. ii. 9–45.
56 Ibid. ii. 59.

this as working-class incomes were stagnating. Investors were increasingly unwilling to sink money in housing when gilts, joint stock companies and local authority bonds all provided better and faster returns.[57]

Historians have differed on how convincing a portrayal this was of a building system in crisis. Avner Offer, concentrating on the role of increasing rates, is inclined to agree. Martin Daunton, on the other hand, sees the Edwardian 'building crisis' as merely a normal down-swing in the building cycle, that would have been reversed.[58] Whatever the case, the urban report is a poor witness for a general shortage of housing of the 'workman's cottage' type. The schedules had not originally been framed to ask this question and 128 'supplementary' forms were sent out to remedy the deficiency.[59] Ninety-two of the replies were categorised as 'reliable' and these split fifty-five to thirty-seven for the existence of such a shortage. This was scarcely a conclusive verdict and suggested a pattern of regional diversity rather than a general trend. But as the enquiry wished to propose a drastic expansion of the state's role in housing provision, it would greatly strengthen their case if they could prove that the existing system of housing provision had irretrievably broken down.

The central problem the enquiry addressed was how to provide better housing for dwellers in 'workman's cottages', without greatly increasing the cost of this housing and putting it beyond the reach of the bulk of the working class. A massive expansion of direct housing provision by local authorities was ruled out. The urban report stated that large-scale council building 'will not be adopted in the lifetime of the present generation'.[60] Nor did it regard this as necessary, whether to stimulate building, improve quality or cheapen rents. Rather, the report proposed to do all this through a partnership between local authorities and private builders.[61] It proposed that local authorities should be given a duty to provide adequate housing for the working class in their area. To fulfil this duty they would be required to draw up preliminary town plans outlining the development of new suburbs. They would be empowered to purchase compulsorily land in these areas, at its current use value rather than its building value, develop it and lease it to private builders or public utility societies to construct new housing. Local authorities would also be empowered to develop new forms of transport, such as electric trams and light railways, between the town centre and the new housing areas. All this new development would prove ultimately beneficial to local authorities because, as they owned the land, they would reap the increment in land values. Should they be deterred by the large capital outlays

---

[57] Ibid. 82–96.
[58] Offer, *Property and politics*, 308–13; M. J. Daunton, *House and home in the Victorian city*, London 1983, 286–307.
[59] *The land*, ii. 66
[60] Ibid. ii. 99–102, 108.
[61] Ibid. ii. 148–57.

required, the enquiry proposed systems of national inspection and 'fines', through the withdrawal of state grants, if local authorities did not meet their duty to provide adequate working-class housing.

This plan was designed to provide a massive increase in the rate of house-building. Furthermore the new houses built under the aegis of the local authorities' town planning rules would be of a much higher quality than those previously constructed.[62] In particular, town planning would provide adequate parks and open spaces, break up the monotonous rows in which most working-class housing was built and ensure that housing was constructed with regard to aspect and landscape. The crucial improvement, though, would be a reduction in the density of housing per acre. The report believed that this could be done without substantially raising the cost of housing for working-class occupiers because it was the high price of land for city sites that produced the need to crowd houses together, so ensuring an adequate return for the builder.[63] If local authorities provided cheap land in the suburbs, builders could significantly lower the density of housing without greatly increasing their costs. The result would be better housing at no significantly greater expense to the working class.

A number of minor measures were proposed to lower the cost of housing, but the core of the programme remained the provision of cheap land by local authorities.[64] This had the advantage of concentrating fire on the landlords, as the group that stood in the way of better housing, by charging high prices for their land, but it failed to cover up a notable ambiguity in the report's plans. Nowhere was it explicitly stated if, or by how much, the price of the new town-planned housing would exceed that of existing housing. This was the weak point in the whole scheme. If the new housing would cost substantially more to build and rent, then most working-class families would not be able to afford it. This problem had been encountered in the existing private experiments in town planning at Letchworth and Hampstead Garden Suburb and the enquiry was well aware of the difficulty.[65] Its answer was that local authorities could provide land more cheaply than any private body, through compulsory purchase. But even the report's authors were confused as to the exact effect this would have. Sometimes Rowntree claimed that the aim was to 'build better houses without increasing the cost above the level of today'.[66] At other times he admitted that rents would be higher, but claimed, rather

---

[62] Ibid. ii. 150–1.

[63] This is most explicitly stated in B. S. Rowntree, 'Notes for Swindon speech', LG, C/28/1/2.

[64] The land, ii. 289–93.

[65] Creese, Garden city, 217, 227; G. Haw to Lloyd George, 14 Apr. 1913, LG, C/9/4/28.

[66] B. S. Rowntree, 'How far is it possible to provide satisfactory houses for the working classes, at rents they can afford to pay?', in B. S. Rowntree and A. C. Pigou, Lectures on housing: the Warburton lectures for 1913, London 1914, 28. This is a reprint of Rowntree's Warburton lecture given at Manchester University on 27 Nov. 1913.

implausibly, that this would be offset by the opportunity to grow food on the allotments provided in the new suburbs.[67]

As explained above, the main outline of the housing chapter was written when the enquiry's information had not been fully collated. This may explain some of the ambiguities in the report. It may also explain the report's reliance on the already existing programme of the town planning movement as a solution to the country's housing problems. The ideas in the report were strikingly similar to those of the town planning enthusiasts and there is ample evidence they were able to influence the report directly. J. S. Nettlefold was interviewed by the committee as early as 13 September 1912 and submitted a memorandum on town planning.[68] Raymond Unwin's book, *Nothing gained by overcrowding*, was read by the committee members and extensively quoted in the report – indeed some of its diagrams were lifted wholesale.[69] Moreover, the most influential figure in the writing of the housing chapter, Seebohm Rowntree, had been heavily influenced by the ideas of the town planning movement through his involvement in his father's building project at New Earswick.[70]

However, the elaboration of this programme based on local authority purchase and town planning, left untouched the estimated 5–10 per cent of the working class who could not afford an 'economic' rent and who were living in 'slums'. Their situation was obviously analogous to that of the agricultural labourers. Suggested solutions followed the same course. Initially, at least, it was mooted that this class should be rehoused by local authorities and their rents subsidised using the income from site value rating.[71] This was rather similar to the rural enquiry's early plans to subsidise the rents of agricultural labourers from a national land tax.[72]

These tentative ideas were not pursued and when Rowntree was able to turn his attention to the housing chapter in August 1913, the rural enquiry had already rejected this method of dealing with the agricultural labourers' case, in favour of Lloyd George's scheme to include a sum to pay an 'economic' rent in their minimum wage award.[73] This idea represented an obvious solution to the problem of the urban 'residuum'. Rowntree saw this rapidly. In October 1913 he wrote to Lloyd George, 'might we not look into a great extension of the Trade Boards Acts in urban areas?'[74]

The reasons for rejecting the rent subsidy policy in the towns were the same as those in the country. It was regarded as a 'financial impossibility' that

67 *The land*, ii. 154.
68 R. Buxton to Lloyd George, 14 Sept. 1912, LG, C/2/1/29.
69 Heath to Lloyd George, 19 Sept. 1912, LG, C/2/1/38; *The land*, ii. 153–4.
70 Briggs, *Social thought*, 95–9.
71 Davies journal, entry for 4 Dec. 1912, E. W. Davies papers, MS 7, fos 68–9.
72 R. Winfrey, memorandum, 27–30 Sept. 1912, in Winfrey, *Great men*, 25–6.
73 R. Buxton to Lloyd George, 17 July 1913, LG, C/2/2/31.
74 B. S. Rowntree, 'Notes for Swindon', LG, C/28/1/2.

would cause serious dissension inside the Liberal Party.[75] Moreover, the committee had the force of the rural enquiry's conclusions in front of them. If trade boards could be applied to farmers, 'it seems inevitable to arrive at a similar decision in dealing with urban employers'.[76] On 5 November 1913 Rowntree, strongly supported by Cross, persuaded the committee to recommend that 'a minimum wage should be fixed for all low-paid wage-earners' and that this sum should include sufficient to pay an 'economic' rent.[77] Lloyd George seems to have been doubtful about this extension of his answer to the rural housing dilemma, but he was sufficiently convinced to include the policy in his speech at Middlesbrough on 8 November.[78]

It was not convincing. The trade boards scheme only made sense in the towns if, as the report asserted, 'probably the largest section' of slumdwellers were in regular, but low-paid work, like agricultural labourers.[79] But no statistics were produced to demonstrate this claim. The report relied on 'the opinion expressed to us by social workers in different parts of the country' and 'enquiries [unspecified] made in London, Manchester, York and other towns'.[80] This was scarcely conclusive and the enquiry itself had to admit that many slumdwellers might be casual workers rather than those in steady, low-paid employment. For these workers, the report could only advocate the 'decasualisation' of their work, though it freely admitted that it had no proposals as to how this might be achieved.[81] Even more intriguingly, the committee thought that, despite all these policies, the towns might still contain a 'residuum' who would be unable to pay an 'economic' rent. Local authorities were advised to buy up old but decent properties to house these people, and charge them 'the best rent they could obtain'.[82] The possibility of a national grant to help local authorities carry out these plans was raised. Thus, as in the rural report, the policy of subsidising rents from national grants was left open, despite all the committee's efforts to disavow this solution.

Although both rural and urban reports recommended a minimum wage and a housing policy, their priorities were different. In agricultural areas the minimum wage was meant to be the centrepiece of the Liberals' appeal. Because so many labourers were low-paid it offered some hope to most of them. The rural report's housing proposals were subsidiary. But in urban areas, better housing for the majority was the central thrust of policy. Trade boards were a means to deal with the inconvenient 'residuum'. Most urban workers

[75] See, for instance, the Liberal divisions over Sir A. Griffith-Boscawen's bill to, in effect, subsidise rents: *Hansard*, 5th ser., 1912, xxxv. 1413–96.

[76] *The land*, ii. 160.

[77] Davies journal, entry for 5 Nov. 1913, E. W. Davies papers, MS 7, fo. 95; *The land*, ii. 161.

[78] Davies journal, 5 Nov. 1913, E. W. Davies papers, MS 7, fo. 95; *Times*, 10 Nov. 1913.

[79] *The land*, ii. 160.

[80] Ibid. ii. 161.

[81] Ibid. ii. 162.

[82] Ibid. ii. 163.

earned above the meagre 'subsistence' level defined as the minimum wage, so that policy could make little appeal to them. The report wished to present the land question to them as a housing question.

The conclusions of the urban report: appealing to the middle class

Logically, it was superfluous to make the following section of the report, 'The acquisition of land' a separate entity. It was an integral part of the housing policy, which depended on the ease and cheapness with which local authorities could purchase land compulsorily. However, the subject had an important place from the inception of the enquiry because it was a traditional grievance that many local authorities held against landowners.[83] The report was certainly able to demonstrate that the various methods of land acquisition local authorities had to use were in some confusion. Even an act of parliament was required in some cases and the vendor of the land was usually in a very favourable position. Under the Land Clauses Consolidation Act of 1845 he was entitled to receive an extra 10 per cent of the value of his land in compensation when compulsory purchase occurred.[84] This situation provided superb ammunition for abusing landlords and accusing them of exploiting urban communities – an opportunity Lloyd George did not allow to go to waste, as in his Glasgow speech on 4 February 1914.[85] The point was worth emphasising because it represented an obvious method of blaming landlords for poor housing and pillorying them as obstacles to improvement. If the working class could be convinced that housing problems were caused by landlords charging high prices for land there was a chance that they would unite behind the Liberals to defeat the landlords, rather than defecting to Labour or the Unionists.

The emphasis on land acquisition also served other purposes. It marked the beginning of the report's attempt to secure middle-class as well as working-class support for the Liberals. Businessmen were offered the chance to compulsorily acquire leases on land, if they could show the land commissioners that they would be putting the land to better use than its current owners.[86] The enquiry justified this policy with some phrases, but no statistics, about the difficulties businessmen had in acquiring land. They were even reduced to saying it was 'common knowledge' that rural landlords were reluctant to sell land for development.[87]

---

[83] *Daily News*, 5 July 1912.
[84] *The land*, ii. 224–83.
[85] *Times*, 5 Feb. 1914. The dukes of Montrose and Sutherland suffered particularly at Lloyd George's hands on this occasion.
[86] *The land*, ii. 333–5.
[87] Ibid. ii. 318.

The emphasis given to land acquisition also served to please the group of Liberals who favoured land nationalisation. The Land Nationalisation Society (LNS) had only three vice-presidents in the 1895 parliament. By 1912 the number had grown to ninety-seven.[88] This growth did not signal the conversion of a large number of Liberal MPs to a policy of immediate state ownership of land. Rather, it meant that the LNS had adopted an interim programme, focusing on the acquisition of land to solve immediate practical problems – particularly smallholdings in the countryside and housing in the towns.[89] On this basis it could mobilise considerable support – 120 MPs signed its memorandum to Lloyd George of December 1912.[90] The chapter on land acquisition served to mollify those who favoured nationalisation, without adding anything substantial to the urban report's programme. The LNS was, in fact, very pleased with the enquiry's conclusions.[91] It contained no group of irreconcilables like the single taxers – Heath noted there was 'no such compact group as those in favour of rating site values'.[92] The LNS could feel particularly happy that so much of the programme of the town planning movement had been adopted by the urban report as the LNS and the town planning movement were closely connected.[93]

The following section of the urban report set out the enquiry's policy to attract the middle class of the towns. The rural report had the minimum wage at its heart, but it had also tried to win support among farmers with its proposals for security of tenure and 'fair' rents. The urban report attempted a similar strategy in the towns. Unfortunately, the towns did not offer a precise equivalent to the farmers. A group in a somewhat similar position, though, who had long attracted the attention of the Liberals, did exist – the short leaseholders. Most of these people were middle-class – the working class usually rented their homes by the week. Short leaseholders could have similar grievances to farmers against their landlords, over compensation for improvements, security of tenure and the level of rent. Lloyd George's idea of a land court to deal with farmers' grievances could be adapted to deal with the relationship between urban short leaseholders and their ground landlords. Lloyd George had mentioned this possibility to Riddell as early as 19 June 1912 and when the enquiry was set up, the Liberal press confidently predicted that this policy would be in the report.[94] It was the section of the urban report that took shape most rapidly – Cross had a draft programme ready by 5 August 1913.[95] This was partly because the enquiry knew the direction in which it

88 LNS, *Annual report, 1909–1910*, London 1910, 12.
89 For LNS gradualism see, for instance, J. Hyder to E. T. John, 20 Aug. 1912, E. T. John papers, NLW, Aberystwyth, John letters, fo. 521.
90 *Daily Chronicle*, 19 Dec. 1912.
91 *Land Nationaliser*, May 1914, 22.
92 Heath to Lloyd George, 4 Dec. 1913, LG, C/2/3/55.
93 Ward, 'Land reform', 184–95.
94 Riddell, *More pages*, 70, entry for 19 June 1912; *British Weekly*, 4 July 1912.
95 'Summary of urban recommendations', 5 Aug. 1913, LG, C/28/1/5.

was heading and partly because Cross himself was an expert on the leaseholds system.

This policy did represent a new departure for the Liberals, though. Before Lloyd George casually arrived at his new policy in June 1912, the Liberals had no clearly defined policy on urban leaseholds. In the mid-1880s they had been associated with leasehold enfranchisement. But this policy was never favoured by the devotees of land taxes or land nationalisation and as the popularity of these ideas increased, the Liberals' association with leasehold enfranchisement waned. By 1912 it was closely connected with Unionist attempts to shore up the bulwarks of property.[96] Lloyd George's land courts idea eschewed the creation of a new group of small property owners, while still dealing with the grievances of short leaseholders.

Such proposals could not have the wide-ranging effects of land courts in the countryside, though. In one of its more valuable pieces of research, the urban report updated the work of the town holdings committee of 1886–9 on the distribution of various forms of urban land tenure. It confirmed the earlier committee's conclusion that 'rather under one third' of the population lived in areas where short leasehold tenure predominated, while 'substantially more than one half' of the population lived in areas of freehold tenure. Short leaseholds were concentrated in a number of specific areas, for example London, south Wales and Liverpool.[97] Thus to the majority of the urban middle class, land courts had no relevance. The response of the enquiry was to widen the application of the policy.

The enquiry was able to do this by extending the land courts programme to cover shopkeepers' business premises. It was usual for retail traders all over the country to lease their premises for a short term – anything from three months to three years.[98] They could harbour grievances against their land-lords similar to those felt by short leaseholders and this had not gone un-noticed by Liberals. In 1906 W. H. Dickinson, Liberal MP for St Pancras North, had set up a body called the Town Tenants League.[99] Its policy was to give 'business tenants' the right to appeal to the courts to gain compensation for all improvements made, fixity of tenure at a 'fair' rent and relief from the 'restrictive' clauses in leases. The League was ostensibly a non-party body and secured the backing of a large number of retail chambers of trade.[100] However, its dominant figure was a Kilburn draper and Progressive London county councillor, B. B. Evans. He not only gave evidence to the urban enquiry, pressing it to adopt the League's policy, he also collected examples of shop-

---

[96] Eight of the twelve sponsors of the 1913 leasehold enfranchisement bill were Unionists.
[97] *The land*, ii. 349. The balance of the population lived mostly in areas of long leasehold i.e. 999-year leases, virtually equivalent to freeholds. There were also a few remaining pockets of copyhold tenure and leases for a number of lives.
[98] Ibid. ii. 446–82.
[99] Town Tenants League, *The town tenants bill*, London 1908.
[100] See B. B. Evans to Lloyd George, 18 Oct. 1913, LG, C/28/1/3.

keepers' grievances for Lloyd George's speeches – on the strict understanding that this activity remained confidential.[101]

Lloyd George showed an early interest in this aspect of leasehold policy and, after some indecision, he overcame Cross's reluctance and extended the land courts policy to include shopkeepers' leases.[102] This greatly increased the number of people who could benefit from the report's leasehold reform proposals, but such a policy could still only reach a minority of the urban middle class. For a policy with a more wide ranging appeal in the towns many Liberals looked to the most complex of all the questions addressed by the enquiry – site value rating and land taxation.

The conclusions of the urban land enquiry: land taxation

When the existence of the enquiry was announced to the press in late June 1912 it was made clear that it would consider land taxation.[103] This was not surprising. The Liberal leadership was committed to at least the principle of this policy and it had widespread support in the party. The rapid rise in rates was creating difficulties for local authorities, unrest among ratepayers and working against the Liberals at the local level. Some sort of reform was becoming urgent.

The report considered site value rating first. On the basis of experience gained from the 1909 budget it rejected the argument that site value rating offered a significant new form of revenue for local authorities.[104] Land taxers argued that it would force contributions from vacant and undeveloped land. But the undeveloped land tax in the budget had produced only £404,066 in total by the end of the fiscal year 1913–14.[105] However, the enquiry did accept the argument that site value rating would encourage house-building, by forcing more land onto the market and relieving buildings of rates.[106] Its evidence, though, was rather thin. The enquiry's informants split 155 to 111 on whether the existing rating system discouraged building. The report was forced to admit that the rating system could only be a factor in the largest towns and among builders operating on the narrowest of margins.[107]

Nevertheless, once the enquiry had reached this conclusion, it was faced with the task of developing a practical scheme of site value rating. Cross could make no progress with this and the matter was in abeyance until Heath was able to give it his attention in June 1913. He decided that the enquiry

101 Ibid.
102 Heath to Lloyd George, 17 Aug. 1912, LG, C/2/1/9; Davies journal, entry for 6 Feb. 1913, E. W. Davies papers, MS 7, fos 78–9.
103 *Times*, 29 June 1912.
104 *The land*, ii. 546–7.
105 Murray, *Budget*, 296.
106 *The land*, ii. 549–53.
107 Ibid. ii. 513, 521–4.

could not produce a policy until it knew what the effect of different levels of site value rating would be.[108] This could be calculated if the enquiry could make use of the national land valuation being carried out by the Inland Revenue. At Heath's request, Lloyd George instructed the valuers to concentrate on providing for the enquiry complete figures on a small group of towns where the valuation was nearly finished (the national valuation was scheduled to end in March 1915).[109] Even then, the enquiry did not receive any figures until 22 November 1913.[110] This was why, when Lloyd George launched his urban policy on 8 and 29 November 1913, he had nothing to say on site value rating.

The enquiry accepted, at the insistent urging of Heath, that if the existing rating system were replaced by site value rating, the whole burden would fall on the landowners.[111] They would not be able to pass it on to occupiers, in the form of increased rent, because site value rating would neither increase the demand for land, nor restrict the supply. This situation was complicated by two factors, though. The enquiry accepted that landowners already paid an undefined percentage of the existing rates, because they had to take the rate burden into account when fixing the level of rent a tenant could afford to pay i.e. rates diminished the landlord's rent. So the effect of site value rating would not be just to transfer rates to landlords, it would redistribute rates between landlords. It would relieve those owning properties where sites were a small percentage of total value and penalise landlords who owned properties where sites were a high percentage of total values.[112]

Broadly, this meant transferring the tax burden from suburban landowners to the owners of central sites, though this process would be most drastic in bigger towns where central site values were very high. If the existing rating system was entirely replaced by site value rating at once, the enquiry estimated, from the Inland Revenue figures supplied, that the owners of central business sites faced a rate rise of at least 33 per cent, while owners of suburban housing would see their rates fall by 56–67 per cent.[113] This level of variation would produce wild fluctuations in the value of properties and a number of anomalies. Moreover, the enquiry accepted that it was most convenient for occupiers to go on paying site value rating, but to deduct it from their rent. These unpredictable variations would therefore initially fall on occupiers. If they were leaseholders under contract to pay all rates, they would have to pay the new rates until their lease expired.[114]

Despite these alarming findings, the enquiry still believed that the argu-

108 Heath to Masterman, 11 June 1913, LG, C/2/2/20.
109 Heath to Lloyd George, 30 Oct. 1913, LG, C/2/3/30.
110 Nathan to Lloyd George, 22 Nov. 1913, LG, C/6/6/3.
111 Davies journal, entry for 14 Jan. 1914, E. W. Davies papers, MS 7, fos 107–8; *The land*, ii. 568.
112 *The land*, ii. 565–8, 574.
113 Ibid. ii. 581–2.
114 Ibid. ii. 568–9.

ments for site value rating were valid.[115] What was needed was a moderate scheme that gradually introduced site value rating. The enquiry finally opted to transfer 1*d.* of the existing rates to site value rating. Local authorities would also be given the option to increase this figure and all future rate increases would be charged to site value rating.[116] It was calculated this would mean, initially, a 4 per cent rate rise for the owners of central business sites and a 2–7 per cent fall for the owners of suburban housing.[117]

To achieve this very modest result, in the rather dubious hope of stimulating house-building, a system of vast complexity would have to be set up. In addition, the enquiry had already assigned the major role in the creation of new housing to its schemes for local authority land acquisition and town planning. Given these circumstances, the problem arises: why did the committee persist in recommending any form of site value rating at all? The answer may lie partly in the ingrained beliefs of influential members of the committee. Heath, for instance, was a persuasive advocate of the case for land taxation.[118] Rowntree, in his book, *Land and labour: lessons from Belgium*, had revealed his firm belief in site value rating.[119] Most important, Lloyd George hinted in the autumn of 1913 that he favoured some form of site value rating.[120] But there were other reasons. If the committee was to produce a policy on rates that would prove popular with most towndwellers, they had to offer a scheme that would definitely reduce rates for most occupiers. The site value rating policy they had adopted could not do this. It offered only a slight and uncertain redistribution of the rate burden.

As an alternative, the committee recommended a £5 million increase in the level of state grants to local authorities. Again, Lloyd George's mind may already have been moving in this direction in late 1913.[121] However, the committee feared that if central grants lowered rates, landowners would benefit by raising their tenants' rents.[122] In effect the government would be subsidising landlords – the traditional Liberal reason for disliking state grants. This was the main thrust of the arguments used by E. R. Cross to justify a national land tax – it would recoup some of this benefit that would otherwise accrue to landlords.[123] The enquiry accepted that this argument was, in theory, 'unanswerable'.[124] But it could not recommend such a policy. The effects of even a 1*d.*/£ land tax were deemed to be predatory from the calcula-

---

[115] Ibid. ii. 591.
[116] Ibid. ii. 591–609.
[117] Ibid. ii. 599–603.
[118] Davies journal, entry for 14 Jan. 1914, E. W. Davies papers, MS 7, fos 107–8.
[119] Rowntree, *Land and labour*, 547.
[120] See *Times*, 13 Oct. 1913, for his remarks at Bedford on 11 Oct. 1913.
[121] Ibid. 9 Nov. 1913.
[122] *The land*, ii. 631–2.
[123] E. R. Cross to Lloyd George, 14 Dec. 1913, LG, C/2/3/61.
[124] *The land*, ii. 632.

tions made using the Inland Revenue figures.[125] This left only the modest site value rate to ensure landowners would not be beneficiaries from the £5 million grant.

The urban report's decision on site value rating also reflected the delicate balance of opinion on the subject inside the Liberal Party. Indeed, when the enquiry was announced, this was one of the most important and difficult subjects on which it was expected to 'harmonize' opinion amongst Liberals.[126] There was undoubtedly still widespread sympathy inside the Liberal Party for site value rating. The land values group's memorial of May 1911, calling for a national land tax and site value rating, was signed by half the Liberal MPs.[127] It was endorsed with barely a dissenting voice at the NLF's annual meeting in November 1912.[128] The efforts of the six or seven single taxing MPs had been redoubled by the adoption of land taxation by the Liberal Government in 1909–10. At the beginning of 1912, they were embarking on a new municipal campaign, emanating from their Glasgow stronghold, and a rural campaign centred around Swindon.[129] The single taxers may have been widely regarded as eccentrics, but they provided pressure to meet the more moderate and widespread feeling in the Liberal Party in favour of land taxation.

On the other hand, the events of 1909–10 had made it clear that land taxation provoked considerable hostility from a section of Liberal MPs. Forty-seven of them had voted against some aspect of the land taxes in the 1909 budget during their passage through the House of Commons.[130] Twenty-one of these MPs were still sitting in 1912. After the land enquiry was launched in July 1912, a small group, including A. C. Murray, Sir Charles Henry and H. H. Raphael spoke out publicly against a land taxing policy.[131] On 21 November 1912 A. C. Murray reported he had collected forty signatures for a petition to Asquith, aimed at preventing the party from being rushed 'blindfold' into support for such a divisive policy.[132]

In this situation the urban report's conclusions were calculated to produce a maximum of Liberal unity. The anti-land taxers could console themselves that there was only a very modest dose of site value rating in the report and that it was not to be the centre of the Liberal campaign. None of the Liberals

[125] Ibid. ii. 634–6.

[126] *Times*, 29 June 1912.

[127] LG, C/15/1/4.

[128] Liberal Publication Department, *Annual meeting of council of NLF, 1912*, 15–16.

[129] *LV*, Oct. 1911, 115–22; UCTLV, *Annual report, 1911–12*, 34. The single taxers had also entrenched their position in Yorkshire: Yorkshire Liberal Federation, executive committee resolutions, 25 Feb. 1913, 4 Mar. 1914, Yorkshire Liberal Federation papers.

[130] Calculated from *LM* xvii (1909), 335–8, 412, 472–3, 612.

[131] *Times*, 20, 24 July, 13 Aug. 1912.

[132] A. C. Murray diary, entry for 21 Nov. 1912, Elibank papers, MS 8814, fos 97–8; B. S. Rowntree to Woollcomb, 4 Nov. 1912, B. S. Rowntree papers, MS 93/XI/1/14, for concern among moderate Liberals in the country at the activities of the single taxers.

who had spoken out against land taxes in 1912 denounced the urban report in public. A. C. Murray was even persuaded to become one of Lloyd George's advisers on the Scottish aspects of the land question.[133]

The land taxers, on the other hand, could hope that the report was the starting point for their programme and that they should confine themselves to persuading Lloyd George to go further, rather than opposing the land campaign outright. The English League for the Taxation of Land Values declared they were 'satisfied' with the urban report.[134] Even among the fanatical single taxers only Wedgwood remained unreconciled and he was unable to secure wider support for a campaign against the land report's moderation.[135] Lloyd George actually played the single taxers very shrewdly. He consulted them throughout the enquiry, leading them to believe that land taxation would be a prominent part of the land campaign.[136] This gave him some influence over them and in August 1912 he was able to persuade them to modify their public campaigns, especially at by-elections, when these aroused the opposition of more conservative Liberals.[137] Despite some grumblings, particularly after the non-appearance of land taxation in his Bedford and Swindon speeches, the land taxers were kept in check until Lloyd George was ready to declare publicly for some form of site value rating at Glasgow on 4 February 1914.[138] This was enough to convince most land taxers that their best hope was to try and push Lloyd George further towards their policies, rather than condemn the land campaign wholesale.[139] Despite this, there could be no doubt that the urban report did not place land taxation at the centre of its approach to the urban land question. This was a marked change from the attitude of the Liberal government in 1906–10, which had climaxed in the 1909 land taxes. Once the enquiry was able to study the effects of those taxes and the projected effects of further taxes they concluded that land taxation was far too difficult and unrewarding a topic to be given a prominent place in the land campaign. Instead, rival policies were promoted to solve the difficulties that land taxation sought to answer. The stimulation of new house-building was assigned to town planning. Increased state grants would solve the local government financial crisis and lower urban rates.

---

133 A. C. Murray diary, entry for 27 Oct. 1913, Elibank papers, MS 8814, fo. 115.
134 LV, June 1914, 2.
135 See LL, 24 Dec. 1913, and J. Wedgwood to S. Wedgwood, 23 Jan. 1914, J. Wedgwood papers.
136 They were consulted over the contents of the schedules: R. Buxton to Lloyd George, 11 Aug. 1912, LG, C/2/1/6. Cross, Heath and Lloyd George then talked extensively to the land taxers in late September 1913: Cross to Lloyd George, 16 Sept. 1913, LG, C/2/3/9.
137 See Outhwaite to Lloyd George, 13 Nov. 1913, LG, C/10/2/32, for Outhwaite's regrets that he had consented to this line of action.
138 P. W. Raffan to C. P. Trevelyan, 7 Nov. 1913, C. P. Trevelyan papers, MS 32.
139 At least initially after the Glasgow speech even Outhwaite was reconciled to Lloyd George: Times, 6 Feb. 1914.

The urban report was far more important than the rural report in developing Lloyd George's ideas for his land campaign. Except in the matter of housing, the latter was largely an elaboration and defence of an outline policy that Lloyd George had already thought up. In the urban report this only applied to the chapter on leaseholds. The enquiry used its freedom in different ways. Its examination of the evidence provided by the Inland Revenue led it to downgrade decisively the importance of land taxation in urban land issues. It was replaced by a housing strategy that was not derived from the study of empirical evidence but stemmed from the already existing programme of the town planning movement, which moved to the centre of Liberal strategy for the first time. Plans for local authorities to assume a duty to house all their working-class residents decently and for a minimum wage for all low-paid workers provided startling new initiatives for the Liberal Party. They also represented a redefinition of what the 'land issue' was. The authors of the urban report claimed that land reform really meant a huge increase in the state's role in welfare provision for the working class. Among the many redefinitions of traditional Liberal language in the Edwardian era this was surely the most sudden and surprising.

6

Breaking Down the 'Relics of Feudalism': The Rural Land Campaign, 1913–1914

The first stage: winning over the cabinet

In the summer of 1913 Lloyd George set in train negotiations with his cabinet colleagues to transform his land policy into the programme of the Liberal government. At this time, although most of the rural report had been drafted, the urban report was in chaos.[1] It was even a struggle to issue the rural report to coincide with the chancellor's object of an autumn launch for the land campaign.[2] This haste did not reflect any hope that the report's conclusions might be turned into legislation prior to the general election due in 1915. The government's timetable was already loaded down with Home Rule, Welsh Church disestablishment and plural voting, let alone its commitments on education and the reform of the House of Lords. Rather, this decision was the outcome of Lloyd George's long-held determination to start the land campaign as soon as possible.

Lloyd George believed that it was vital to distract attention from unpopular policies like Home Rule and national insurance and force the Unionists onto the defensive. Time would also be required to familiarise the electorate with the new proposals and create the hoped-for wave of support.[3] Indeed, the original intention was to start the campaign in October 1912. A hall had even been booked for a great inaugural speech by the chancellor.[4] However, this had to be cancelled after the enquiry committee met for a weekend conference with Lloyd George at de Forest's Leicestershire home, Gaddesby Hall, on 27–30 September 1912.[5] The committee were forced to conclude that they were 'almost snowed under' by the information sent in by the investigators.[6] Consequently, no progress at all had been made in writing either of the land reports. As he had no organised material to support the policies he

---

[1]   Heath to Lloyd George, 4 July 1913, LG, C/2/2/26.
[2]   The first print run of the rural land report was finally made on 10 Oct. 1913: Hodder to Lloyd George, 10 Oct. 1913, LG, C/10/1/16.
[3]   Riddell, *More pages*, 70, entry for 19 June 1912; *The political diaries of C. P. Scott, 1911–1928*, ed. T. Wilson, London 1970, 68–9, entry for 16 Jan. 1913.
[4]   Heath to Lloyd George, 12 Sept. 1912, LG, C/2/1/22.
[5]   The conference is described in Davies's journal, entries for 27–30 Sept. 1912, E. W. Davies papers, MS 7, fos 52–9, and in Winfrey, *Great men*, 25–6.
[6]   Winfrey, *Leaves*, 202–3.

already favoured, and no new ideas had been produced to fill the gaps in his programme, Lloyd George had no option but to postpone the campaign.[7]

But he continued to hope for an early start. On the basis of optimistic reports that the enquiry had 'practically completed their work' a January 1913 campaign launch was planned.[8] Similar wishful thinking in the new year made Lloyd George contemplate making his inaugural speech in spring 1913.[9] The state of the enquiry did not permit either date and for Lloyd George to embark on a new initiative when he was still trying to implement national insurance and was under the shadow of the Marconi investigations would have been the height of folly. However, by mid-1913 these false starts had produced considerable impatience among Liberals at the land campaign's non-appearance. The loss of the rural seat of Newmarket on 19 May 1913 led Liberal newspapers, and some of Lloyd George's closest allies, to press him to start the campaign at once.[10] Shortly after this, Lloyd George could feel he had just enough backing from the enquiry to take action. On 4 July 1913 he received a draft of all but the superfluous section V of the rural report.[11] This freed Rowntree to solve the difficulties confronting the urban enquiry. The chancellor could hope that in the autumn of 1913, the traditional platform season, he would be able to announce the enquiry's major conclusions.

Further delay might prove fatal to the whole project. 1913–14 would see the crisis over Home Rule and a sudden dissolution might forestall the campaign. Moreover, Lloyd George needed to restore his radical credentials after the Marconi scandal and he was anxious to hit back at his Unionist detractors – to 'give them snuff' as he put it.[12] He had occasionally remarked that he was willing to start the campaign on his own, without government backing.[13] But throughout 1912–13 Lloyd George had been careful to keep the prime minister and senior cabinet colleagues informed of the enquiry's progress in the hope and expectation that he would receive their approval.[14]

Lloyd George continued to pursue these tactics when he had finally decided to launch the land campaign. He knew that if he could convince a handful of the most senior cabinet members he would probably win the day in the full cabinet. In 1909, on the 'People's Budget', the support of Asquith,

[7] *Manchester Guardian*, 10 Oct. 1912.
[8] *Daily Chronicle*, 16 Dec. 1912.
[9] Lloyd George's speech at the National Liberal Club, 31 Jan. 1913, reported in the *Times*, 1 Feb. 1913.
[10] *Nation*, 17 May 1913; *Daily News*, 19 May 1913; *British Weekly*, 22 May 1913; *Daily Chronicle*, 2 June 1913. See Riddell, *More pages*, 151–2, entry for 21 May 1913, for pressure from Masterman and Harold Spender.
[11] Heath to Lloyd George, 4 July 1913, LG, C/2/2/26.
[12] Riddell, *More pages*, 167, entry for 6 July 1913.
[13] Ibid. 63–4, entry for 27 May 1913; *Diaries of C. P. Scott*, 70, entry for 16 Jan. 1913.
[14] Riddell, *More pages*, 70, 76, entries for 19 June, 2 July 1912; Lloyd George to A. H. D. Acland, 8 Oct. 1912, LG, C/2/1/52.

Churchill and Haldane, and Grey's neutrality, had allowed Lloyd George to over-ride the objections of the rest of the cabinet.[15] On 18 July 1913 the chancellor gave a dinner to some of his more influential colleagues, to sound out their attitudes.[16] Asquith was reported to be 'considering' the matter and studying papers that Lloyd George had given him. But Crewe, on whose judgement he most relied, was hostile. Churchill, as author of the 1909 Trade Boards Act, was enthusiastic about the minimum wage. Grey was also favourable. The real enigma was Haldane. 'I really don't know where he is. I never know where he is. He is the most confusing clever man I have ever met' as Lloyd George complained.[17]

Haldane might well hold the key to the cabinet's approval. Asquith trusted him and he was the only member of the cabinet with an alternative plan of campaign for a 1915 election. Haldane wished the Liberals to fight on the basis of a great scheme to reform the education system from elementary to university level.[18] In this he had the support of Crewe and Pease. But his efforts to win over his other colleagues revealed a startling lack of political finesse. On 10 January 1913 Haldane had made a much-publicised speech at Manchester, stating that Asquith and Lloyd George had authorised him to say that education would be the government's next major task.[19] In fact, he had merely mentioned to the prime minister and chancellor that he would touch on education in his speech. This sort of behaviour produced irritation rather than agreement.[20] Haldane, Crewe and Pease made a number of speeches during 1913 on the need for a 'National System' of education. But, as Haldane later admitted, 'too few people were keenly interested in Education to afford us the requisite breeze for our sails'.[21] They only succeeded in arousing the wrath of the Nonconformist lobby, who demanded that the government deal with the 'single school' issue before any other education reforms.[22] This issue concerned those areas where the only school available for children to attend was a Church of England school, taken within the state system in 1902. Nonconformists insisted that these schools should be subjected to full local authority control, or alternative schools be built. In view of the need to retain Nonconformist enthusiasm when fears of 'Rome Rule' in Ireland were causing it to waver, the cabinet, in a series of discussions

15 Murray, *Budget*, 150.
16 Riddell, *More pages*, 171, entry for 19 July 1913.
17 Ibid.
18 R. B. Haldane to M. E. Haldane, 9 Jan. 1913, Haldane papers, NLS, Edinburgh, MS 5989, fo. 5.
19 *Times*, 11 Jan. 1913.
20 *Diaries of C. P. Scott*, 68–9, entry for 16 Jan. 1913.
21 R. B. Haldane, *An autobiography*, London 1929, 218–19.
22 W. Robertson Nicoll to Asquith, 17 Nov. 1913, Board of Education papers, PRO, Kew, MS 24/630.

during 1912–14, gradually abandoned Pease's initial education proposals in favour of a simple 'single schools' bill.[23]

Thus, Haldane could have little hope for his plans by July 1913. This may explain why he accepted instead Lloyd George's offer to co-operate in, and influence the course of, the land campaign. In a crucial interview on 23 July 1913, Haldane agreed to endorse all of the rural enquiry's major conclusions (the urban enquiry had not come to any conclusions by then).[24] In return, Lloyd George accepted Haldane's suggestion that wages, rents and land acquisition should be determined by land commissioners, rather than a series of boards and courts. Lloyd George had acquired a useful ally and stymied the only alternative scheme before the cabinet. With Grey, Churchill and Haldane on his side, he could be more confident of gaining Asquith's approval. At the final summer cabinet of 13 August 1913, the prime minister told his colleagues that the land campaign would be discussed at the first autumn meeting on 14 October. Until then, ministers were requested to maintain public silence on the matter. But it may be an indication of the way Asquith's views were tending that he agreed to Lloyd George's urgent request to make one speech on the land issue before then (at Bedford on 11 October).[25]

In the recess, interested members of the cabinet, like Sydney Buxton, Hobhouse and Runciman circulated their views on 'the land' to their colleagues in the form of memoranda.[26] But Lloyd George struck first. In an ingenious move to neutralise one of his foremost opponents in the cabinet, he offered McKenna the chance to influence the land campaign, by co-operating with Lloyd George, Grey and Haldane in writing a cabinet memorandum on the subject.[27] The result, published on 21 August 1913, was a masterly document. It revealed that, in return for a studiously moderate tone, presenting the rural enquiry's proposals as attempts to improve agricultural productivity and to make economic laws apply to wages and rents where social pressures prevented this, McKenna had actually been persuaded by his colleagues to accept all of its proposals.[28] Crucially, any mention of land courts was abandoned in favour of the 'Haldane Arbitration Panel' i.e. the land commissioners plan.[29] This proved useful in reassuring the cabinet that

[23] J. Clifford to Pease, 24 Oct. 1911, ibid. MS 24/624. See also G. Sherington, *English education, social change and war, 1911–1920*, Manchester 1981, 22–38.

[24] 'Notes of interview with Haldane', 23 July 1913, LG, C/4/17/3.

[25] *Diaries of Charles Hobhouse*, 146, entry for 19 Aug. 1913.

[26] W. Runciman, 'Rural land', 13 Sept. 1913, cabinet papers, MS 37/116/58; S. Buxton, 'The land question', 3 Oct. 1913, MS 37/116/64–5; C. Hobhouse, 'The land question', 2 Oct. 1913, MS 37/116/66.

[27] 'Land', 21 Aug. 1913, ibid. MS 37/116/56. The document was anonymous, but its authorship was admitted at the cabinet meeting of 14 Oct. 1913: J. Pease diary, entry for 14 Oct. 1913, Gainford papers, MS 39.

[28] See 'Land', 5–7.

[29] This was the description used in W. Runciman to Asquith, 18 Aug. 1913, Runciman papers, MS 82.

there was no intention of replicating the Irish system of 'dual ownership' of agricultural land – a matter that worried Asquith – without conceding anything substantial.[30] The whole document was ideally designed to soothe the nerves of any timorous spirits in the cabinet and to reassure them that nothing unreasonable was planned.

After some hard study of the land question, Lloyd George then travelled up to Arran on 27 September 1913 to meet Asquith at Brodick Castle, and gain his approval of the land campaign.[31] After lengthy discussions, involving Illingworth and Runciman, Asquith consented. As in 1909, the prime minister supported a radical initiative by Lloyd George to revive the Liberals' electoral fortunes, while he concentrated on chairing the cabinet and the pressing problems of high politics. But he questioned Lloyd George closely on the merits of his scheme and it was here that the enormously detailed and cohesive plans worked out by the land enquiry proved their worth, convincing Asquith of the viability of the land programme.[32]

Lloyd George then presented the conclusions of the rural enquiry, as modified by his discussions with colleagues, to three successive cabinet meetings on 14–16 October 1913.[33] He proposed that a new land ministry should be set up. It would fix agricultural wages 'by wages board or order of the Land Ministry acting through the Land Commissioners'.[34] The commissioners would also deal with tenancy, rents and land acquisition. There would be state-built housing for the labourers 'as far as possible' at an economic rent. The commissioners would also handle urban leaseholds. But as the urban enquiry had come to no other conclusions, the programme considered by the cabinet was almost entirely rural. Given the fact that Asquith, Grey, Haldane, Churchill and McKenna had already approved this package, the cabinet was presented with a virtual *fait accompli*. But there was none of the bitter and prolonged argument that had characterised discussions of the 1909 budget.[35] As Hobhouse noted, 'no one took much objection to any particular point' and 'it was much more that we debated details than that we differed on principles'.[36] John Burns spoke against subsidised rents, but as they had not been proposed, he only succeeded in annoying the rest of the cabinet.[37] The

---

[30] Davies journal, entry for 8 Aug. 1913, E. W. Davies papers, MS 7, fo. 90.

[31] *Times*, 29 Sept., 1 Oct. 1913. Rather inappropriately, Illingworth had hired Brodick Castle for the shooting.

[32] *Daily News*, 2 Oct. 1913. See also Spender, *Life, journalism and politics*, i. 159, where Spender describes preliminary discussions between Asquith and Lloyd George in London.

[33] Described in J. Pease diary, entry for 14 Oct. 1913, Gainford papers, MS 39; *Diaries of Charles Hobhouse*, 147–8, entry for 17 Oct. 1913; Asquith to George V, 18 Oct. 1913, Asquith papers, MS 7, fos 67–8.

[34] The cabinet's decisions were embodied in 'Cabinet note on ministry of land', 18 Oct. 1913. A copy is preserved in Harcourt papers, MS 443, fos 201–5.

[35] Murray, *Budget*, 148–71.

[36] C. Hobhouse to Pease, 22 Oct. 1913, Gainford papers, MS 90.

[37] Riddell diary, entry for 17 Oct. 1913, Riddell papers, MS Add. 62973, fo. 56.

only serious critic was Runciman, who was worried that a minimum wage would lead to the dismissal of labourers and more land converted to pasture.[38] Runciman had developed his own plans for the board of agriculture to build some 90,000 cottages at a projected rent of 3s. per week, and he believed that the creation of this mass of non-tied housing would free the labourers to demand higher wages.[39] To mollify Runciman, Lloyd George adapted the enquiry's proposals to fit in with this scheme – primarily by giving the responsibility for constructing new cottages to a land ministry (i.e. a greatly expanded board of agriculture) rather than to local authorities.[40]

On 16 October 1913 the cabinet unanimously sanctioned the land campaign.[41] This was a tribute to Lloyd George's skill in handling his colleagues. But the fragmentary and unco-ordinated discussions of 14–16 October also revealed how difficult it was for ministers to make detailed criticism of the carefully worked out land programme. The discussion rambled as ministers threw out ideas – Churchill even suggested that incompetent farmers and landowners should have their land expropriated.[42] Even the president of the board of agriculture, with all the resources of his department behind him, was unable to make any significant alterations in Lloyd George's proposals. The other members of the cabinet, absorbed in running their departments, had no alternative plans for a 1915 election.[43] Perhaps, also, Lloyd George's proven success with the land issue in 1909–10 helped convince his colleagues. They hoped that he would be able pull off the same feat again.

After 14–16 October 1913 little further discussion of the rural campaign occurred in the cabinet. Its main outlines had been agreed, but there was little prospect of immediate action. In January 1914 Runciman circulated some proposals on how the proposed land ministry might be constituted, but it provoked little interest amid the furore over the naval estimates.[44] However, the land proposals were not forgotten or abandoned by the cabinet. As 1914 wore on, and a general election came closer, interest in them revived. By May 1914 the organisers of the land campaign were pressing Lloyd George for a 'clear definition' of some of the points left obscure in October 1913, particularly the machinery to fix a minimum wage and the limitation of the labourers' hours of work.[45] Lloyd George brought these matters up with Asquith on 11 June 1914 and proposed that a cabinet

[38] J. Pease diary, entry for 14 Oct. 1913, Gainford papers, MS 39.
[39] See *Times*, 12 July 1913, for Runciman's speech to a Young Liberal conference outlining these plans.
[40] See 'Cabinet note on ministry of land', 18 Oct. 1913, Harcourt papers, MS 443, fos 201–5.
[41] Asquith to George V, 18 Oct. 1913, Asquith papers, MS 7, fos 67–8.
[42] For example, J. Pease diary, entry for 14 Oct. 1913, Gainford papers, MS 39.
[43] Haldane, *Autobiography*, 216–17.
[44] 'Ministry of land', 9 Jan. 1914, cabinet papers, MS 37/118/9.
[45] B. S. Rowntree to Lloyd George, 12 May 1914, LG, C/2/4/16.

committee should discuss future legislation. Two committees, on land and housing, respectively, were duly appointed to look at future bills on 'Land & Wages Reform'.[46] The cabinet note embodying the decisions of 14–16 October 1913 was recirculated and a list was drawn up of precisely which policies ministers had proclaimed in public.[47] The enquiry submitted its detailed plans for the new ministry of land.[48] Thus, far from abandoning the land proposals, the cabinet was contemplating putting them into more concrete form when World War One ended all these discussions.

However, the overcrowded legislative timetable allowed only one item of the rural campaign to appear in a bill. This was the plan for state-built cottages, foreshadowed in the kings' speech of 10 February 1914 and finally given a second reading on 24 July 1914.[49] This did not mean that the cabinet regarded the housing proposals as the most important part of the rural campaign. Partly, it reflected Runciman's enthusiasm for this approach. But mainly, it was a response to the considerable embarrassment the government had suffered over the housing bills introduced each year in 1912–14 by the USRC. These bills provided for a state grant of £1 million to local authorities to subsidise house construction – £500,000 each for urban and rural areas.[50] This provoked the sustained hostility of John Burns, the land taxers and all Liberals who feared that subsidised rents would prevent wages from rising.[51] But other Liberal and Labour MPs deplored Burns's inactivity and demanded action on housing, whatever the side-effects of government grants might be.[52] The result was a series of splits and recriminations, although the majority of the party were willing to follow Burns. On 15 March 1912 fifteen Liberal and seventeen Labour MPs voted with the Unionists, thus allowing the housing bill a second reading, only for Burns to kill it in committee. On 18 April 1913 Burns advised Liberals to abstain on the second reading, intending to use the same tactics. But thirty-six Liberals insisted on dividing the House and voting against the bill to register their objections.[53] It was again read a second time in 1914, only to expire in committee.[54]

These scenes allowed the Unionists to charge the government with insincerity in its plans for housing reform in the land campaign.[55] They also provoked demands from Liberals for the government to produce its alterna-

46 Montagu to Lloyd George, 12 June 1914, LG, C/1/1/18; Joseph Rowntree Social Service Trust, minute book, 6 July 1914.
47 'Formation of ministry of land and forests, June 1914', 19 June 1914, cabinet papers, MS 37/120/71; 'Land policy declarations of ministers', 29 June 1914, MS 37/120/78.
48 'Ministry of Land', 25 June 1914, ibid. MS 37/120/75.
49 Hansard, 5th ser., 1914, lviii. 52–3; lxiii. 809–26.
50 Sir A. Griffith-Boscawen, Memories, London 1925, 154.
51 For example, Hansard, 5th ser., 1912, xxxv. 1413–96.
52 See J. Sutton in the above debate, ibid. xxxv. 1465–7.
53 Ibid. 1913, li. 2236–320.
54 Ibid. 1914, lix. 2388–471.
55 For example in the adjournment debate on rural housing: ibid. lxii. 2093–100.

tive if it could not accept the Unionist bill.[56] The final incentive to action was provided by the admiralty's plans to build housing for government workmen at the new naval base of Rosyth.[57] To legislate for this and still ignore the agricultural labourers would be too embarrassing. But it proved to be almost impossible to find a niche in the legislative timetable. Plans to include labourers' housing in the revenue bill were dropped at the last moment.[58] Finally, a clause was added to the Rosyth housing bill, enabling the board of agriculture to borrow up to £3 million to start building at least some of the promised cottages. But the bill did not receive its second reading until 24 July and as the Unionists would not accept its clause on rural housing as 'non-controversial' it had no chance of becoming law.[59] This incident illustrates why more of the land campaign did not achieve legislative shape – there was simply no parliamentary time available. The government's actions on the 1914 housing bill showed it could only make expressions of good intent until after the next election.

The organisation of the rural land campaign

The campaign itself was launched by Lloyd George in a blaze of publicity in two great set-piece speeches at Bedford on 11 October 1913 and Swindon on 22 October.[60] The cabinet's agreed rural programme was mixed in with his usual assault on the landlords. The rural land report finally appeared on 15 October 1913, when 15,000 copies were put on sale.[61] The Liberal press was supplied with advance copies and then primed with snippets of information by the enquiry.[62] But it was emphasised throughout that the campaign launched by Lloyd George was not a private venture and that it was the policy of the cabinet. In fact, the government's new policies on a minimum wage and state-built housing for agricultural labourers were announced by Churchill and Runciman, respectively, on 18 October, before Lloyd George spoke on them at Swindon.[63] Thereafter, cabinet ministers added 'the land' to the usual agenda of their speeches, with notable effusions by Crewe at

---

56 *Westminster Gazette* and *Manchester Guardian*, 21 Mar. 1914.
57 'Housing of government employees', 26 May 1914, cabinet papers, MS 37/119/65.
58 Samuel announced that rural housing would be in the revenue bill in a speech at Cheltenham reported in the *Daily Chronicle*, 15 June 1914, but when the bill was printed on 18 June 1914, the proposals had been removed.
59 See *Hansard*, 5th ser., 1914, lxv. 877–89, for Long's speech.
60 Though Bedford was not representative of government policy as the cabinet had not then met to approve the land proposals, it is usually counted as the start of the land campaign.
61 Hodder to Lloyd George, 7 Nov. 1913, reported that the report was 'selling well': LG, C/10/2/20.
62 Heath to Lloyd George, 25 Oct. 1913, LG, C/2/3/26.
63 *Times*, 19 Oct. 1913.

Royston (24 October), Pease at Rotherham (1 November), Churchill at Alexandra Palace (15 November), Grey at Bradford (4 December) and Simon at Manchester (11 December).[64] Asquith definitively endorsed the campaign in a speech at the National Liberal Club on 9 December 1913.[65] In addition, Liberals with rural seats, like Sir Harry Verney, Edwin Montagu and Cecil Harmsworth, hastened to make the land campaign the central feature of their speeches.[66]

However, the Liberal leadership could not take time off from government to conduct a campaign that might last well over a year. Moreover, they naturally had many other concerns and had to deal with immediate events, as well as future plans, in their speeches. In fact, as the crisis over Home Rule gathered momentum during 1914, the land proposals receded from the foreground of Liberal speeches. Lloyd George's attempt to reassert the position of the campaign at Huddersfield on 21 March 1914 was overtaken by news of the Curragh mutiny.[67] The land campaign did not achieve Lloyd George's aim of displacing Ireland from the forefront of political controversy. But this does not mean that the campaign had ground to a halt or failed to make an impact in rural areas, merely that it was being conducted at a much more local and detailed level than the high politics of Westminster.

Lloyd George had emphasised to C. P. Scott that a land campaign 'was not a case for speeches alone; the country must be flooded with pamphlets and relevant facts'.[68] What was needed was an organisation to carry out a constant campaign of propaganda. The responsibility for setting up such an organisation, once the land campaign was launched as government policy, fell on the chief whip, Percy Illingworth. He had plenty of precedents in front of him. The Edwardian era had seen an explosion of organisations campaigning for particular policies which were actually extensions of a political party. The Tariff Reform League and its mirror image, the Free Trade Union, had started the trend.[69] The Budget League of 1909 had raised campaigning to a new degree of sophistication, even using the gramophone to play the leaders' speeches to remote audiences.[70] In 1911–12 Elibank had set up the Home Rule Council and the National Insurance Committee to campaign for these Liberal policies.[71] In November 1913 Illingworth began to

---

[64] See *LM* xxi (1913), 623–4, 700, 762.
[65] Ibid. 770–2.
[66] *Daily Chronicle*, 18 Oct. 1913; Montagu to Lloyd George, 21 Oct. 1913, LG, C/4/1/7; Harmsworth to W. Runciman, 19 Oct. 1913, Runciman papers, MS 82.
[67] *Nation*, 21 Mar. 1914, said that Lloyd George would be 'reopening' the land campaign. But *Times*, 23 Mar. 1914, reveals that most of the speech was devoted to Ireland.
[68] *Diaries of C. P. Scott*, 68–9, entry for 17 Jan. 1913.
[69] Sykes, *Tariff reform*, 41, 43, 180–1.
[70] Murray, *Budget*, 189.
[71] Elibank to Asquith, 2 Feb. 1912, Elibank papers, MS 8803, fos 16–18.

create a similar organisation, eventually named the Central Land and Housing Council, to carry on the land campaign.

Initially, the regional Liberal federations were instructed to appoint regional land and housing councils.[72] These bodies were largely ceremonial. They were composed of the same sort of Liberal stalwarts who sat on the regional federations, with the later addition of all MPs and candidates in the region.[73] The actual work of organising the campaign fell on each federation's full-time staff, with extra help from constituency agents.[74] The regional councils were not even allowed to elect freely delegates to the Central Land and Housing Council – the names were 'suggested' by Illingworth.[75] This body in turn elected an executive committee which had responsibility for the national direction and organisation of the land campaign. Its chairman was a member of the cabinet, Lord Beauchamp.[76] The president was the marquess of Lincolnshire (as Carrington had become) and the two honorary secretaries were the Liberal MPs, Cecil Beck and Sydney Arnold, one representing a rural and the other an urban seat, to signify the campaign's dual nature. It was, perhaps, indicative that the Central Land and Housing Council operated from 38 Parliament Street – in the same building as the whips' organisation, the Liberal Central Association. The whole elaborate structure was a rather thin disguise for a campaign set up and organised by the Liberal whips.

Certainly, the finance for the land campaign seems to have come from the whips' 'war chest', though Lloyd George did solicit a few specific contributions from sympathetic Liberal magnates like Lever, Cadbury and Rowntree.[77] By December 1913 eight years of dealing in political honours had provided the Liberals with sufficient funds to launch a massive and continuous campaign of propaganda. Whiteley had managed to collect £500,000 in 1906–8 alone and his methods had been followed by his successors as chief whip. Finance was, therefore, never a problem for the land campaign and in just the two or three months before May 1914 it was able to spend over £40,000.[78] At the national level, the central council's literature committee, chaired by Seebohm Rowntree, produced at least twenty-one

[72] For example, Midland Liberal Federation, executive committee, 14 Nov. 1913, Midland Liberal Federation papers.
[73] Ibid. 2 Dec. 1913.
[74] Ibid. 14 Nov. 1913. For help from agents see Lancashire, Cheshire and North-Western Liberal Federation, executive committee, 10 July 1914, Lancashire, Cheshire and North Western Liberal Federation papers, Central Reference Library, Manchester, MS M 390/3.
[75] Midland Liberal Federation, executive committee 14 Nov. 1913, Midland Liberal Federation papers.
[76] For the composition of the executive committee see LM xxi (1913), 770–2.
[77] Lloyd George to W. H. Lever, 3 Oct. 1913, LG, C/2/3/14; B. S. Rowntree to Lloyd George, 6 Oct. 1913, LG, C/2/3/16; Joseph Rowntree Social Service Trust, minute book, 22 Dec. 1913.
[78] Whiteley to Asquith, 29 May 1908, Asquith papers, MS 11, fos 139–40; Riddell diary, 11 May 1912, Riddell papers, MS Add. 62970, fo. 102; Joseph Rowntree Social Service Trust, minute book, 11 May 1914.

different pamphlets and ten different booklets for distribution.[79] It also produced a monthly, then weekly, publication from 7 February 1914, entitled *The Homeland*, to inform Liberals of the campaign's progress and aims, and carried on the enquiry's role in feeding information to the Liberal press.[80]

But the main burden of organisation fell upon the central council's paid secretary, G. Wallace Carter, who moved over from performing the same role at the Home Rule Council (and before that at the Free Trade Union).[81] His first task was to train an army of speakers and he recruited no fewer than eighty full-time paid speakers and 150 volunteers through the regional councils.[82] During the first two weeks of December 1913 they were put through a rigorous training course at the National Liberal and Eighty Clubs. Mornings were devoted to lectures and afternoons to discussions. The training was supervised by Rowntree and lectures were delivered by the major figures in the enquiry.[83]

The speakers were launched onto the country in the new year. Initially, they followed the precedent of the national insurance campaign and concentrated on giving courses of lectures to local Liberals, informing them of the nature of the campaign and arguments to be used in its support.[84] But in the spring, the emphasis shifted to holding public meetings. After a conference between the federation secretaries and the officers of the central council, the campaign was stepped up in April and May 1914.[85] Each region formed a 'Plan of Campaign' to cover its whole area with meetings by August 1914. The usual procedure was to select one manageable area at a time and then deluge it with meetings addressed by land speakers in conjunction with the local MP or candidate.[86] In rural areas this meant rejecting large rallies in favour of ensuring that each and every village had at least one meeting. Meetings were accompanied by a staggering distribution of literature. On 28 May 1914 Carter reported to Lloyd George that not only were 90–120 meetings occurring each day, but 1.45 million booklets and 1.5 million leaflets had been distributed on rural matters alone.[87] The campaign organisers also took care to utilise other adjuncts of the party, like the National League of Young Liberals and the Eighty Club, to provide speakers and distribute literature.[88]

79 *The Homeland*, 4 Apr. 1914.
80 G. W. Carter to Lloyd George, 24 Nov. 1913, LG, C/2/3/49.
81 Elibank to Asquith, 2 Feb. 1912, Elibank papers, MS 8803, fos 16–18.
82 Lloyd George to Asquith, 5 Dec. 1913, Asquith papers, MS 25, fos 63–6.
83 *Daily Chronicle*, 4 Dec. 1913.
84 Midland Liberal Federation, executive committee, 29 Jan. 1914, Midland Liberal Federation papers; Leeds Liberal Federation, cabinet committee, 16 Jan., 1 May 1914, Leeds Liberal Federation papers, WYAS.
85 Carter to Lloyd George, 28 May 1914, LG, C/2/4/20.
86 See LG, C/15/1/22–32, for detailed reports on the rural campaign in Thirsk and Malton in May 1914. See also the *Taunton Echo*, 23 June 1914, for the close co-operation between Philip Rowsell, the Liberal candidate in Bridgwater, and the rural land campaign.
87 Carter to Lloyd George, 28 May 1914, LG, C/2/4/20.
88 See the *Young Liberal*, April 1914, for the launch of their land campaign and the issues for

This vast effort was the beginning, not the climax, of the campaign. Its organisers were well aware of the need to hammer the message home and overcome the suspicions of sceptical audiences.[89] The aim was to campaign continuously in the country until the projected 1915 election.[90] In June 1914 the central council were planning an even bigger effort for the autumn – the traditional platform season.[91] Naturally, this sort of campaign could not attract much attention in the national press. Nor could it change the substance of national debate while civil war threatened in Ireland. But it did mean that the campaign was not necessarily a failure, simply because it was not the centrepiece of ministers' speeches or leading articles in the *Times*. Instead, it was being prosecuted vigorously in the country: the ground was being prepared for the forthcoming general election.

'We rustics will fight like tigers': the Liberal Party and the rural land campaign

The ultimate effectiveness of the campaign could only be judged from the results of that election. But some conclusions can be attempted. The first is that it was a remarkably good method of unifying and enthusing the Liberal Party. This was a great help when so many issues, from Home Rule and women's suffrage to industrial unrest, opened up divisions within the Liberal ranks. It is scarcely surprising, given the leadership's dominance of the party, that the main body of Liberals received the land campaign with approval. The NLF conference of 26–7 November 1913 showered praise on the campaign.[92] The enthusiasm of the *Daily News, Daily Chronicle* and *Westminster Gazette* was echoed at local level by papers like the *Liverpool Daily Post, South Wales Daily News* and *Birmingham Gazette*.[93] Moreover the rural campaign succeeded in firing the enthusiasm of the radicals without alienating the party's more conservative supporters. This was not an easy task in a party as heterogeneous as the Liberals and revealed how well Lloyd George had chosen his ground.

On the party's social-reforming wing, the journalists grouped around the *Nation* and *Daily News* were particularly enthusiastic about the campaign. Far from viewing it as a distraction from the pressing social problems of the towns, they saw it as a fulfilment of their desire to extend the boundaries of

June and August for some accounts of its progress. See also *Eighty Club year book, 1914*, London 1914, 13–14, for the club providing and training speakers.

[89] For example, W. Crook to Lloyd George, 31 May 1914, LG, C/2/4/27.

[90] B. S. Rowntree to Lloyd George, 25 May 1914, LG, C/2/4/19.

[91] B. S. Rowntree to Lloyd George, 19 June 1914, LG, C/2/4/30.

[92] Liberal Publication Department, *Proceedings of the annual meeting of the council of the NLF, 26–7 Nov. 1913*, London 1913, 55–9.

[93] See the 23 Oct. 1913 editions of all these newspapers.

traditional Liberalism to include significant social reform. The *Nation* was ecstatic in its praise.[94] L. T. Hobhouse wrote a series of articles in the *Manchester Guardian* lauding the new rural policy.[95] J. A. Hobson delivered a paper to the Rainbow Circle on the vital need for a rural minimum wage.[96] This reflected the long-standing commitment of this group to rural land reform. But the specific nature of the proposals – especially the minimum wage – fitted very well their concept of how Liberalism should develop.[97] Other radicals in the party shared their approval of the land campaign. Chiozza Money wrote to Lloyd George of his 'delight' at the proposals.[98] Addison declared that 'They are exactly the kind of thing we want and they will evoke real enthusiasm.'[99]

Even from the party's more cautious members there was barely a murmur of complaint against the land campaign throughout 1913–14. Indeed, some of the party's wealthiest and least progressive figures displayed considerable enthusiasm for the land proposals. The executive committee of the Central Land and Housing Council included men like Sir Courtney Warner (honorary treasurer), Cecil Beck (honorary secretary), Sir Walter Runciman and Lord Strachie.[100] Sir Charles Nicholson wrote fulsomely to Runciman of his delight at the new policies.[101] Even those who had opposed the land enquiry in 1912, when they feared it would be dominated by the single taxers, were won over. Sir Charles Henry had denounced the enquiry in 1912, but by 1914 he was hosting land campaign meetings on his own estate in Berkshire.[102] Even the ultra-Gladstonian, F. W. Hirst, wrote to Lloyd George after his Bedford speech that the land report was 'full of meat and well sustains your speech'.[103] These reactions illustrate the campaign's dual nature as a combination of social reform with an attack on the citadel of privilege. It may also indicate that any Liberals who could not reconcile at least some social reform with the old Liberal shibboleths had already left the party by 1913. Certainly, there is no record of any defections over the land campaign.

This unity was reflected amongst rural Liberals. MPs and candidates rushed forward in the autumn of 1913 to condone and promote the campaign. This applied to more conservative figures like Sir Richard Price, A. W. Soames and Sir Richard Mathias, as well as to enthusiastic social reformers

---

94 *Nation*, 11, 18, 25 Oct. 1913.
95 *Manchester Guardian*, 2–10 Oct. 1913.
96 J. A. Hobson, 'Rural wages', 12 Nov. 1913, in *Minutes of the Rainbow Circle, 1894–1924*, ed. M. Freeden (Camden 4th ser. xxxviii, 1989), 234–5.
97 Clarke, *Liberals and social democrats*, 155–63; Collini, *Liberalism and sociology*, 104–5.
98 Chiozza Money to Lloyd George, 23 Oct. 1913, LG, C/10/1/65.
99 C. Addison to Lloyd George, 23 Oct. 1913, LG, C/10/1/62.
100 *LM* xxi (1913), 770–2.
101 Sir C. Nicholson to W. Runciman, 21 Oct. 1913, Runciman papers, MS 82.
102 *Times*, 24 July 1912; *Daily Chronicle*, 15 July 1914.
103 F. W. Hirst to Lloyd George, 13 Oct. 1913, Lloyd George papers, MS 22525.

like Phillips Price and Noel Buxton.[104] Even the remaining Liberal land-owners produced only a few 'subdued murmurs' about the campaign.[105] Some of them, like the marquess of Lincolnshire and Lord Beauchamp, Lord Ashby St Ledgers, Lord Saye and Sele and Lord Lucas even took a prominent part.[106] The only difficulties arose in some areas of the south-west and north of England, where significant numbers of smaller, Nonconformist farmers regularly voted Liberal. Many Liberals in these areas, like George Lambert, were enthusiasts for the land campaign.[107] But a few feared it would alienate Liberal farmers. George Schuster, candidate for Eskdale, decided to avoid mentioning the campaign in his speeches.[108] Sir Luke White, MP for Buckrose, chose to emphasise his 'independence' on rural matters.[109]

But instead of opposing the campaign, most Liberals from these areas sought to emphasise its benefits to farmers. In this they received the cordial help of the leadership. Agar Robartes, MP for St Austell, was able to gain an audience with Lloyd George for a deputation from the Cornish Farmers Union on 26 February 1914. The chancellor was notably amiable and conciliatory.[110] Sir Luke White's bill, allowing tenant farmers to claim compensation for disturbance if evicted when their land was sold, was rushed through parliament in 1914, settling a grievance outstanding since a 1910 court case.[111] On the whole, those farmers' leaders who had remained Liberals, like E. M. Nunnelly of Northamptonshire, found enough in the campaign to their liking to cancel out their disapproval of the minimum wage.[112]

One immediate effect of the land campaign and the enthusiasm it created among rural Liberals was that it helped to redress the enormous disadvantages that the Liberals suffered in agricultural seats because of weak organisation. The extension of the franchise in 1884 had made it imperative to create electoral machinery to win over the new voters. But the long distances and scat-

---

[104] *Eastern Daily Press*, 16, 24 Oct. 1913; *Gloucester Journal*, 20 Dec. 1913; M. P. Price, *My three revolutions*, London 1969, 233–4; *Eastern Daily Press*, 24 Oct. 1913.

[105] See Lord Beauchamp to Crewe, 19 Jan. 1913, Crewe papers, MS C/2, describing the reaction of Lord Sheffield and Lord Courtney to Lord Ashby St Ledgers's forthright speech in favour of an agricultural minimum wage.

[106] Lincolnshire, Beauchamp and Saye and Sele were all on the executive committee of the Central Land and Housing Council. For Ashby St Ledgers see his speech in the Lords: *Hansard*, 5th ser., 1913, xiii. 307–19. For Lucas see Gage to Runciman, 23 Oct. 1913, Runciman papers, MS 82.

[107] Lambert collaborated closely with Lloyd George over the land issue: Lloyd George to R. Buxton, 22 Sept. 1912, C. R. Buxton papers, Rhodes House, Oxford, MSS Brit. Emp. S 405 1/1, fos 11–12.

[108] G. Schuster to W. Runciman, 11 Dec. 1913, Runciman papers, MS 82.

[109] *Times*, 15 Oct. 1913. White was fairly openly opposed to the minimum wage: *Yorkshire Herald*, 3 Feb. 1914.

[110] *Times*, 27 Feb. 1914.

[111] *LM* xxii (1914), 207, 514.

[112] For Nunnelly's activities see A. Steel-Maitland to Bonar Law, 28 Oct. 1913, Bonar Law papers, MS 30/3/62.

tered populations in rural seats made them expensive to contest. In addition, each village had to be 'nursed' by means of donations to chapels, village halls and clubs. After the Whig defections of 1886, the Liberals could not count on the support of many wealthy men in the countryside to subsidise the required scale of activity.[113] As one rural Liberal bemoaned, 'Money is not easy to get in the country as the Liberals are mainly the working classes.'[114]

As a result, no Liberal organisation at all was founded in some rural areas until the early 1900s.[115] It proved difficult to find men like R. W. Perks, who had to spend £40,000 on Louth in 1892–1910, and many rural seats went uncontested.[116] After the Liberal recovery in the early 1900s, increased subventions from the whips allowed more contests (although twenty-three agricultural seats were still unfought in December 1910) but the Unionists retained their overwhelming superiority in organisation and finance.[117] The land campaign contested this by allowing meetings to be held in every village all over the country. Funds, propaganda and speakers were provided to proclaim a policy specifically tailored to rural voters, and to fight a long-drawn-out campaign against the Unionist hegemony.

The prospect of success definitely raised the morale of rural Liberals. 'We rustics will fight like tigers behind you and the Government' as Cecil Beck wrote.[118] They began to organise themselves from below to meet the initiative from the Liberal leadership. In 1911, rural Liberals had founded the NLHL, largely from the amalgamation of two societies – the Central Smallholdings Society and the Land Club League – devoted to encouraging smallholdings.[119] But the new League soon began to turn its attentions to electoral matters. In November 1912 an organising secretary was appointed 'to work primarily at the question of Local Elections' and the League promoted a series of conferences to interest rural Liberals in standing for their local councils.[120] In 1913 the League raised an election fund and endorsed and provided help to more than a hundred county council candidates in rural England, provoking a contest for the first time in many of these seats. Some 50,000 leaflets were printed for the elections and propaganda continued into

113 See T. Jenkins, 'The funding of the Liberal Unionist Party and the honours system', *EHR* cv (1990), 920–38, for the wealth concentrated in the ranks of the Liberal Unionist defectors.

114 Harker to Crook, 4 Mar. 1904, H. Gladstone papers, MS Add. 46024, fo. 103.

115 For example, Crook to H. Gladstone, 14 Apr. 1904, ibid. fo. 144, on St Augustine's, Kent.

116 Perks, *Autobiography*, 133.

117 This allowed rural Unionists to make regular gains over Liberals when the electoral register was updated each year. See, for example, Barkston Ash Conservative Association, executive committee, 1 Mar. 1910, 7 Feb. 1911, Barkston Ash Conservative Association papers, WYAS.

118 C. Beck to Lloyd George, 22 Oct. 1913, LG, C/4/1/8.

119 NLHL, *Annual report, 1911*, 4.

120 NLHL, *Annual report, 1912*, 6.

1914 with pamphlets, lecture tours, meetings and a regular magazine, *For Land and Home*.[121]

The Liberals were, therefore, well-placed to exploit any increase in their popularity in rural areas. Liberal and Unionist politicians who observed the agricultural scene were convinced that it was the land campaign's proposals for a minimum wage and state-built housing that had produced such an increase in support among agricultural labourers. In late May 1914 G. Wallace Carter held a meeting with the secretaries of the regional Liberal federations who reported to Lloyd George on the progress of the campaign in their areas. Finnemore of the Midlands stated that the labourers were 'pathetically keen' on the minimum wage, and Hughes of the eastern counties that 'the Wages Question appeals to the labourer with a force that can hardly be imagined'.[122] Storey of Yorkshire wrote that the labourers were 'undoubtedly impressed and favourable' and Crook from the home counties that the campaign had 'taken on well' in low wage areas.[123] Other rural Liberals shared this assessment. Oliver Brett, candidate for Tavistock, declared that the campaign was 'taking like wildfire'.[124]

Perhaps more significantly, Unionists were also impressed by the campaign's impact. Agents like E. Hely and MPs like Robert Sanders warned Steel-Maitland that the campaign was steadily winning votes in the countryside.[125] Steel-Maitland was forced to conclude that the deluge of propaganda was 'having an effect' in rural seats and that the autumn would see 'a setback rather than an improvement' for the Unionists. [126] Charles Bathurst insisted on the campaign's popularity in the south and west of England when writing to Bonar Law.[127]

In addition, the Liberals could hope to benefit from the 'Agrarian Awakening' i.e. the rash of strikes, lockouts and demonstrations staged by agricultural labourers right across rural England, from Lancashire to Wiltshire and Kent, in the spring and summer of 1914.[128] As prices rose, the labourers'

---

121 *Westminster Gazette*, 8 May 1913.

122 W. Finnemore to Lloyd George, 29 May 1914, LG, C/2/4/22; Hughes to Lloyd George, 29 May 1914, LG, C/2/4/25.

123 H. Storey to Lloyd George, 29 May 1914, LG, C/2/4/26; Crook to Lloyd George, 31 May 1914, LG, C/2/4/27.

124 O. Brett to Lloyd George, 26 Oct. 1913, LG, C/10/1/71. For clear expectations of gains in rural seats see Yorkshire Liberal Federation, executive committee, 4 Mar. 1914, 14 July 1916, Yorkshire Liberal Federation papers.

125 E. Hely (agent, West Country) to J. Boraston, 12 Jan. 1914, Steel-Maitland papers, GD 193/119/5/60; Steel-Maitland to Lord Lansdowne, 22 Jan. 1914, GD 193/119/5/54–6.

126 'Memorandum', 6 Apr. 1914, ibid. GD 193/119/5/1–2; Steel-Maitland to Bonar Law, 23 June 1914, Bonar Law papers, MS 39/4/40.

127 Bathurst to Bonar Law, 4 Dec. 1913, ibid. MS 31/1/6.

128 The phrase is from the *Nation*, 14 Mar. 1914. The best accounts of this phenomenon are still F. Green, *History of the English agricultural labourer, 1870–1920*, London 1920, 195–232, and R. Groves, *Sharpen the sickle! The history of the Farmworkers Union*, London 1949, 127–51.

meagre cash wages were left behind. This was one reason why the minimum wage was so popular, but it also produced a distant echo of the great industrial upheavals in the towns. One difference in the countryside was that the labourers found it as difficult as ever to organise themselves and significant unionisation only occurred in Norfolk and parts of the West Midlands.[129] Instead, local Liberals provided leadership and representation. Examples of this included the Northampton MPs, McCurdy and Lees-Smith, spearheading the campaign against Lord Lilford's dismissal of labourers for trade union membership in June 1914, and Cecil Beck and E. N. Bennett working for the strikers imprisoned during the Helion Bumpstead dispute in North Essex in July 1914.[130] Even where trade unions were active they remained closely linked with Liberalism. In Herefordshire, the Workers Union received financial help from Liberal tradesmen and support from Liberal newspapers, and at least one of its rural organisers was also a speaker for the land campaign. In Norfolk, George Edwards, the best known agricultural trade unionist, also spoke for the land campaign.[131] Moreover, though the labourers' union was becoming more independent from Liberal tutelage, there was no indication it had either the funds or the inclination to promote any Labour candidates in 1915.[132] Thus, in a 1915 election, the Liberals could feel confident of an upsurge of support amongst agricultural labourers.

Their standing with the farmers was, however, much more dubious. Championing striking labourers was scarcely likely to endear the Liberals to the farmers. The federation secretaries reported to Lloyd George that the farmers' attitudes ranged from 'an absence of marked ill will' in the Midlands, to 'suspicious and hostile' in Yorkshire, when confronted with the campaign's proposals.[133] After observing some forty campaign meetings in the Thirsk and Malton division of Yorkshire, Bruno Lasker, Rowntree's secretary, believed that the Liberals would gain no further support from farmers through the land campaign. The 'Minimum Wage will mean for them diminished profits', he wrote bluntly, and 'they are not, as a rule, exploited by cruel and wicked land-

---

[129] By 1914 the National Agricultural Labourers and Rural Workers Union had possibly 15,000 members, concentrated in Norfolk: Groves, *Sharpen the sickle!*, 144. The Workers Union, which recruited labourers in the West Midlands, probably did not equal this total: R. Hyman, *The Workers Union*, Oxford 1971, 45–8.

[130] See *Times*, 20 Apr. 1914, for the Lilford dispute. For Bennett and Beck taking up the Helion Bumpstead case see the *Daily Citizen*, 29 July 1914, and C. Jenkinson to MacDonald, 28 July 1914, Labour Party letter files, Labour Party archive, London, MS LP/PA/14/1/4.

[131] For Herefordshire see S. Box, *The good old days: then and now*, Hereford 1955, 2–3, and *Rural World*, Mar. 1914, 55; for Norfolk see G. Edwards, *From crow-scaring to Westminster*, London 1922, 186.

[132] A. Howkins, *Poor labouring men: rural radicalism in Norfolk, 1870–1923*, London 1985, 112, suggests, on the basis of a newspaper interview by Edwards, that the union might have sponsored a candidate at a 1915 election, but this is not supported by any firmer evidence.

[133] Finnemore to Lloyd George, 29 May 1914, LG, C/2/4/22; Storey to Lloyd George, 29 May 1914, LG, C/2/4/26.

lords. Some of them know they are under-rented.'[134] Farmers might, therefore, dislike the idea of a land court because it would actually raise rents, rather than lower them. As John Wallop, a Liberal landowner, wrote of the farmer, 'in practice he distrusts all legislation'.[135]

Certainly, the National Farmers Union adopted a stance very close to the Unionist position of land purchase schemes and relief of the rates, rather than the campaign's proposals.[136] But there are indications that the promise of security of tenure at least prevented the Liberals from facing a tidal wave of hostility from farmers and did divide them over the merits of the Liberal and Unionist schemes. Reports survive of pro-security of tenure resolutions being passed in the Farmers Unions of North Herefordshire, Northamptonshire, Yorkshire and Cornwall and the Hertfordshire chamber of agriculture.[137] This might suggest that the Liberals had a chance of not losing the support of those farmers who had remained Liberals in 1910. When Richard Reiss addressed the Norfolk Liberal farmers on 18 April 1914, he was able to persuade them to endorse the campaign.[138]

The electoral impact of the rural land campaign

The electoral impact of a pronounced pro-Liberal swing among agricultural labourers is a difficult matter to judge, but some general comments can be made on the changing significance of the agricultural vote since the mid-1880s. First of all, although numbers employed on the land had fallen by nearly half a million between 1881 and 1911, it still remained a major employer, with 1,065,101 people working in agriculture in 1911.[139] Moreover, as there was no redistribution of seats between 1885 and 1918, the decline in agricultural employment did not lead to a reduction in the representation of rural areas in the Commons. Agriculture was even more over-represented in parliament in 1914 than it had been in 1885. Labourers remained the majority of those employed in agriculture – some 656,337 in 1911, while farmers and their relatives accounted for 383,333.[140] Most significantly for the land campaign, labourers were still concentrated on the large arable farms in the south and Midlands, where they outnumbered the farmers by up to ten to one, as in Hertfordshire.[141] These were precisely the areas in

134 B. Lasker to Lloyd George, n.d., but May 1914, LG, C/15/1/27.
135 Crewe to Lloyd George, enclosing a letter from Wallop, 22 Nov. 1913, LG, C/4/1/12.
136 See *Times*, 7 Feb. 1914, reporting the reactions of NFU delegations to Lloyd George and Bonar Law.
137 These are collected in *The Homeland*, 18 Apr. 1914.
138 Ibid. 2 May 1914.
139 See the interpretation of census figures in Howkins, *Reshaping rural England*, 171–2, 201–4.
140 *Census of England and Wales*, 1911, x, p. xlv.
141 Ibid. x, p. xlviii.

which the Liberals needed to make a substantial improvement in their electoral performance. In the south-west or north, the ratio was much closer. But these were the areas where the Liberals retained some support among the smaller, Nonconformist farmers as well as the labourers and had done reasonably well even in 1910. In December 1910, for instance, they still won two of the three Cornish 'agricultural' seats.[142] Thus, even a small pro-Liberal swing among labourers in these areas might help to retain seats, or make gains in marginals. This process would, naturally, be assisted if the Liberals could retain their support among the farmers – hence the importance of the pro-farmer element in the land campaign.

Overall then, although agriculture employed a diminishing percentage of the English workforce, it retained considerable electoral significance, and the key to mobilising this bloc was the labourer's vote. An increase in Liberal support in this group might not 'sweep the rural constituencies', but Robert Sanders was probably correct in thinking it would put marginal Unionist seats at risk in the countryside.[143] Both Liberals and Unionists believed that 'a lot of votes . . . and some seats' would change hands in the rural areas and that Lloyd George was right to be 'very pleased' with the land campaign's progress in the countryside.[144]

For more precise evidence the only source available is the Liberal government's by-election record of 1911–14. During 1911–12 there was a marginal reaction against the government in rural seats (a swing of 1.7 per cent) similar to that in all seats (1.6 per cent).[145] On 31 May 1912 the Liberals retained the almost entirely agricultural seat of Norfolk North-West on a small anti-Liberal swing of 2.8 per cent – a good result coming between the heavy anti-government swings at Manchester South (11 per cent) and Ilkeston (9.1 per cent). There was, therefore, no advance warning of the result at Newmarket on 16 May 1913, when the Unionists gained a rural Liberal seat on a swing of 6.6 per cent.

This result indicates that just prior to the launch of the land campaign the Liberals faced a difficult task in the English rural seats. Newmarket was a division with only three towns (Soham, Ely and part of Newmarket itself) and 70 per cent of the voters lived in small villages, most of them engaged in some form of agriculture.[146] There was a strong tradition of Nonconformity and Liberalism in these villages and the seat was won by the Liberals in 1885–95,

---

142 See appendix.

143 Carter to Lloyd George, 28 May 1914, LG, C/2/4/20; Steel-Maitland to Lord Lansdowne, 22 Jan. 1914, Steel-Maitland papers, GD 193/119/5/54–6.

144 E. Hely to J. Boraston, 12 Jan. 1914, ibid. GD 193/119/5/60; Lucy Masterman diary, entry for 2 Dec. 1913, in Masterman, *Biography*, 261.

145 This is calculated from the swings in Horncastle, Wellington, South Somerset, Hitchin and Norfolk North-West, and compared with national swing: Clarke, 'Electoral position', 834.

146 *Times*, 13 May 1913. Ely had 1,500 electors, Soham 950 and Newmarket 850, out of a total of 10,731.

1903–January 1910 and in December 1910. The result of the by-election, when compared with the relatively good Liberal performance at Norfolk North-West – a seat that was similar in being heavily agricultural with a strong Liberal tradition – therefore requires some explanation.[147] It is hard to see why the traditional Liberal handicaps in Newmarket – the influence of Ely cathedral and Newmarket racecourse, the outvoters and 'the giant Fear' – should have been more potent in 1913 than in December 1910.[148] Possibly, the Liberal candidate, George Nicholls, was a poor choice. Though a Nonconformist and an ex-labourer he was a stranger to the seat and was not a wealthy man.[149] The division's four previous MPs and Denison-Pender, the Unionist victor in 1913, were all very rich, and a number of local Liberals pointed to the significance of Denison-Pender's conspicuous generosity in nursing the constituency.[150] However, Norfolk North-West had been won by a carpet-bagger in financial difficulties so this cannot be the whole explanation.

The most likely reason behind the poor Liberal performance was the introduction of national insurance payments on 15 July 1912 (a month and a half after the Norfolk North-West by-election). The deduction of 4d. per week was naturally unpopular with labourers who earned as little as 12s. per week in the winter. The legislation also forced the dissolution of the village sick clubs that played such an important role in rural life. Unionists were very active in schemes to save these clubs by federating them into county-wide approved societies.[151] In the Newmarket campaign Denison-Pender entirely ignored Tariff Reform in favour of an all-out assault on the insurance act.[152] Every commentator on the by-election, from the *Daily Herald* to the *Daily News* and the *Times*, agreed that the insurance issue had alienated the labourers.[153] Nicholls had little to hit back with, as the land proposals were not yet government policy. The messages he received from Lloyd George, Asquith and Churchill were studiously vague.[154] Nicholls attempted to propound his own scheme of voluntary conferences to raise wages, in return for rate relief to farmers. This alienated the farmers without convincing the labourers, and Nicholls was duly beaten.[155] The *British Weekly* concluded that while 'the Government measure was still in the clouds' similar results could be expected from the rest of rural England.[156]

---

147 Pelling, *Social geography*, 97–8. The seat was only won by a Unionist in 1886.
148 See H. Spender's article in the *Daily News*, 16 May 1913.
149 Illingworth had pushed him on a reluctant constituency: Riddell diary, entry for 17 May 1913, Riddell papers, MS Add. 62972, fo. 172.
150 The *British Weekly*, 22 May 1913, published letters from three local Nonconformist ministers emphasising this factor.
151 R. Prothero [Lord Ernle], *From Whippingham to Westminster*, London 1938, 254–60.
152 See *Times*, 10 May 1913.
153 See the 19 May editions of all these newspapers.
154 See *Times*, 7 May 1913, for Churchill; 8 May 1913 for Lloyd George and Asquith.
155 At a farmers' meeting Nicholls was shouted down: *Daily News*, 13 May 1913.
156 *British Weekly*, 22 May 1913.

The only by-election in rural England after the launch of the land campaign indicated that the campaign had at least had the effect of counteracting the disillusionment felt with the Liberals in the countryside in early 1913. That by-election was in the Buckinghamshire division of Wycombe on 18 February 1914. In contrast to Newmarket, the Liberals had only won Wycombe in 1906 and did not even contest the seat in December 1910, against an excellent Unionist organisation.[157] In January 1910 the Unionist majority was 2,556 and a majority of over 3,000 was confidently predicted for the by-election.[158] In addition to the unpopularity of national insurance and the usual anti-government swing in a by-election, local factors were strongly in the Unionists' favour. The new Great Western and Central railway line to Marylebone, opened in 1906, had brought a flood of commuters into the seat around Gerards Cross and Beaconsfield. The rise of 1,800 in the electorate in 1910–14 was largely attributable to this phenomenon, and most of these new voters were reckoned to be Unionists.[159] The core of the Liberal vote was the working class of High Wycombe, mainly engaged in chairmaking. But since November 1913, the whole town had been riven by a lock-out in the chairmaking industry. By February 1914 some 2–3,000 men were idle and there had been a number of riots in which factories and the metropolitan police had been stoned. The chairmakers were estimated to be 75–80 per cent Liberal and the dispute deprived the Liberals of the help of some of their keenest supporters. The strike leader, Councillor Forward, advised his followers to abstain.[160] Efforts at mediation could not solve the dispute before polling day and the local press reported 'light' voting in Wycombe, while the Unionists were able to poll successfully the commuters at the eastern end of the seat.[161]

Yet, instead of a humiliating reverse, the Liberals achieved a small pro-government swing of 1.2 per cent from the January 1910 result. It is true that the Liberals had an excellent candidate in Tonman Mosley, a barrister and businessman from a landed background and an ex-Unionist, who had bought a country house in the seat and become chairman of the county council. But it is hard to believe that he had enough 'influence' to counter the factors working against him, or more appeal than the Unionist candidate, Du Pré, who was a popular landlord from a family long-established at Beaconsfield.[162] A more likely explanation for the good Liberal performance was the intensive campaign in the rural villages run by the Central Land and Housing Council. The marquess of Lincolnshire consulted the council's officials on how to conduct the by-election on 14 January 1914 and he initiated

---

157 Lord Parmoor, A retrospect, London 1936, 61.
158 Daily Chronicle, 20 Feb. 1914.
159 Times, 16 Feb. 1914.
160 Ibid. 3 Jan. 1914. Speculation about a Labour candidate came to nothing however.
161 South Bucks Free Press, 20 Feb. 1914.
162 Times, 13 Jan. 1914.

the council's campaign at a meeting on 2 February.[163] Then a specially imported staff of lecturers was reported to be 'scouring the countryside' pressing the land policy.[164] The result was a pro-Liberal swing sufficient to wipe out the enhanced commuter vote, the problems in Wycombe itself and the usual anti-government swing.

Though some Liberals had even higher expectations, Rowntree believed that this result 'indicates the strength of the Liberal position'.[165] It demonstrated that an intensive land campaign could, by cancelling out any anti-government swing, save the thirty English rural seats won by the Liberals in December 1910. In addition, if the pro-government swing of 1.2 per cent at Wycombe was repeated in all English rural seats, the Liberals would gain a further nine seats.[166] But the Liberals might hope to do even better than this if the general election was held after the plural voting bill became law. This possibility worried the Unionist leadership, and with good reason.[167] The Liberal and Unionist organisations both made estimates of which seats the Unionists had won in December 1910 because of plural voting.[168] Each concluded that the Unionists had won twenty-nine seats in this way, and they agreed on the names of twenty-five of these seats.[169] This remarkable congruity, based on entirely different sources, suggests a high degree of accuracy, especially as both parties made great efforts to track down and poll sympathetic pluralists.[170] Of the twenty-five English seats both parties agreed on, no fewer than seventeen were agricultural, and they included eight of the nine seats that would be won on the 'Wycombe' swing of 1.2 per cent.[171]

These statistics provide an additional reason why the Liberals might hope to make gains in rural England in a 1915 general election. If the land campaign could cancel out any anti-government swing in the rural areas, the abolition of plural voting alone would hand the government nearly twenty seats. Moreover, in July 1914, the land campaign was only just beginning to build up to a 1915 election and its full impact can only be surmised from the

163 CD, entries for 14 Jan., 2 Feb. 1914.
164 *Times*, 7 Feb. 1914. The most detailed account of the campaign is in the *South Bucks Free Press*, 6 Feb. 1914.
165 B. S. Rowntree to J. Rowntree, 30 [*sic*] Feb. 1914, B. S. Rowntree papers, MS 6(a).
166 Mid-Norfolk, Stowmarket, North Lonsdale, Bodmin, Ramsey, North Dorset, Chippenham, Ross and Bassetlaw: see appendix.
167 Long to Bonar Law, 31 Dec. 1913, W. Long papers, BL, MS Add. 62404.
168 LM xviii (1910), 645; W. A. Gales, memorandum, n.d. but 1917, Steel-Maitland papers, GD/193/202/62.
169 Altrincham, Eddisbury, Bodmin, Egremont, Eskdale, High Peak, Tavistock, Torquay, North Dorset, Tewkesbury, Ross, Huntingdon, Darwen, Newton, North Lonsdale, Melton, Stamford, Mid-Norfolk, Bassetlaw, Woodstock, Stowmarket, Woodbridge, Isle of Wight, Chippenham and Droitwich.
170 G. Jones, 'Further thoughts on the franchise', *P&P* xxxiv (1966), 134–8.
171 Eddisbury, Bodmin, Eskdale, Tavistock, North Dorset, Tewkesbury, Ross, Huntingdon, North Lonsdale, Melton, Stamford, Mid-Norfolk, Bassetlaw, Woodstock, Stowmarket, Woodbridge and Chippenham.

events of 1913–14. A gain of twenty or so seats was probably the absolute minimum the government could look forward to in rural England at the next election.

Therefore, despite the campaign's failure to dominate national political debate, it cannot be said that it made no positive impact. Observers believed that the rural campaign was popular with the labourers and Liberal organisation was in a better position than ever before to take advantage of this popularity. Together with the abolition of plural voting it meant that the Liberals could look forward to gains rather than losses in the English rural seats. In this area at least there was no sign of the 'Strange Death of Liberal England'.

7

The Urban Land Campaign, 1913–1914

In contrast to the rural land campaign, it is far more plausible to present the urban land campaign as a failure. Indeed, some historians, like Bruce Murray, Bentley Gilbert and George Bernstein have judged it to have been a more or less unmitigated disaster.[1] Criticism has focused on two points: first, that Lloyd George had misjudged the political temper of the towns and 'in the urban areas his land program was failing to ignite the anticipated enthusiasm' and that this is confirmed by the by-election results of 1913–14; second, that the difficulties the government experienced with its 1914 budget were a serious setback for the urban campaign.[2] Bentley Gilbert believes that the budget 'caused a rebellion' among Liberal MPs which 'clearly defined the limits of the Party's tolerance for social and economic change' and that, as a result, 'land reform had died'.[3] This chapter tests out these views by looking in some detail at the urban campaign and its relationship to the 1914 budget.

'our people have very little to say': the 'failure' of the urban land campaign

There can be little doubt that the land campaign did not make much progress in the towns during 1913–14. This was the opinion, not just of hostile commentators, but of those conducting the land campaign. When G. Wallace Carter, the secretary of the Central Land and Housing Council, reported to Lloyd George on 28 May 1914, after his conference with the regional federation secretaries, he had to admit that 'the campaign in the boroughs has been disappointing'.[4] The secretaries confirmed this in the reports they sent directly to Lloyd George. Storey of Yorkshire wrote that 'generally speaking, the town meetings have been small and dull and little enthusiasm has been aroused'.[5] Crook of the home counties believed that 'In urban areas the Government's proposals have so far failed to catch on' and

---

[1] B. Murray, 'Lloyd George, the navy estimates, and the inclusion of rating relief in the 1914 budget', WHR xv (1990), 58–78, and ' "Battered and shattered": Lloyd George and the 1914 budget fiasco', Albion xxiii (1991), 483–507; Gilbert, 'Budget of 1914'; Bernstein, Liberalism and Liberal politics, 4, 145–7.
[2] Murray, 'Budget fiasco', 506.
[3] Gilbert, 'Budget of 1914', 139, 141, 140.
[4] Carter to Lloyd George, 28 May 1914, LG, C/2/4/20.
[5] Storey to Lloyd George, 29 May 1914, LG, C/2/4/26.

that 'Greater London is quite unmoved. The Land Question has not touched it at all.'[6] Lloyd George accepted the accuracy of these reports. He wrote to Runciman that 'it is quite clear that something more has to be done to educate the urban population'.[7] It would be erroneous, however, to conclude from these reactions that the policies devised by the urban land enquiry had been rejected by the towns. In fact, this programme was never presented to the country in 1913–14. The reasons for this lay in the delays in developing policies within the urban enquiry and then gaining the approval of the cabinet. By the time this process had been completed it was too late to make any impact on the country before World War One intervened.

When Lloyd George brought his proposals on the land to the cabinet meetings of 14–16 October for approval, he was able to present an outline of the entire rural programme. But this was impossible for the urban side of the enquiry, which had fallen far behind its rural counterpart. When, in June 1913, Lloyd George decided to launch the land campaign in the autumn, he knew that, as the rural enquiry was virtually completed, Rowntree would be able to devote his time to producing an urban strategy. On 25 August 1913 Rowntree was 'working on the evidence' for the housing chapter, though 'nothing' had been written on rating.[8] Unfortunately, the chancellor failed to provide Rowntree with enough time to evolve a coherent set of policies from the mass of urban data. At the cabinet meetings of 14–16 October 1913, Lloyd George was only able to present two urban proposals to go alongside the rural programme.[9] The first was that leaseholders and business tenants should have legal protection against eviction, rent rises and restrictive covenants. The second was that local authorities should be able to purchase land at its true market value in advance of any immediate need for such land. This latter policy was later to form a crucial plank in the enquiry's housing plans, but such proposals did not yet exist in early October 1913. The cabinet duly approved Lloyd George's leaseholds and land acquisition schemes. When ministers spoke on 'the land' in autumn 1913, they coupled these policies with the rural programme in their speeches, as Churchill did at Alexandra Palace on 15 November and Asquith at Oldham on 6 December.[10] In the prime minister's definitive speech on the government's land policy on 9 December 1913, leaseholds and land acquisition were included (together with a call for a national survey of the nation's housing needs).[11]

It is clear, therefore, that both Lloyd George and the cabinet believed that the land campaign should have an urban dimension and wished to promote this aspect of the campaign. However, the urban elements in the programme

---

6 Crook to Lloyd George, 31 May 1914, LG, C/2/4/27.
7 Lloyd George to W. Runciman, 12 June 1914, LG, C/7/5/8.
8 B. S. Rowntree to Lloyd George, 25 Aug. 1913, LG, C/2/2/48.
9 'Cabinet note on ministry of land', 18 Oct. 1913, Harcourt papers, MS 443, fos 201–5.
10 *Times*, 17 Nov., 8 Dec. 1913.
11 Ibid. 10 Dec. 1913.

approved in October 1913 were so meagre that the land campaign appeared to be a largely rural affair. On the vital areas of housing, rates and wages, the government had literally nothing to say. This continued to be the case, despite the fact that by early November Rowntree had produced a sketch of most of the urban programme.[12] This was embodied in two speeches by Lloyd George, at Middlesbrough on 8 November and Holloway on 29 November.[13] He outlined the enquiry's proposals to allow local authorities to promote high-quality working-class housing on land they would acquire in the suburbs and to develop transport schemes to the town centres. For the lowest paid there would be wages boards to raise their earnings and so allow them to occupy better housing. The leasehold proposals were expounded in greater detail at Holloway. But the proposals remained vague outlines. The wages board policy was referred to in a single sentence at Middlesbrough. The chancellor still had nothing to say on rates beyond a few hints, as the enquiry still had not come to any conclusions on this matter.[14] Most important, the policies Lloyd George presented for the first time at Middlesbrough and Holloway did not have the approval of the cabinet. There had not been sufficient time to present them at a cabinet meeting and the proposals were, in any case, a mere outline. Therefore, they were not taken up in the speeches of other ministers and the campaign continued to present a largely rural aspect.

That most of the urban programme did not have cabinet approval had a serious effect on the campaign launched by the Central Land and Housing Council in 1914. Because this body was the creation of the chief whip and was under his authority, rather than that of Lloyd George, it could only promote those items in the urban programme that had been endorsed by the cabinet. As, initially, this only included leaseholds and land acquisition, Rowntree was at a loss as to what to say to the council's urban speakers when he was supervising their training in December 1913.[15] The speakers were sent out into the country with no policy at all to propound on housing, rates or wages. Reiss wrote on 4 February 1914 that 'as regards housing, it is impossible for us to prepare or issue any literature. This means that we can produce practically nothing that appeals to workers in the towns'.[16] Carter believed that 'we are seriously handicapped by the fact that on the urban side our people have very little to say'.[17] As a result of this paucity of relevant policies, public meetings in support of the urban campaign were noticeably absent

---

[12] The last important principle to be approved by the enquiry was the urban minimum wage on 5 Nov. 1913: Davies journal, entry for 5 Nov. 1913, E. W. Davies papers, MS 7, fo. 95.

[13] *Times*, 10 Nov., 1 Dec. 1913.

[14] The enquiry did not receive the information needed to evaluate the effects of various land taxation schemes until late November: Nathan to Lloyd George, 22 Nov. 1913, LG, C/6/6/3.

[15] B. S. Rowntree to Lloyd George, 23 Nov. 1913, LG, C/2/3/48.

[16] Reiss to B. S. Rowntree, 4 Feb. 1914, LG, C/2/4/6.

[17] Carter to B. S. Rowntree, 4 Feb. 1914, ibid.

from many towns: 'In some areas they will not have either meetings or lectures until they know what the Government's urban policy is. In London they have seriously discussed abandoning the whole Campaign until we have more to tell them' Carter informed Lloyd George.[18] In fact, many big cities, like Manchester, Leeds and York saw nothing of the land campaign until June and July 1914.[19]

Where the urban campaign did make an appearance, it was this lack of positive proposals for audiences in the towns and consequent rural bias that the campaign's organisers identified as the cause of the campaign's failure. As Crook wrote, 'the rural programme was first in the field, was better formed, was more emphatically and authoritatively stated and therefore caught on'.[20] Finnemore of the Midlands Liberal Federation wrote that while 'less emphasis had been placed on the urban than on the rural side' there could be no hope of the urban side of the campaign picking up.[21] Some of the speakers did not help in dispelling the impression of a largely rural campaign. Christopher Addison thought the London speakers 'know more about cabbages than slums' and 'They appear to have been great on Wat Tyler but he has fallen flat.'[22] But the real difficulty lay in the fact that the speakers had few policies to propound that would interest the towns. The urban campaign had not so much failed as failed to happen.

By-elections, 1913–14, and the urban land campaign

Similarly, it is not possible to argue that the by-elections held during 1913–14 prove that the urban policies of the land enquiry had no appeal to the towns, because these policies were never prominent in any Liberal campaign. Even the rural proposals were conspicuous by their absence after, and quite possibly because of, the Reading by-election of 8 November 1913. Reading was a very marginal seat, which Rufus Isaacs had held for the Liberals by only ninety-nine votes in December 1910. With the normal anti-government swing in a by-election, the Liberals must have been very doubtful of holding the seat. In addition, local factors were against them. The Unionists had an established and wealthy candidate in Leslie Wilson, who ran a vigorous campaign against the National Insurance Act, which was generally agreed by

[18] Ibid.
[19] Manchester Liberal Federation, executive committee, 14 May 1914, Manchester Liberal Federation papers, Central Reference Library, Manchester, MS M 283/1/3/3; Leeds Liberal Federation, cabinet committee, 23 June 1914, Leeds Liberal Federation papers; *Yorkshire Gazette*, 27 June 1914.
[20] Crook to Lloyd George, 31 May 1914, LG, C/2/4/27.
[21] Finnemore to Lloyd George, 29 May 1914, LG, C/2/4/22.
[22] C. Addison, *Four and a half years*, London 1934, i. 20, 26, entries for 30 June, 14 July 1914.

commentators to be unpopular in a low-wage town like Reading.[23] On the other hand, the Liberals were unable to find a local candidate and, after some difficulties, settled on the wealthy and radical outsider, G. P. Gooch. But this decision provoked the threat of an anti-vaccinationist candidate from within the local party. This was only narrowly avoided and Gooch's candidature was slow to gather momentum. [24] The Liberals were also hampered by the appearance of a British Socialist Party (BSP) candidate, J. G. Butler, to split the radical vote. Though Butler's campaign was desperately short of money he had a considerable local base on which to build.[25] He received the backing of the local ILP and the trades council – which had sponsored five independent Labour councillors in Reading – and the BSP had an active local branch.[26]

Entering the last week of the campaign, Gooch's prospects of victory looked remote. Local Liberals therefore decided on a change of tactics. At this time, in early November, Lloyd George had announced the government's new rural land policy, but there was no indication as to most of the accompanying urban policy. As a last resort, Gooch's campaign attempted to convince the workers of Reading that the proposed rural reforms would benefit them too. Leaflets appeared proclaiming, 'Vote for Gooch and the new Liberal land policy – the wage raising policy for Reading.'[27] The Liberals argued that higher agricultural wages would lead to higher wages being set in the towns. A revived rural economy would stop labourers migrating to the towns and causing unemployment, and a more prosperous countryside would buy more of Reading's products.[28] These arguments were on the same lines as those used by Joseph Chamberlain in 1885 to convince urban workers of the benefits to them of his allotments policy.[29] But, as in 1885, the workers of Reading were not persuaded. Gooch lost the by-election, with the Liberal poll declining 10 per cent on its December 1910 figure. Local reports suggested that votes were lost about equally to the Unionist and BSP candidates.[30]

This was not, however, a setback for the urban campaign. The Liberal effort at Reading had focused on the government's rural proposals. But, perhaps as a result of the Reading by-election, the Liberals did not repeat the tactic of attempting to convince urban voters of the benefits of rural reform.

[23] *Daily Chronicle*, 24 Oct. 1913; *Times*, 29 Oct. 1913.

[24] *Daily Chronicle*, 23 Oct. 1913.

[25] *Justice*, 25 Oct. 1913. Butler was secretary of the United Government Workers Federation, but this union's election fund only amounted to £19 and the union was, anyway, divided over Butler's candidature: *Westminster Gazette*, 3 June 1912; *Government Workers Advocate*, Dec. 1913.

[26] *Justice*, 25 Oct., 1 Nov. 1913; A. Alexander *Borough government and politics: Reading, 1835–1985*, London 1985, 174; C. Tsuzuki, *H. M. Hyndman and British socialism*, Oxford 1961, 278–9.

[27] *Daily News*, 4 Nov. 1913.

[28] *Times*, 4, 5, 7 Nov. 1913.

[29] Simon, 'Chamberlain and the unauthorised programme', 240–3.

[30] *Our Flag*, Dec. 1913, 196. For the accuracy of agents' calculations see J. Irvine, 'Forecasting by-election results', *NR* lxiii (1914), 765–74.

Gooch said of this strategy, 'I cannot say of my own knowledge that it won me any votes', and if this assessment was widely shared in the Liberal Party it is obvious why the rural campaign made no further appearances at urban by-elections.[31] But, as the urban proposals were still not government policy, the urban campaign was also absent. This was true even when the candidate would seem to have been ideally suited to run a campaign on land reform. In the Durham North-West by-election of 30 January 1914, the Liberal candidate was Aneurin Williams, one of the most prominent figures in the land nationalisation and garden city movements.[32] Yet, land reform received no prominence in this by-election. Williams confined himself to a defence of the government's record and the usual quarrel with the Labour candidate over who was the more genuine representative of the workers.[33]

Even when Lloyd George's close ally, C. F. G. Masterman, stood at Ipswich on 23 May 1914, the land campaign did not enter his strategy. This was despite the fact that Masterman had an extremely difficult task in attempting to retain the seat for the Liberals. The deceased Liberal MP's majority in December 1910 had been only 1.6 per cent. While Masterman was unknown in the area, the Unionist candidate, 'Union Jack' Ganzoni, had carefully nursed the seat.[34] The Unionists worked the Insurance Act issue very strongly against Masterman and he believed it did him great harm in the town's poorest quarters.[35] He also had to put up with the nuisance of a 'rebel' candidate, Jack Scurr, who had pursued him from Bethnal Green to campaign against the Insurance Act. Yet at no stage did Masterman turn to 'the land' to help him. He kept to his defence of the Insurance Act and the government's programme.[36] Lloyd George spoke for Masterman on 22 May,[37] but he centred his appeal on the threat to constitutional government posed by the Unionists' behaviour over Ulster and the many benefits Ipswich had received from old age pensions, national insurance and his new 'luck-sharing' budget. The Central Land and Housing Council opened an office in Ipswich to distribute propaganda, but it remained in the background and did not attempt to launch a campaign like that at Wycombe in February 1914.[38] It is not, therefore, possible to conclude from this, or any other by-election in 1913–14, that the urban campaign had no appeal to the voters – for such a campaign was never attempted.

31 *Westminster Gazette*, 10 Nov. 1913.
32 Williams was chairman of the executive committee of the LNS and a director of the First Garden City Ltd.
33 *Daily Citizen*, 8–30 Jan. 1914, especially issues for 21–24 Jan.
34 Ganzoni claimed to have had a haircut in every barber's shop in Ipswich: *Eastern Daily Press*, 18 May 1914. This was a sensible approach to politics in Ipswich, where elections were of a traditional and personal nature: *Manchester Guardian*, 18 May 1914.
35 Riddell, *More pages*, 213, entry for 24 May 1914.
36 See his speeches reported in the *Daily News*, 16, 18 May 1914.
37 *Times*, 23 May 1914.
38 *East Anglian Daily Times*, 16 May 1914.

'a very small part' of the urban campaign: leasehold reform, 1913–14

The only policy of the urban programme that was consistently promoted throughout 1913–14 was leasehold reform. This had been approved by the cabinet on 14–16 October 1913, included in ministers' autumn campaign speeches and formed part of the Central Land and Housing Council's propaganda.[39] It was designed to appeal to two distinct groups: middle-class families who occupied their homes on a short leasehold of between twenty-one and ninety-nine years; and shopkeepers who leased their premises for a much shorter period. It can be argued, however, that Liberal attempts to appeal to middle-class voters on these lines were futile because the middle class was moving wholesale into the Unionist fold. The reasons for this are usually defined as fear of the organised working class and rising taxes, increased social segregation and economic difficulties.[40] However, this view cannot be wholly sustained for the Edwardian era. The 1910 elections revealed considerable regional variations in middle-class voting patterns, with the middle class of northern England, Scotland and Wales still relatively favourable to the Liberals.[41] Local research and statistical evidence have confirmed the role of Nonconformity in keeping middle-class Liberals in the fold.[42] Moreover, it can be argued that the occupational grievances of groups like shopkeepers played a significant role in their lives and gave them a separate identity that both parties might hope to exploit.[43] In fact, the Edwardian middle class can be presented as divided on regional, religious and occupational lines, much like the working class. This gave the Liberals the opportunity to appeal to different segments of the middle class, rather than facing an undifferentiated Unionist mass.

Liberals had taken up the grievances of leaseholders with some vigour since the early 1880s, initially on the basis of 'leasehold enfranchisement', i.e. compelling landowners to sell buildings to their lessees.[44] It is difficult to determine, though, whether the leaseholds issue had produced any electoral dividends for the Liberals in middle-class areas that would otherwise have tended to Unionism. It is not possible to determine the percentage of leaseholders per constituency and it is hard to separate the effects of the

---

[39] *Liberal land policy and the shopkeeper* (Central Land and Housing Council leaflet, no. 4), London Feb. 1914.

[40] G. Crossick, 'The emergence of the lower middle class in Britain: a discussion', in G. Crossick (ed.), *The lower middle class in Britain, 1870–1914*, London 1977, 11–60.

[41] Blewett, *Peers*, 400–6.

[42] J. Cox, *The English churches in a secular society: Lambeth 1870–1930*, Oxford 1982, 151–76; H. McLeod, *Class and religion in the late Victorian city*, London 1974, 176–81; K. Wald, 'Class and the vote before the First World War', *British Journal of Political Science* viii (1978), 441–57.

[43] C. Hosgood, 'A "brave and daring folk"? Shopkeepers and trade associational life in Victorian and Edwardian England', *Journal of Social History* xxvi (1992), 285–308.

[44] Reeder, 'Urban leaseholds'.

leaseholding system from other factors. For instance, the seat of Christchurch (actually largely consisting of Bournemouth) had a lower than average Unionist vote over 1885–1910 for a middle-class seat in the Wessex region. This might have been due to the leasehold system – Bournemouth was partly built on land leased from the Tapps-Gervis-Meyrick family. But it might also have been due to the strength of Nonconformity – a factor that could produce relatively high Liberal votes in middle-class seats with any form of land tenure.[45] In his general survey of English constituencies, Henry Pelling identified only eight middle-class seats where he felt the leasehold system had benefited the Liberals.[46] In December 1910 the Liberals held only one of these seats (Rochester), but a small swing of 2.8 per cent would carry another four (Southport, Christchurch, Torquay and Hastings). Using the experience of 1885–1910, it is therefore possible to conclude that more attention to the domestic leaseholds issue might be of some benefit to the Liberals, but only in a handful of constituencies. At best, it could only be a marginal factor in a general election.

The appeal to business tenants was a new initiative, though, with the advantage of aiming at a group which was not confined to a minority of seats. The shopkeepers' grievances had been vigorously promoted since 1906 by the Town Tenants League.[47] Despite its thinly disguised partisan nature, the League commanded impressive support. A total of 106 trade associations and retail chambers of trade passed motions in support of its policies, which were later to be taken over by the urban report and the Liberal government.[48] Lloyd George placed some weight on this issue. He received a Town Tenants League deputation on 30 October 1913 and arranged for his speech in reply, endorsing its programme, to be printed as a pamphlet.[49] The opinion of Liberal and Unionist observers was that the new policy was very popular with shopkeepers. Lloyd George told Asquith that they were 'delighted' and Frank, Knight and Rutley, advisers to the Unionists on urban policy, wrote that 'the Party would lose many votes' on the issue because it was 'necessarily very popular with shopkeepers'.[50] The 'disquieting' reports of London Unionists on the headway the Liberals were making with their business tenants policy led to Walter Long's Holloway speech of 17 January 1914, when he attempted to match the Liberals' promises.[51] But although 'the shopkeeper

---

45 For example the freehold city of Salisbury: Pelling, *Social geography*, 131–2.
46 For Croydon, Rochester, Hythe, Hastings, Eastbourne, Christchurch, Torquay and Southport see ibid. 65, 81, 84, 131, 170, 279.
47 Town Tenants League, *Town tenants bill*.
48 Evans to Lloyd George, 18 Oct. 1913, LG, C/28/1/3.
49 D. Lloyd George, *The urban land problem: the case of the town tenants*, London 1913.
50 Lloyd George to Asquith, 5 Dec. 1913, Asquith papers, MS 25, fos 63–6; Frank, Knight and Rutley, 'Leasehold enfranchisement scheme', 7 May 1914, Steel-Maitland papers, GD 193/119/5/3–7.
51 Lord Lansdowne to R. Cecil, 20 Jan. 1914, Cecil of Chelwood papers, BL, MS Add. 51161; *Times*, 19 Jan. 1914.

... is a person not to be lightly passed over when a General Election is imminent', business tenancies were still a sectional interest with limited appeal.[52] They could only be 'a very small part' of an urban programme, as the *Nation* pointed out.[53] The leaseholds policy could bring the Liberals some benefits, but not enough to sweep the towns.

The cabinet and the urban land campaign, 1913–14

However, there are indications that if the First World War had not intervened, the Liberal government would have been able to launch a far more comprehensive urban policy in the autumn of 1914. Between December 1913 and June 1914 the cabinet endorsed all the major elements of the land enquiry's urban report, thus providing the government with a far-ranging and radical programme to appeal to the towns. When the Ministry of Reconstruction summarised the proposals to which the Asquith government had consented, it revealed that the cabinet had agreed that local authorities should have a statutory duty to ensure that adequate housing existed in their areas.[54] They would have powers to acquire land, subject it to town planning and lease it out for building. They could develop new transport schemes and obtain a fair price for land through the land commissioners. The government would 'extend the operations of the Trade Boards to other low paid industries' to allow their workers to afford better housing. There would be state grants to assist local authorities and a measure of site value rating. Yet 'further proposals' were 'under the consideration of the Government' when war broke out.

The cabinet did not approve all these measures as a single package, as with the rural proposals on 14–16 October 1913, but dealt with them as they forced their way to the government's attention and when they could spare the time from the many crises of 1913–14. First, when Lloyd George decided that he wished to include plans for increased state grants and site value rating in his 1914 budget, he gained the cabinet's authority to announce at Glasgow on 4 February that site value rating would be government policy.[55] Then, in late February, Seebohm Rowntree wrote to his father that the cabinet was to be circulated with copies of the enquiry's sections on housing, with Lloyd George's 'recommendation that they shall be approved' at its next meeting.[56] There is no record of when this occurred, but on 14 and 19 May, Herbert Samuel, president of the local government board, made speeches identifying the housing policies of the government with those outlined by the urban

---

[52] Frank, 'Leasehold enfranchisement', Steel-Maitland papers, GD 193/119/5/3–7.

[53] *Nation*, 3 Jan. 1914.

[54] 'Summary of the chief proposals of the late government to improve urban housing conditions', n. d. [1917], Ministry of Reconstruction papers, PRO, Kew, MS 1/552.

[55] *Times*, 5 Feb. 1914.

[56] B. S. Rowntree to J. Rowntree, 30 [sic] Feb. 1914, B. S. Rowntree papers, MS 6(a).

enquiry.[57] Some Liberal propaganda at this time, especially *100 points in Liberal policy* and two Central Land and Housing Council leaflets, also suggest that the enquiry's proposals on housing had been accepted by the government.[58]

Finally, the cabinet came under intense pressure from the organisers of the land campaign, transmitted *via* Lloyd George, to endorse the minimum wage in urban areas. Carter believed that this 'would place our urban campaign on an entirely different level, more nearly approaching the rural campaign'.[59] After Rowntree and Cross visited the chancellor at Criccieth at Whitsun, Lloyd George took the matter up.[60] On 11 June 1914 Asquith consented to extend the wages board policy to the towns.[61] This meant that the government had accepted, albeit in piecemeal fashion, all the major items in the urban report. But, amidst the crisis over Ireland, the urban programme remained without a ringing public endorsement from the government, whatever had been decided in 10 Downing Street. To the public, the land campaign remained a predominately rural affair.

However, the programme which the government had accepted by June 1914 represented a bold new initiative in social reform that touched the central concerns of working-class life. The idea of a minimum wage was crucial to worries over the relationship of wages and prices in a boom era.[62] It was not aimed at higher paid, unionised workers, who might fear that 'minimum wage' would soon come to equal 'maximum wage', but at the lowest paid who had little hope of raising their wages through organisation. The labour movement had accepted the need for wage regulation for this group by supporting the 1909 Trade Boards Act and some trade unions covering low paid occupations, like the agricultural workers, had come to advocate the minimum wage policy.[63] The Liberals chose housing, though, as the route to appeal to the bulk of town workers. This was certainly a vital area of concern. Even if the approach of the urban report was somewhat oblique – focusing on land acquisition, town planning and new transport schemes – its impact could probably be heightened by skilful presentation. Avoiding a commitment to state construction and subsidies for housing also had its bonuses. It

---

[57] For Samuel's speeches to the Yorkshire Land and Housing Council at Sheffield and the Imperial Health League at South Kensington see *Times*, 15, 20 May 1914.

[58] Liberal Publication Department, *100 points in Liberal policy and of the Liberal record*, London 1914, 89; *Housing the town worker* (Central Land and Housing Council leaflet, no. 17), London 1914; *The town worker's rent and his wage* (Central Land and Housing Council leaflet, no. 18), London 1914.

[59] Carter to Lloyd George, 28 May 1914, LG, C/2/4/20.

[60] Lloyd George to B. S. Rowntree, 14 May 1914, LG, C/2/4/15.

[61] Montagu to Lloyd George, 12 June 1914, LG, C/1/1/18.

[62] See Gourvish, 'Standard of living', for the pressure on working-class standards of living.

[63] See *Hansard*, 5th ser., 1909, iv. 393–6, for T. Richards giving the act Labour and trade union support. See also *Report of proceedings at the 46th Trades Union Congress*, London 1913, 310 (5 Sept. 1913).

avoided charges of burdening the rates and creating 'charity' housing. It also reflected the fact that because local authority housing was so minimal before 1914, and the breakdown of the private rented sector was not universally accepted, state construction and subsidy did not seem to be the only solution to housing problems.[64] Generally, anti-landlordism plus social reform had rallied the working class to the Liberals in 1910. The government hoped to perform the same feat in 1915.

The urban campaign was also designed to appeal to the middle class of the towns. Leasehold reform would probably have brought the Liberals some benefits, though its appeal was strictly limited. The main Liberal appeal would have to be through site value rating and relief to the rates from central grants. Rate relief could not help but be popular. More land taxation would probably alienate those middle-class groups closely connected with the management and ownership of land, but the Liberals had probably lost all the support they were going to on this issue in 1910. Then, they had still retained considerable middle-class support, especially among Nonconformists outside the south of England. The Liberals hoped that a further assault on landlordism would again touch their radicalism.

The 1914 budget

Only one aspect of the urban campaign achieved legislative form before August 1914 though – the provision of rate relief and site value rating in the 1914 budget. This did not mean that the government regarded these proposals as the most significant element in the Liberal approach to urban land problems. One of the most important achievements of the urban report was to displace rating from the forefront of the Liberal view of the urban land question and install housing and wages instead. These were the central features of the programme endorsed by the cabinet during the period from December 1913 to June 1914. That the rating proposals appeared first in 1914 was entirely due to Lloyd George's attempts to produce a popular budget out of a difficult situation. The land campaign and the budget became entangled because the chancellor was the author of both projects.

Some hints about Lloyd George's longer-term financial plans had become evident to those closely observing the political scene in the autumn of 1913. The first element derived from the steadily worsening financial crisis facing local authorities. After continual pressure from this quarter, the whole subject had been referred to a departmental committee in 1911. Lloyd George, though, had little faith in its deliberations and during 1913 he had several times hinted at the need to restructure the grants system entirely.[65]

The second element in Lloyd George's plans was discernible from his

---

64 See the response of the land enquiry's informants: *The land*, ii. 66.
65 'Local taxation projects', 20 Apr. 1912, Nathan papers, Bod. Lib., MS 429, fos 52–3;

remarks, both in the House of Commons and in some of his land campaign speeches, that he favoured some form of site value rating.[66] This policy retained its popularity with many of the Liberal rank and file and pronouncements on reform of the rates helped keep the enthusiasts for land taxation satisfied. Moreover, it offered a chance to make use of the land valuation set in train in 1910, which would be completed in 1915. But an interest in site value rating was not necessarily separate from long-term plans to reform and increase local authority grants. It was a commonplace of Liberal thought that grants in relief of rates benefited landowners by allowing them to raise rents. This view was reinforced by the conclusions of the urban enquiry.[67] But, if increased grants were combined with site value rating, then any benefit to the landlord could be wiped out. The fact that the land enquiry produced such a plan in 1913–14 may be an indication of the way Lloyd George's mind was moving.

But the chancellor's hints did not suggest that he had any plans for the immediate future. Reform of the grants and rating system would require complex legislation and the government's timetable was already overloaded. Lloyd George put no such proposals to the cabinet in the autumn of 1913, nor did he initially provide for such a scheme in his 1914 budget. In fact, his main aim for that budget was to make it as non-controversial as the previous three. Since the infamous 'People's Budget' a buoyant economy had provided a steadily increasing revenue to cover rising current expenditure. The chancellor had been able to report regular surpluses and no new taxation. However, on 17 November 1913 he was obliged to tell the cabinet that, without cuts in the estimates, he faced a deficit of some £10 million.[68] But he was not willing to admit to the need for new taxes. The main victim he proposed was education, which would have its demand for an extra £2 million refused. The other important contender for more expenditure was the admiralty. The chancellor proposed more lenient treatment there. Admiralty estimates would only be pared down, while the sinking fund was raided to provide the rest.[69] This attitude could have been linked to Lloyd George's gratitude to Churchill for his support over the Marconi scandal and his need for a like-minded ally over the Ulster negotiations.[70] But Riddell, at least, claimed it was the result of a deal whereby Churchill supported the land campaign, and, in return, Lloyd George supported the naval estimates.[71]

Whatever the truth of the matter, Lloyd George failed to spearhead the

---

Hansard, 5th ser., 1913, l. 132–52; Times, 10 Nov. 1913 (report of speech at Middlesbrough).

66 Hansard, 5th ser., 1913, lvi. 366–80; Times, 13 Oct. 1913 (report of speech at Bedford).
67 The land, ii. 629–31.
68 J. Pease diary, entry for 17 Nov. 1913, Gainford papers, MS 39.
69 Asquith to George V, 18 Nov. 1913, Asquith papers, MS 7, fos 74–5.
70 P. Rowland, The last Liberal governments, London 1968–71, ii. 274–5.
71 Riddell diary, 31 Oct.–1 Nov. 1913, Riddell papers, MS Add. 62973, fos 59–60.

campaign against increased naval expenditure in the cabinet in December 1913. He only asked the admiralty to shave their estimates, so he could avoid raising taxes, rather than demanding wholesale cuts. This strategy was, initially, successful and Churchill agreed to find some savings for 1914–15.[72] He did not clash with the chancellor until he refused to postpone laying down four extra dreadnoughts from January to June 1915 – something that would crucially affect expenditure in 1915–16. In a heated exchange of notes over the cabinet table, Lloyd George insisted he had only promised to support increased spending for 1914–15, but had always said he would fight to reduce the naval estimates in 1915–16.[73]

The explanation for Lloyd George's curious behaviour is that he had long-term plans for his 1915 budget. The most likely course of action he had charted was to use the money freed from a decrease in naval spending for 1915–16, probably with some extra taxation, to finance an overhaul and expansion of state grants to local authorities. Site value rating would be introduced at the same time to prevent landowners benefiting from the change. The chancellor obviously hoped for a non-controversial budget in 1914, as major changes were foreseen for the following year. If Lloyd George did have such a scheme in mind it would explain the very hasty production for the cabinet of two memoranda on land taxation, on 13 and 24 December 1913.[74] Possibly the chancellor hoped to use them to explain and justify his plans for a 1915 budget if only he could reduce naval spending in 1915–16. The memoranda make most sense when read in conjunction with his other cabinet memorandum of 24 December opposing Churchill's demands for four dreadnoughts in 1914–15.[75] Such a scheme would also help to explain some of the passages in Lloyd George's famous *Daily Chronicle* interview of 1 January 1914, where he contrasted rising naval expenditure with the pressing need for rate relief. It is also noticeable that, on the same day, he wrote a letter that was intended for publication to P. W. Raffan of the land values group, in which he promised that site value rating was possible in the near future.[76]

But Churchill did not moderate his demands – in fact he increased them in a cabinet memorandum of 10 January 1914.[77] With the prime minister's support, and making full use of the threat of resignation, he prevailed. The cabinet of 27 January agreed to a further rise in naval spending and the

---

[72] Asquith to George V, 20 Dec. 1913, Asquith papers, MS 7, fos 84–8.

[73] Churchill, *Churchill*, ii. 660–2.

[74] Nathan to Lloyd George, 11 Dec. 1913, Inland Revenue papers, MS 63/35, N22.1, fo. 33, reveals that Harper was asked for the data on 10 December. It became 'The rating and taxation of land values', 13 Dec. 1913, cabinet papers, MS 37/117/92, and 'Taxation and rating of site values', 24 Dec. 1913, MS 37/117/96.

[75] 'Navy estimates, 1914–15', 24 Dec. 1914, ibid. MS 37/117/97.

[76] Lloyd George to Raffan, 1 Jan. 1914, LG C/2/4/1, published in *Times*, 14 Jan. 1914.

[77] 'Naval estimates, 1914–15', 10 Jan. 1914, Asquith papers, MS 25.

construction of all four dreadnoughts in 1914–15.[78] This decision finally destroyed any hope of avoiding tax rises in the 1914 budget. But Lloyd George's plans were not necessarily in ruins because of this development. The comfort for the chancellor was that Churchill promised to find major savings for 1915–16, despite the new dreadnoughts. Lloyd George hoped to save £4 million from the navy estimates (though Churchill definitely promised only £2 million). Moreover, he thought he could find a further £2.25 million from juggling the insurance fund and the increased revenue from existing taxes would no doubt provide even more.[79] This meant that the chancellor had hopes of finding enough money in 1915–16 for his scheme for reforming rates and grants without raising taxes in 1915 as well as 1914.

However, Lloyd George was reluctant to present a 1914 budget whose only feature was to increase taxes to pay for more dreadnoughts. As he later told Riddell, 'while we were about it there was no reason why we should not provide for other things beside the Navy'.[80] In other words, the chancellor intended to bring forward to 1914 his announcement of major increases in state grants in 1915–16. The new taxes in 1914 would help pay for the grants when naval expenditure fell. Site value rating would be introduced in 1915 as well. As early as 28 January he told Nathan, chairman of the Inland Revenue, to start preparing a scheme for tax increases in 1914 to cover increased naval spending and, subsequently, increased state grants.[81] On 4 February he told his audience at Glasgow that site value rating would be government policy and on 19 February he announced in the Commons that the government intended to 'take steps, and to take them this year, for the relief of local taxation'.[82]

The exigencies of rising national expenditure had produced a curious situation. The urban land report had not even been written, let alone approved by the cabinet. Yet Lloyd George was proposing to take advantage of the need to raise taxes in 1914 to implement one section of the urban land strategy on grants and rating. But this did not mean that these ideas were the most important section of the urban land campaign. When it appeared in April 1914 the urban report made it quite clear that housing development had replaced rating reform at the forefront of the Liberal approach to the land question in the towns. Lloyd George seized on the reform of rates and grants in February 1914 as a way of producing a social-reforming budget when he was faced with the need to increase taxes, rather than because he was obsessed with the significance of land taxation or believed it should be at the forefront of Liberal social policy. Thus the urban land policy did not stand or fall on the fate of the 1914 budget.

78 Asquith to George V, 29 Jan. 1914, ibid. MS 7, fos 93–4.
79 'Memorandum of interview, 28 January 1914', Nathan papers, MS 429, fos 268–70.
80 Riddell, *More pages*, 214–15, entry for 14 June 1914.
81 'Memorandum of interview, 28 January 1914', Nathan papers, MS 429, fos 268–70.
82 *Times*, 5 Feb. 1914; *Hansard*, 5th ser., 1914, lviii. 1176–87.

The budget was not finally unveiled until 4 May. It provided for a bevy of new taxes on the very wealthy, including a 2d. rise in the top rate of income tax to 1s.4d. on earnings over £2,000 *per annum*. The new taxes would pay for an £11 million scheme of central grants to local authorities in 1915–16. In 1914–15 they would cover Churchill's increased naval budget and also provide 'provisional' extra grants of £2.55 million for the period 1 December 1914–31 March 1915. The grants scheme was inextricably linked to the introduction of site value rating to ensure that landlords did not benefit from any reduction in the rate burden. Lloyd George proposed that the land valuation should be adapted to provide local authorities with separate valuations for the land and the improvements on it in their districts. In the future they would levy both a combined rate on land and improvements and a site value rate on land alone, but they would only be able to reduce the combined rate. This would prevent the rate relief in the budget from aiding landowners.[83]

Unfortunately for the chancellor, the government was forced to withdraw its scheme for provisional grants covering 1914–15 on 22 June 1914 – though this did not affect the planned grant increases for 1915–16.[84] It is this event that has led some historians to claim that the urban campaign was in serious difficulties in 1914, particularly because Lloyd George's plan was opposed by a number of backbench Liberal MPs. Actually, the dropping of these grants was a minor matter and it was certainly not occasioned by a backbench revolt, but rather by procedural difficulties in the Commons. There was, in fact, an obvious flaw in Lloyd George's plan. He had insisted on providing a scheme of grants for 1914–15, even though they would be distributed on the old, inefficient basis and would, according to Liberal theory, benefit landlords as there would be no site value rate in place when they were paid. This was obviously only acceptable if it was a temporary arrangement, to be replaced by a new system of grant allocation and the introduction of site value rating. But these plans might be held up by the House of Lords for up to two years. In the meantime, the Liberals might lose an election and they would, effectively, have set up a system of benefit to landlords for the Unionists to extend.

To prevent this, Lloyd George proposed that the finance bill containing the taxation to pay for the provisional grants should be kept in the House of Commons until it was certain that the House of Lords would pass the scheme to allocate grants on a new basis and to provide for site value rating.[85] Lloyd George decided that it was not imperative to give local authorities immediate power to levy site value rates. All that was necessary immediately was a measure to provide for the future separation of land and improvement values and to ensure that when the valuation was complete, relief would only go to

[83] Details taken from Lloyd George's budget speech, ibid. lxii. 56–94.
[84] For Herbert Samuel's speech announcing the withdrawal of the provisional grants see ibid. lxiii. 1575–92.
[85] The best explanation of this is Lloyd George's still somewhat opaque speech to the Commons on 11 May 1914: ibid. lxii. 774–801.

improvements. These provisions and the new system of grant allocation were placed in a proposed revenue bill which would have to pass through parliament before the taxes to pay for the provisional grants for 1914–15 were approved by the Commons.

Yet this ingenious scheme could not succeed. Under the Provisional Collection of Taxes Act of 1913 the finance bill had to follow a strictly defined timetable. In particular it had to be passed by both houses of parliament by 5 August. That meant that the revenue bill had to be written, passed by the Commons and debated by the Lords by the time the finance bill was sent to the upper house for them to pass it by 5 August. This was an impossible timetable. The cabinet only agreed even to attempt it because they were under the impression that the finance bill had until 5 September to pass.[86] When they learned the true position they had to accept there was no possibility of sending the revenue bill to the Lords for early August.

In these circumstances, partial retreat was the only option. The provisional grants for 1914–15 were abandoned as they could not be combined with measures to ensure the introduction of site value rating and a reformed method of grant allocation. As this knocked nearly £3 million off proposed expenditure for 1914–15, the top rate of income tax was reduced to 1s.3d. from 1s.4d.[87] Despite the claims of the Unionists, and historians like Bruce Murray and Bentley Gilbert, this was not actually a serious setback for the budget. As Lloyd George said in the Commons on 24 June, 'whereas our original intention was that part of the grants should become payable on 1 December, we now propose that they should become payable in the next financial year'.[88] The new grants had merely been postponed for some four months, not abandoned. By dropping the provisional grants, the government freed the revenue bill from the need to pass before the finance bill, but they still intended to introduce it in time to become law by March 1915. This would allow the new grants for 1915–16 to be distributed on the reformed basis of allocation and enable the Inland Revenue to start work on adapting the 1909 valuation, to be completed in 1916–17.

Thus, Lloyd George's grant and rating schemes had merely been delayed by a procedural miscalculation. This can scarcely be described as a major set-back for the urban land campaign, especially as these schemes were not even the central elements of that campaign. Nor was the postponement announced on 22 June in any way occasioned by backbench discontent among Liberal MPs.[89] Whatever anybody in the Liberal Party thought about Lloyd George's plans, the parliamentary timetable did not allow them to be

---

86 Ibid. lxiv. 395; Asquith to V. Stanley, 18 June 1914, in H. H. Asquith: letters to Venetia Stanley, ed. M. Brock and E. Brock, Oxford 1985, 89.

87 Hansard, 5th ser., 1914, lxiii. 1575–92.

88 Ibid. lxiii. 1869.

89 This point is made more fully in I. Packer, 'The Liberal cave and the 1914 budget', EHR cxi (1996), 620–35.

introduced for 1914–15. But some historians have seen the objections of a group of backbench MPs, dubbed 'the cave', to the provisional grants as a sign of widespread opposition within the party to further Lloyd Georgian social reform, including the land campaign.

This group first appeared in May 1914 and deputations saw Lloyd George on 22 May and Asquith on 15 June.[90] Not satisfied with their responses, the cave published its case in the *Times* on 18 June. Basically, they objected to voting on taxes in the finance bill before they had had an opportunity to approve the object of expenditure contained in the revenue bill. The 'constitutional and businesslike' course would be first to pass the revenue bill and then provide for the new taxation to pay for the increased grants. The government adopted this course, but because of procedural difficulties, rather than the cave's objections. This was not the end of the cave, though, for on 7 July twenty-two Liberal MPs abstained on the government motion to guillotine the finance bill. Asquith offered the group an enquiry into the anomalies of the operation of income tax and they promised to cause no further trouble that session.[91]

This sudden change of direction from local government grants and rating to income tax reform indicates that the cave was not only interested in questioning Lloyd George's schemes. In fact, it was a loose and unco-ordinated body of MPs, whose motivation and interests varied enormously. Some were perennial malcontents. Others had grievances that varied from the government's failure to arrest Sir Edward Carson to the Commons' adjournment on 6 July as a mark of respect on the death of Joseph Chamberlain, when MPs had been ordered to attend that day on a three-line whip.[92] Much of the hostility to the form of the grants and rating scheme for 1914–15 was not provoked by any dislike of the scheme itself but by the fear that if the Commons voted taxation which could not be used for grants because the revenue bill was not passed, then the money would be used for more naval expenditure.[93] In fact, the cave was much more a continuation of the argument over naval spending that had engulfed the government in December 1913–February 1914 than a revolt against Lloyd Georgian social reform.

The existence of the cave was certainly not evidence of widespread disaffection with the land campaign in the Liberal ranks. In fact, some MPs who took a prominent part in organising the cave's activities, like A. G. C. Harvey and Sir Charles Nicholson, were enthusiastic supporters of the campaign.[94] The cave's leader, Richard Holt, had his doubts, but these were kept to himself. He agreed to take the chair on the occasion of Lloyd George's

[90] *Times*, 23 May, 16 June 1914.
[91] *Hansard*, 5th ser., 1914, lxiv. 1127–9; *Times*, 9 July 1914.
[92] *Daily News*, 8 July 1914; *Westminster Gazette*, 8 July 1914.
[93] *Pall Mall Gazette*, 16 June 1914.
[94] A. G. C. Harvey to Lloyd George, 23 Oct. 1913, LG, C/10/1/63; Sir C. Nicholson to W. Runciman, 21 Oct. 1913, Runciman papers, MS 82.

Middlesbrough speech of 8 November and found some things at least in the campaign to his liking.[95] Other members of the cave, like G. H. Radford and Thomas Lough, had also appeared on Lloyd George's platform at urban land campaign speeches.[96] The cave included at least nineteen enthusiasts for land nationalisation or land taxation. Only one MP associated with the cave had spoken out against the land campaign, and that was H. H. Raphael in 1912, when it was feared that the enquiry would be a stalking horse for the single taxers.[97] It is, therefore, very difficult to see the cave as a revolt against the land campaign.

The final verdict on the urban land campaign must remain open. The proposals of the urban enquiry, though accepted by the government, were never effectively presented to the electorate. Its reaction cannot, therefore, be judged. The urban campaign was a Liberal initiative that was cut short by the outbreak of the First World War, rather than a sign of the Liberals' failure to appeal to the towns. What can be asserted, though, is that the land campaign and the government's radical direction were not seriously hampered by the events surrounding the 1914 budget. These difficulties were due to the parliamentary timetable and did not represent a major setback for the plans outlined in the budget. The revolt of the Liberal cave had no serious effects and was very far from being a concerted backlash against the government. Its fluctuating membership and diffuse aims made it one of the cabinet's least difficult problems in 1914.

[95] R. Holt diary, entry for 18 Nov. 1913, R. Holt papers, Liverpool City Library, Liverpool, MS 920 DUR 1/10, contains his strictures on Lloyd George's economics, but in his entry for 21 Dec. 1913, he found a Runciman speech on the land 'excellent'.
[96] Both spoke for Lloyd George at Holloway: *Times*, 1 Dec. 1913.
[97] Ibid. 13 Aug. 1912.

8

Confusing the Enemy: The Unionist Party and the Land Issue, 1912–1914

Traditionally, the strength of the Tory Party had lain in the English counties. But the Third Reform Act and the success of the Liberals in 1885 in many former Conservative bastions had a long-lasting effect on the party's perceptions. Like the Liberals, they came to regard rural England as a 'swing' area that could be won by either party, and the agricultural labourers as the key to results in these seats. Conservatives dared not rely purely on the influence of landowners to produce a favourable verdict in the countryside. Chamberlain had seemed to demonstrate in 1885 that policies to please the new voters were needed too. The Tories had pursued two basic strategies. First, they had emphasised their identity as the 'party of rural England', which would revive agriculture, providing work and prosperity for all in the countryside, while the Liberals were an urban party, only interested in cheap food for the towns. Thus the Conservatives lowered rates on agricultural land in 1896 and included some proposals for agricultural protection in their tariff reform policies from 1903 onwards.

But this approach was always intertwined with a determination to compete with the Liberals' proposals for land reform. It was the Conservatives who produced the first legislation on allotments and smallholdings, in 1887 and 1892 respectively. In 1909–10 Balfour had countered the Liberals' smallholdings programme with promises of his own. The major difference between the parties by the Edwardian era was the Tories' insistence on providing land for sale to new owners, rather than renting land to council tenants. This flexibility over land reform had caused some heart-searching in the Conservative ranks, especially over granting powers of compulsory purchase to local authorities. But these doubts had been swept aside by the need to retain the electoral allegiance of rural England.

This twin strategy had been generally successful. Only in 1906 had the Liberals won a majority of English rural seats. But the party leadership was always uneasy about the allegiance of the agricultural labourers. After 1910 this disquiet was compounded by new doubts about the party's umbilical link with landownership. Though the Unionists had successfully transformed themselves into a broadly-based party of property with significant popular support, landowners still occupied an important role in the party, symbolised by the leadership of the 'Hotel Cecil' in 1885–1911 and the use of the House of Lords to frustrate Liberal governments.[1] The great achievement of the Liberals with the 'People's Budget' and their assault on the House of Lords was to launch a successful attack on the Unionists, and win two elections, by turning their opponents' links with the landlords into an electoral handicap. As Lord Balcarres confided to his diary in 1910 after a shadow cabinet meeting on future policy, 'I fancy we should be unwise to reopen the land question more than we can help.'[2]

The announcement of Lloyd George's land enquiry therefore found the Unionists very sensitive about how they should respond. The chairman of Central Office, Sir Arthur Steel-Maitland, admitted in a memorandum written in the summer of 1912 that he was worried whether any such initiative would be 'very effective'.[3] But, given the party's long-established willingness to promote allotments and smallholdings, the lines along which Unionists should react seemed clear enough. A re-affirmation of their commitment to provide land for would-be peasant proprietors would maintain their support in the countryside and prevent them being labelled as reactionary defenders of the landlords. This strategy was outlined in two speeches by Lord Lansdowne in July 1912 and June 1913.[4] In the first he re-emphasised the party's devotion to the cause of promoting small-scale landownership and added a definite pledge of state loans to tenant farmers when their landlord sold his estate. In the second this promise was extended to cover all those who wished to buy their farms if the landowner was willing to sell.

However, in contrast to the 1880s and 1890s, the Unionists' response to Liberal proposals for land reform neither united their party, nor provided them with an adequate antidote to the Liberals' promises. A number of historians have pointed out the extreme difficulty the Conservatives experienced in 1912–14 in either rallying around the 'peasant proprietors' strategy or producing an alternative.[5] No fewer than three committees were appointed to look into the party's land policy in these years and after intense disagreements its stance was still not clear by August 1914. Lloyd George's land campaign succeeded where all its predecessors failed in seriously discomforting the Unionist Party.

---

[1] The best summaries of this process remain J. Cornford, 'The transformation of Conservatism in the late nineteenth century', VS vii (1963), 35–65, and 'The parliamentary foundations of the Hotel Cecil', in R. Robson (ed.), *Ideas and institutions in Victorian Britain*, London 1967, 268–311.
[2] *Crawford papers*, 166–7, entry for 14 Nov. 1910.
[3] Memorandum by Steel-Maitland, n.d. [mid-1912], Steel-Maitland papers, GD 193/80/5/44–9.
[4] *Times*, 25 July 1912, 23 June 1913.
[5] Sykes, *Tariff reform*, 262–4, 277–84; Fforde, *Conservatism and collectivism*, 126–59; E. Green, *The crisis of Conservatism: the politics, economics and ideology of the British Conservative Party, 1880–1914*, London 1995, 289–94; I. Packer, 'The Conservatives and the ideology of landownership, 1910–14', in M. Francis and I. Zweiniger-Bargielowska (eds), *The Conservatives and British society, 1880–1990*, Cardiff 1996, 39–57.

The reasons behind this confusion were themselves fairly straightforward. There was a certain amount of scepticism in the Unionist leadership, particularly among landowners, about the economic viability of small owners, the cost of state loans to create them and the problems that compulsory purchase of land would produce.[6] But the fundamental difficulty with pursuing this strategy was that many Unionists simply did not believe that it would be popular enough to combat the appeal of the minimum wage to agricultural labourers. As Rowland Prothero, a prominent land agent and adviser to the Unionists wrote to Steel-Maitland in 1913: 'Against such a policy the Unionist programme would have no chance.'[7]

These fears were confirmed when Lloyd George launched his land campaign in October 1913. The best the Tory leadership could do was to issue instructions to 'treat Lloyd George's land policy with ridicule or contempt' and to focus on Ulster instead.[8] But the Unionist whip, Robert Sanders, noted in his diary that this was 'not very practicable in county divisions'.[9] His fellow MP, J. F. Hope, agreed that 'I dare say we can laugh Lloyd George out of court about deer and pheasants, but we can't treat wages in this fashion' and C. H. Simpson, agent for East Dorset, confirmed that 'In rural districts Mr Lloyd George's proposals must be dealt with to the exclusion of almost every other topic.'[10] The Conservatives were convinced that the rural land campaign represented a serious threat to their hold on rural England and that they had to produce a policy to counter its effectiveness. As F. B. Mildmay's agent in Totnes noted, it was 'absolutely necessary' to have a policy on wages boards and E. Hely, agent for the West Country, told Central Office that if such a policy was not forthcoming, 'this is going to lose us a lot of votes among the agricultural classes and some seats'.[11]

If the Tories followed the example of their reaction to the Liberals' allotments and smallholdings policies, the obvious solution was to produce their own scheme for a minimum wage. This was the line taken by the MPs in the USRC. They believed that as Lloyd George's proposals were so popular, there was no point in opposing them and the only way to neutralise their appeal was to make the minimum wage a cross-party issue.[12] Behind this opinion lay the assumption that the landlords were a waning asset for Unionism. The

6   Packer, 'Ideology of landownership', 46–9.
7   Prothero to Steel-Maitland, 4 Feb. 1913, Milner papers, Bod. Lib., MS 39, fos 74–8.
8   Lansdowne to Steel-Maitland, 31 Oct. 1913, Steel-Maitland papers, GD 193/119/599.
9   *Real old Tory politics: the political diaries of Robert Sanders, Lord Bayford, 1910–35*, ed. J. Ramsden, London 1984, 67, entry for 13 Nov. 1913.
10   J. F. Hope to Steel-Maitland, 1 Jan. 1914, Bonar Law papers, MS 31/2/3; C. H. Simpson to J. Boraston, 21 Jan. 1914, Steel-Maitland papers, GD 193/119/5/59.
11   F. Mildmay to Lord Salisbury, 16 Feb. 1914, 4th marquess of Salisbury papers, Hatfield House, MS (4)74/78; Hely to Boraston, 12 Jan. 1914, Steel-Maitland papers, GD 193/119/5/60.
12   Leslie Scott's letter, *Times*, 12 May 1913.

party could only win the next election and save the Union (and the Welsh Church) by convincing working men that it was in earnest about social reform. The Tories' attitude to wages boards was a test case for their willingness to embrace state welfare.

However, it has not been appreciated how far the USRC were prepared to carry their strategy of co-operating with Lloyd George over wages boards. The main organisation for rural Liberals, the NLHL, already contained some prominent USRC figures, including Lord Henry Bentinck as its president and C. B. Bathurst and Christopher Turnor as vice-presidents. In 1912 two other USRC members, Sir Arthur Griffith-Boscawen, Unionist MP for Dudley, and Philip Lloyd-Greame, candidate for Buckrose, joined the NLHL's executive committee. Between March and September 1913 Lloyd-Greame chaired a committee of the League set up to investigate low agricultural wages, which duly reported in favour of statutory wages boards.[13] The USRC could scarcely go any further to demonstrate its willingness to jump aboard Lloyd George's bandwagon and it continued to champion the main proposals of the land campaign throughout 1913–14.[14]

But matters were not so simple for the leadership, which had to take into account the feelings and prejudices of a wide variety of Unionist supporters. It was, for instance, obvious that the adoption of a wages board policy would alienate many Tory farmers. They would be unlikely to defect to the Liberals, but they might be tempted to support independent farmers' candidates at the next election. It was widely known that some agricultural protectionists were so livid at the dropping of 'food taxes' by the Unionists in January 1913 that they were considering opposing rural Tory MPs at the next election.[15] Moreover, the NFU was keen to run its own candidates to secure direct representation for farmers in the Commons.[16] These might just be rumours and aspirations, but they gave weight to those Tories who argued that Bonar Law should 'stick to the farmer who is on our side and never mind the labourer whose vote you won't get anyhow'.[17] The most vigorous exponent of this view was the redoubtable Walter Long – scarcely a negligible figure in the party.

Long emphasised that landowners, too, would be alienated by an endorsement of wages boards, especially as farmers would be bound to claim rent reductions to compensate for paying higher wages.[18] This was obviously an important factor to take into account as landowners were still a formidable

13 NLHL, *Annual report*, *1911*, 3; *1912*, 1; *1913*, 4–5.
14 See the USRC's draft bill for statutory wages boards, introduced on 21 Apr. 1914: *Hansard*, 5th ser., 1914, lxi. 776.
15 J. Fraser to Bonar Law, 28 Mar. 1913, Bonar Law papers, MS 29/2/44.
16 C. Campbell and G. Bellwood, memorandum, 24 Oct. 1913, describing a meeting with Bonar Law: ibid. MS 30/3/51.
17 See *Real old Tory politics*, 67, entry for 13 Nov. 1913, reporting Lord St Audries's opinion.
18 Long to Bonar Law, 31 Oct. 1913, Bonar Law papers, MS 30/3/77.

force in Edwardian Unionism.[19] But Bonar Law was well aware of the need not to appear as the mere tool of landed interests. Paradoxically, that was one pressing reason why the Unionist leadership had to be cautious about making concessions on the wages boards issue. In 1913–14 Tory landowners were worried not just by the land campaign but by the imminent possibility of Irish Home Rule. Bonar Law had entered discussions with Asquith in October 1913 about a compromise settlement, based on Ulster's wish to be excluded from rule by a Dublin parliament.[20] If the Liberals made any gestures towards Ulster, these would have to be included in a separate amending bill, as the Home Rule bill could only overcome the Lords' two-year veto by passing in the form in which it was introduced in 1912. Bonar Law was anxious that his party should not appear to reject any reasonable offer from the Liberals out of hand and wished to put down Unionist counter-proposals to any amending bill, rather than just using the Tory majority in the Lords to bring about its defeat. But such a move would be bound to enrage diehard landowners in the Lords as it would mean that the party had implicitly accepted the need to abandon southern Irish landlords to rule from Dublin. In early 1914 Lord Willoughby de Broke was organising a covenant among the peers, pledging them not to accept any form of Home Rule before an election had been called. The shadow cabinet feared that if the Lords rejected a generous amending bill this would 'transfer the battle ground from the case of Ulster to that of the House of Lords' and Asquith would 'dissolve on the cry that the Lords had for Party purposes insisted on Civil War'.[21] At all costs, the leadership had to keep control of its troops in the Lords and that meant not antagonising them by any betrayals of the landed position in the face of the land campaign.

The Unionist leadership was, therefore, caught on the horns of an excruciating dilemma by the land campaign. Bonar Law did his best to avoid mentioning the matter at all, but by April 1914 Steel-Maitland was becoming ever more concerned. The Curragh mutiny had made the coercion of Ulster most unlikely and the summer of 1914 would see the climax of negotiations for an Irish settlement. He believed that it seemed 'suicidal that we should let our whole attention be monopolised by the Irish crisis . . . if the Irish crisis should be settled, we shall at once be confronted by the fact that the land question will come into great prominence'.[22] Eventually, a new policy was announced by Lord Salisbury and Lord Lansdowne in the Lords on 21 April 1914.[23] They suggested that a future Unionist government would

[19] J. Ramsden, *The age of Balfour and Baldwin, 1902–40*, London 1978, 94–5, 97–8.
[20] For the Home Rule imbroglio in 1912–14 see D. Dutton, *'His Majesty's loyal opposition': the Unionist Party in opposition, 1905–15*, Liverpool 1992, 203–50.
[21] Lord Midleton, memorandum, 23 June 1914, Salisbury papers, MS (4)75/112–15; Lord Selborne to Lady Selborne, 17 June 1914, in *The crisis of British Unionism: the domestic political papers of the second earl of Selborne, 1885–1922*, ed. G. Boyce, London 1987, 111–13.
[22] Steel-Maitland, memorandum, 6 Apr. 1914, Steel-Maitland papers, GD 193/119/5/1–2.
[23] *Hansard*, 5th ser., 1914, xv. 942–55, 976–89.

institute 'voluntary wages boards' – bodies that would set local minimum wages for agricultural labourers, but with no legal power to enforce their recommendations, which would rely on 'public opinion' for their effect.

This announcement signalled that the Unionists had finally been driven to accept the need to compete with Lloyd George's promises. But Salisbury and Lansdowne failed notably in their attempt to unite the party around this new policy. As Lord Carrington noted after the brief debate, 'The Tory Peers, however, do not seem to relish the idea very much and they showed their dislike by staying away.'[24] The only other Tory peers to speak, Lord Parmoor and Lord Malmesbury, were both hostile and Walter Long was soon denouncing the new policy to Bonar Law.[25] The Unionist Press was disdainful or 'crochety'.[26] From the other end of the Unionist spectrum, the USRC continued to insist on wages boards with compulsory powers. It was no wonder that the Salisbury–Lansdowne policy was not given much publicity in the summer of 1914. But it was Steel-Maitland who articulated the real difficulty with the strategy, noting that voluntary wages boards might not 'avoid falling between two stools, i.e. irritating farmers on our side who are already jumpy and yet not providing labourers with sufficient counter-attraction to Lloyd George's proposals'.[27] By June 1914 he was even more gloomy, declaring that as the importance of debates on the land increased this could only harm the Tories.[28]

Thus, the land campaign proved a particularly shrewd political thrust by Lloyd George. It placed the Unionist leadership in an almost impossible position, torn between the need to match the chancellor's promises and the fear of internal party strife. But this was only possible because the Tories shared so much of Lloyd George's analysis. They, too, thought that the political allegiance of the English rural seats was volatile and that an effective appeal to the interests of agricultural labourers would swing them towards the Liberals. They, too, believed that the minimum wage policy was such an appeal and that the Liberals would make important gains in the English counties. In the closely-fought election which Unionist whips expected in 1914 or 1915 the land campaign might make all the difference between success and failure.[29]

---

[24] CD, entry for 21 Apr. 1914.
[25] *Hansard*, 5th ser., 1914, xv. 965–76; Long to Bonar Law, 6 May 1914, Bonar Law papers, MS 32/3/13.
[26] Steel-Maitland to Salisbury, 25 Apr. 1914, Salisbury papers, MS (4)74/167.
[27] Steel-Maitland, memorandum, 6 Apr. 1914, Steel-Maitland papers, GD 193/119/5/1–2.
[28] Steel-Maitland to Bonar Law, 23 June 1914, Bonar Law papers, MS 39/4/40.
[29] See *Real old Tory politics*, 72–3, entry for 24 Feb. 1914, for a sober assessment of the by-election trends.

9

Labour and the Land Issue, 1912–1914

The land campaign was mainly an attempt to improve the Liberals' position at the expense of the Unionists. But it also aimed to maintain Liberal support against any challenge from Labour. The pre-1914 Labour Party was still perceived by many contemporaries as an adjunct to the Liberals. In fact, at the national level, the two parties had grown closer together in 1910–14 as Labour MPs provided consistent support for the minority Liberal government. But this co-operation did not obscure the fact that in some regions Labour was attempting to expand at the Liberals' expense and this could cause a serious division in the 'progressive' vote, resulting in Unionist gains. In 1910 this had not been a great problem. In January 1910, in twenty-seven three-cornered contests, Labour had won none and the Unionists only five (Bow and Bromley, Camlachie, Cockermouth, Whitehaven and Manchester South-West). But the Liberals would be seriously handicapped at the next election if Labour attacked Liberal seats on a significantly wider front and the Labour vote increased over its 1910 level. The Liberals had been warned of this danger by the fourteen three-cornered by-elections in Liberal seats in 1911–14. The Unionists won six of these seats on a minority vote (Oldham, Crewe, Midlothian, Lanarks South, Leith and Derbyshire North-East).

The exact number of Labour candidates in Liberal seats in a 1915 election is, of course, impossible to estimate. But even the Labour NEC's lists prepared for their meeting on 23 June 1914 showed that the Lib.–Lab. pact of 1903 was holding in many places. The NEC did not foresee any extra candidates in any of the twelve double-member seats shared by Labour and Liberal MPs, or clashes between Liberal and Labour candidates in cities like Birmingham, Sheffield, Liverpool, Nottingham or Wolverhampton.

However, some Liberal–Labour clashes were unavoidable in a 1915 election, and, given the strengthening of Labour's organisation (however unevenly) in 1911–14 it is unlikely that there would have been fewer conflicts than in January 1910. Not all of these possible three-cornered contests were equally dangerous for the Liberals. More Labour candidates in rock-solid Liberal areas like Durham, south Wales or west Yorkshire were of less concern because the Unionist vote was so low in these regions that they were unlikely to win many three-cornered contests. But in more marginal areas it would be worrying for the Liberals if they lost a significant number of votes to Labour.

The Liberals had to aim to reproduce the situation of 1910. The January 1910 election had shown that non-Unionist voters were willing to indulge in a degree of tactical voting in three-cornered contests to ensure that the

Unionist did not win. Obviously, this mainly benefited incumbent Liberal MPs. In the nine seats with three-cornered contests in 1906 and 1910 (Huddersfield, Leeds South, Portsmouth, Eccles, Camlachie, Ayrshire North, Lanarks, Govan, North-East and North-West), the Liberals' average share of the vote rose from 37.7 per cent to 42.9 per cent while Labour's fell from 27.2 per cent to 18.5 per cent. This ensured that only two of these seats were won by Unionists in 1910 (Portsmouth and Camlachie). The Liberals had once again to dissuade wavering voters from switching to Labour and so letting Unionist candidates win three-cornered fights.

The land campaign was not the great constitutional drama of 1910, but it might help convince working-class voters that the Liberals were still a party worth keeping in office. This was not wholly implausible. The competition for working-class votes was not a simple matter of proposing the most social reform. The older tradition of working-class radicalism still retained considerable purchase, especially in Liberal-dominated areas, and the land campaign was designed to stimulate the traditional hostility to 'privilege' that had been so effective in 1910. But, as in 1910, the land campaign offered radicalism plus the hope of material benefits for working-class voters. Moreover, it sought to avoid the mistakes of national insurance by offering social reform that would be attractive to the working class.

The Labour land enquiry, 1912–14

The Labour leadership were certainly aware of the threat posed to them by the land campaign. They responded by setting up their own enquiry in mid-August 1912, on the initiative of Arthur Henderson. After sounding out the NEC's views, the Labour MPs appointed a committee to produce a new rural programme for the party.[1] George Roberts, the MP with the closest rural connections, chaired the enquiry with Henderson as secretary. The other members were the keen land taxer, George Barnes, and James Parker, who had served on the 1911–12 Haversham committee on the sale of landed estates.[2]

The decision to set up the enquiry was not unanimous. When Jim Middleton, the party's assistant secretary, had asked NEC members for their reactions, six had been favourable and one wanted a decision postponed. But Ben Turner and Pat Walls were opposed to the idea, on the grounds that 'it is an imitation of the Liberal move and that it is time for campaigning rather than enquiry'.[3] The decision to over-rule this view reflected two main points. First that Labour, as the third party in British politics, could not determine the agenda. It had to be ready to respond to disputes between the two main

---

1   Middleton to A. Henderson, 14 Aug. 1912, Labour Party papers, HEN/08/1/59.
2   *The Labour party and the agricultural problem*, London 1914, 1.
3   Middleton to Henderson, 14 Aug. 1912, Labour Party papers, HEN/08/1/59.

parties with its own distinctive contribution. But Labour's decision to hold an enquiry also showed that most Labour leaders regarded the land issue as one of great significance. This does not mean that there was much interest in the countryside in the party – only one Labour election address mentioned agriculture in 1910.[4] Rather, it was a measure of Labour's hostility to landlords. The budget of 1909 and the struggle against the House of Lords evoked so much commitment in the Labour ranks because landlords were still seen as one of the most powerful reactionary elements in society. It was only in 1911 that, 'the first great crack appeared in the battlemented structure of modern feudalism', as J. R. Clynes put it.[5] Labour was also committed to the idea that the land belonged to the people and should be used for their benefit.[6] This was an old radical tradition but it still had some purchase among early twentieth-century socialists. Most notably, some Labour leaders remained enthusiastic about land settlement as a cure for unemployment – something of an obsession with Hardie, Lansbury and Jowett.[7] Thirty of the thirty-seven Labour MPs sitting in 1914 were vice-presidents of the LNS and land nationalisation was a ritual part of ILP and TUC policy.[8]

But Labour was an almost entirely urban party. It had no plans at all for an assault on rural landlordism. The enquiry was meant to remedy this defect. *Labour Leader* declared that the land question was 'urgent and arresting. It is a question which the Labour and Socialist movement must study at close quarters, and in regard to which we must formulate precise and constructive remedies'.[9] In response, the newspaper's letter pages were flooded in the following months with proposals ranging from state farms to smallholdings.[10] The Labour enquiry was designed to produce a coherent policy from this babel of ideas.

The enquiry worked intermittently from August 1912 to September 1913. It took evidence from sources as diverse as Joseph Fels, the National Agricultural and Rural Workers Union and the LNS, and would even have interviewed the Unionists' Rural League had they agreed.[11] An interim report was published on 16 June 1913 with the aim of pre-empting the land enquiry's

---

4   Blewett, *Peers*, 317.
5   J. R. Clynes, *Memoirs*, London 1937, i. 146.
6   M. Tichelar, 'Socialists, Labour and the land: the response of the Labour Party to the land campaign of Lloyd George before the First World War', *TCBH* viii (1997), 127–44, emphasises the significance of the ILP's long-standing commitment to land reform in determining its response to the land campaign, but is weaker on the immediate political context in 1912–14 and the input of bodies like the Fabians and trade unions.
7   I. Maclean, *Keir Hardie*, London 1975, 46; Lansbury, *My life*, 142–6; K. Laybourn, 'The defence of the "bottom dog": the ILP in local politics', in J. Jowitt and D. Wright (eds), *Victorian Bradford*, Bradford 1982, 230–3.
8   D. Howell, *British workers and the ILP, 1888–1906*, Manchester 1983, 344; Barry, *Nationalisation*, 64–5.
9   *LL*, 13 June 1912.
10   Ibid. June–Oct. 1912.
11   *Times*, 15 Oct. 1912; *Rural World*, Sept. 1912.

conclusions. Subsequent trips by the Labour committee to Ireland and Denmark did not substantially affect the final report published in January 1914. The NEC ordered 25,000 copies to be printed to disseminate Labour's views.[12] The report's first point was to emphasise that 'the ultimate aim of public ownership' was the only way to appropriate land values, develop production and raise wages.[13] Central and local authorities must have full powers to buy land with the aim of eventual land nationalisation. This was a clear difference of emphasis from the Liberal report, which contained no such aim (though de Forest's dissenting memorandum did).

But once the Labour committee considered immediate problems it became clear that it anticipated the Liberal report in almost every detail. It recommended a minimum agricultural wage, set by county or district boards. A nationally-determined figure was ruled out as impossible, and each board would take local factors into account.[14] Farmers would be able to claim the required wage increases back from landlords through fair rent courts. More smallholdings and agricultural co-operation were recommended. Only on housing was there a difference from the Liberal report. Labour believed that to include a sum for an 'economic' rent in the minimum wage award was to 'incur the risk of completely disrupting the agricultural industry'.[15] Local authorities should therefore be encouraged to build cottages by central subsidies that would be gradually reduced as wages rose. This option had much support in the Liberal Party, but it had not appeared in the land enquiry's report because it was deemed too expensive and divisive.[16] But it had not been conclusively rejected either, and as Labour favoured a subsidy that would be phased out, it cannot be said that the two reports were far apart.

This remarkable congruity was based on two factors. First, it was natural for the Labour Party to concentrate on the labourers' plight and to take the advice of their representative, the labourers' union. That union favoured extending trade boards to agriculture and the TUC had passed a resolution to this effect at each meeting since 1910.[17] The union believed that only state action could raise wages in agriculture because effective organisation was almost impossible amongst such a scattered and low-paid workforce. It also favoured a policy of state subsidies for rural cottages and had a long history of advocating smallholdings. However, the union disliked rent courts. George Edwards believed that 'The large farmers have nothing to complain of'.[18]

Secondly, whenever socialists had considered rural problems before 1912, their views had been very close to those of radical Liberals, and there had

---

12 NEC minutes, 24 Jan. 1914, Labour Party papers. The visits to Ireland and Denmark are described by Roberts in *Typographical Circular*, Oct., Dec. 1913.
13 *Labour and agricultural problem*, 3.
14 Ibid. 3–4.
15 Ibid. 5.
16 *The land*, i. 133–5.
17 *Proceedings at 46th TUC, 1913*, 310.
18 *Times*, 24 May 1914; *LL*, 19 Sept. 1912.

often been co-operation between the two groups. In 1907, when Lord Carrington had consulted Labour on his smallholdings legislation, he had received a memorandum emphasising the very themes of council tenancy, compulsory purchase and central powers that he intended to include in his bill.[19] 'I am glad to think we are not very far apart', he wrote to MacDonald.[20] Later, George Roberts, chairman of the Labour land enquiry, was on the executive committee of the NLHL, the main Liberal organisation working in the countryside.[21] It advocated a minimum wage and state-subsidised cottage building, just as the Labour enquiry was to recommend. This was not a surprising situation. The Labour movement had not divided from the Liberal Party over rural land reform any more than it had over Home Rule, Free Trade or licensing reform. The parties were divided by urban, industrial conflicts, not by any chasm of outlook that affected every issue. On many matters, the Labour Party held the same opinions as most Liberals.

Moreover, the direction Liberals were taking in rural matters coincided with the kind of approach Labour was taking towards urban social problems. From 1910, Labour's stance began to shift from its emphasis on the right to work. The ILP and the Fabians collaborated in a campaign for a 'National Minimum', also known as the 'War Against Poverty'.[22] In boom years unemployment was less of a concern than the struggle to maintain working-class living standards as prices rose. A central plank in the demand for a minimum standard of welfare was the call for a minimum wage. Labour's amendment to the address, moved by Snowden on 13 March 1913, was concerned with this subject.[23] On 9 April 1913, Will Crooks introduced a bill for Labour, to extend the Trade Boards Act to all low-paid occupations.[24] By recommending a minimum wage for agriculture the Labour enquiry was extending this approach into the countryside. The similarity in the Liberal and Labour reports was a clear demonstration of how close many Liberal and Labour leaders were in their attitudes to social reform. But the result for Labour was that, far from providing a suitable riposte to the Liberal initiative, they had endorsed it in advance.

The Fabians and the land enquiry

A possible source of alternative ideas for Labour was the Fabian society. This too held a rural enquiry in 1912–13. It did not have its origins in the announcement of Lloyd George's enquiry, however. Rather, it was the child of

---

[19] 'Smallholdings bill: memorandum re Labour Party's position', n.d.[1907], Ramsay MacDonald papers, PRO, Kew, MS 30/69/1220.
[20] Carrington to MacDonald, 26 Mar. 1907, ibid., MS 30/69/1151.
[21] NLHL, Annual report, 1911, 3.
[22] See the Daily Citizen, 12, 21 Oct. 1912.
[23] Hansard, 5th ser., 1913, l. 458–574.
[24] Ibid. li. 1280–324.

the Webbs' renewed interest in the Fabian society on their return to England in March 1912. The *New Statesman* was one fruit of their attempts to push Fabian ideas into the centre of politics. Another was the decision of the finance and general purposes committee on 20 June 1912 to set up two enquiries to determine future policy.[25] The first and more important was on industry, and was chaired by Beatrice Webb. It launched a lengthy and complex investigation and eventually provided the kernel of the Labour Research Department in later years.[26] The second enquiry was assigned to study 'Land problems and rural development'. The Fabian executive appointed the chairman and nucleus of the enquiry from among its own members, while ordinary Fabians with an interest in the subject could also join the committee, until it grew to 'about twenty five in all'.[27] The committee defined eight topics for investigation and members were each assigned to one of these. They wrote papers, gathered evidence and, at weekly meetings in London, discussed their findings. Land experts like Christopher Turnor, Josiah Wedgwood and Joseph Hyder were interviewed.[28] Draft conclusions were given as a lecture to the Fabian society as early as 28 February 1913, but a draft report did not appear, in a special supplement to the *New Statesman*, until 2 August 1913.[29]

The most important figures in the enquiry were its chairman, H. D. Harben, and the two veteran Fabians, Edward and Margery Pease.[30] Harben was a very wealthy man (his grandfather had built up the Prudential Assurance company) and a substantial landowner in Buckinghamshire. A long-term disciple and friend of the Webbs, he had pursued a gradual political pilgrimage from right to left. A Unionist candidate in 1900, he had stood as a Liberal in 1906 and again in 1910. On 5 July 1912 he resigned as Liberal candidate for Barnstaple over the women's suffrage issue and by December 1912 he was the major financial backer of the *Daily Herald*.[31] The Peases were more conventional middle-class Fabians – Edward was the Fabians' secretary from 1890 to 1913.[32] They had long been interested in rural matters through

[25] Fabian Society, finance and general purposes committee, 20 June 1912, Fabian society papers, Nuffield College Library, Oxford, MS C/12.

[26] *The diary of Beatrice Webb*, ed. N. Mackenzie and J. Mackenzie, London 1984, iii. 176–7.

[27] *Fabian News*, Oct. 1912.

[28] Ibid. Oct. 1912, Jan. 1913.

[29] Ibid. Apr. 1913.

[30] Harben organised the committee and wrote the draft report of 2 Aug. 1913, as well as *The rural problem*, London 1913, the final conclusions. Edward Pease arranged the publication of the draft, and the Peases were the committee's most assiduous attenders. They received the largest number of commendations for influential memoranda submitted to the committee: Fabian society, executive committee, 6, 27 June 1913, Fabian society papers, MS C/12; *Fabian News*, Jan. 1913.

[31] *Diary of Beatrice Webb*, iii. 179; *Times*, 6 July 1912; G. Lansbury, *The miracle of Fleet Street*, London 1925, 15–16.

[32] See J. Bellamy and J. Saville (eds), *Dictionary of Labour biography*, ii, London 1974, 293–8.

their involvement in the affairs of the Surrey village of Limpsfield – home to many artists and socialists since the 1890s.[33] Other significant figures on the enquiry included Reginald Bray, a Surrey landowner, close friend of Masterman, and Progressive member of the LCC;[34] Harold Aronson, a Liberal barrister active in various smallholdings and rural housing movements;[35] and G. P. Blizard, a young Fabian accountant and Progressive candidate for the LCC in 1913.[36]

Despite this committee's greater experience of rural matters than its Labour or Liberal counterparts, its conclusions were broadly similar. The committee recommended a minimum wage, which would include a sufficient sum to pay an 'economic' rent, though in contrast to the other reports it preferred a nationally determined minimum figure.[37] Rather surprisingly, rent courts were not endorsed, although farmers would be given the option to quit, if they wished, when their wages bill rose to meet the national minimum standard. Even more surprising was the report's equivocal attitude to game preservation – an unheard-of concession to the landlord's point of view from a radical organisation.[38] It may not be fanciful to attribute these two elements in the report to the prominence of landowners like Harben and Bray on the committee. On rural housing, the committee favoured a state subsidy to local authorities, though more cautiously than in the Labour report. The grant would only be enough to cover the sinking fund and half of any deficit.[39] Smallholdings were strongly recommended and there was a reference to the need for eventual land nationalisation.

In his *History of the Fabian Society*, Edward Pease cautiously noted that the Fabian report 'cannot be said to have been epoch-making'.[40] Instead of providing Labour with new ideas on the land question, the Fabians had merely provided further support for the Liberal land report. This was not surprising. Most of the figures on the Fabian enquiry were ex-Liberals, or used to working closely with Liberals. In particular, Edward and Margery Pease

---

[33] Ibid. Margery Pease was elected to the rural district council in 1911. Other prominent residents of Limpsfield included Edward and Constance Garnett, Ford Madox Hueffer [Ford], Sydney Olivier and Stephen Crane. See F. E. Green, *The Surrey hills*, London 1915, 9–13.

[34] All were mentioned in *Fabian News*, Jan. 1913, and the preface to *The rural problem* as submitting influential memoranda. For Bray see P. Brandon, 'A twentieth-century squire in his landscape: Reginald Bray of Shere, Surrey', *Southern History* iv (1982), 191–220.

[35] Aronson was author of *Our village homes* (London 1913), and *The land and the labourer* (London 1914). He worked for both the NLHL and the land campaign: NLHL, *Annual report, 1912*, 3, and *The Homeland*, 7 Mar. 1914.

[36] *Fabian News*, Apr. 1914.

[37] Harben, *Rural problem*, 25–8.

[38] Ibid. 32–4, 97–104.

[39] Ibid. 36–43.

[40] E. Pease, *History of the Fabian Society*, 3rd edn, London 1963, 228.

were central figures in the NLHL.[41] But the Fabian enquiry's approach also grew out of the society's own traditions. Since the 1890s Fabians had advocated wages boards for sweated industries as part of their concept of a 'national minimum'. In 1905–9 they were an important component of the Anti-Sweating League – a particular interest of Beatrice Webb's.[42] In Fabian Tract No. 123 of 1905, *The revival of agriculture: a national policy*, a Fabian civil servant called H. W. Macrosty had brought this idea to bear on agriculture. He advocated a national minimum wage for labourers, including enough for an 'economic' rent, rent courts, smallholdings and gradual land nationalisation. Sidney Webb thought enough of the minimum wage idea to include it in his 'intercepted letter' of 1906, advising the new Liberal government on a suitable programme.[43] Thus, the Fabian enquiry already had the central feature of its approach to rural problems mapped out for it even before it began work – a policy which anticipated the contents of the Liberals' land report. When Lloyd George launched his land campaign in October 1913, the *New Statesman* could only declare, somewhat lamely, that it was 'generally satisfactory'.[44]

'checkmated by Lloyd Georgeism':
Labour and the land campaign, 1913–14

This response was not, however, much different from that of the Labour leadership. As they had commissioned a report on rural policy that had endorsed most of Lloyd George's programme they perhaps had little choice. On 16 October 1913, MacDonald reviewed the land report in the *Daily Chronicle*. He described it as 'masterly' and pointed to the 'striking harmony' between the Liberal and Labour reports. His only criticism was that the land report did not make clear its attitude to state subsidies for cottage-building. Even this criticism was tempered by MacDonald's remarks that 'theoretically' there was nothing to say for subsidies, though they might be necessary as a 'temporary expedient'. This was a shrewd analysis of one of the report's obscurities, but scarcely a swingeing criticism. Other leaders did not even go this far. In a speech at Middleton on 20 October 1913 Arthur Henderson said that if the government carried out its land programme, 'they would have no more loyal supporters than those in the ranks of the Labour Party'.[45] In a press interview after Lloyd George's Swindon speech, George Roberts said that, 'if the Government legislates on the lines and in the spirit of his speech last

---

41 NLHL, *Annual report, 1911*, 3, 14. Margery Pease was the League's honorary secretary and Edward Pease drafted its constitution.
42 A. McBriar, *Fabian socialism and English politics, 1884–1918*, Cambridge 1962, 259–61.
43 S. Webb, 'The Liberal cabinet: an intercepted letter', *NR* xlvi (1906), 789–802.
44 *New Statesman*, 25 Oct. 1913.
45 *Manchester Guardian*, 21 Oct. 1913.

night, Mr. Lloyd George will deserve and receive the whole-hearted support of George Roberts, and, in my opinion, that of the whole Labour Party'.[46] Similar statements were made by the rank and file in the Commons. Albert Smith said on 6 November 1913 that 'if the Chancellor intended to improve wages paid to agricultural labourers he would have no more ardent supporters than the members of the Labour Party'.[47]

In taking this line, the leadership had overwhelming support from the trade union movement. The engineers' journal called the land initiative Lloyd George's 'crowning achievement' and stated that 'one feels that the Labour Party in Parliament will back this . . . for all it is worth'.[48] To general admiration of the chancellor's radicalism, many trade unions added a deep-seated, if atavistic, concern for the welfare of agricultural labourers. They felt that measures to improve labourers' conditions would dry up a potential source of blackleg labour. At the 1913 TUC, £500 was voted to the labourers' union to employ two extra organisers precisely for this reason. The railway clerks, moving the motion, declared that 'it is largely from this class of worker that blackleg labour is recruited in times of dispute'.[49] The dockers union also believed that 'During times of strike it is from farm areas that much of blackleg labour is recruited.'[50]

Many in the trade-union movement also believed that low agricultural wages held down urban wages and that migration from the countryside increased competition for jobs. The NUR delegate, seconding the 1913 motion at the TUC, said that low agricultural wages, 'persistently stood in our way when we have tried to raise the wages of our people'.[51] G. H. Stuart, of the postmen, believed that 'the influx of countrymen being stemmed, wages must go up in the towns'.[52] Many trade-union officials who had become MPs believed the same. George Barnes referred to labourers, 'invading the towns and intensifying the competition for employment' and Joseph Pointer to 'a steady migration to the already overcrowded towns.' which had to be stemmed.[53] These beliefs were deeply enough ingrained for trade unions to spend money and their officials' time on helping the labourers' fight for higher wages. Sympathetic action from the NUR and the dockers was crucial to the success of the farm labourers' Lancashire strike of 1913.[54] Railwaymen often provided branch secretaries for the Workers Union's agricultural section and the dockers' union sent the labourers on strike in north Essex in

---

[46] *Eastern Daily Press*, 24 Oct. 1913.
[47] *Daily Citizen*, 7 Nov. 1913.
[48] *ASE Monthly Journal and Report*, Feb. 1913.
[49] *Proceedings at 46th TUC, 1913*, 313.
[50] *Dockers Record*, Aug. 1914.
[51] *Proceedings at 46th TUC, 1913*, 314.
[52] *Postman's Gazette*, 1 Nov. 1913.
[53] *Glasgow Herald*, 26 Jan. 1914; *Sheffield Guardian*, 17 Oct. 1913.
[54] Green, *Agricultural labourer*, 195–9.

June 1914 £20 per week, and the help of their organisers.[55] The National Union of Boot and Shoe Operatives (NUBSO) offered the labourers' union £50 *per annum* in 1917 to help its organisation and a NUBSO activist (and then official) was president of the labourers' union from 1911 to 1923.[56]

By offering general support to the land campaign, the Labour leadership was, therefore, just expressing the views of the Labour movement's most important component. As Beatrice Webb said of MacDonald, 'In his old-fashioned Radicalism, in his friendliness to Lloyd George, he represents the views and aspirations of the bulk of Trade Unionists.'[57] But the leadership's stance was also part of their general approach to the Liberal government. They believed that there was no point in opposing Liberal reforms that were reasonable and popular with the Labour movement. Labour had to prove itself the better party of reform by criticising the details of Liberal plans and producing its own proposals. In the long term, Labour had to hope the Liberals would baulk at further social reform and stand open to attack as reactionaries, or split, with the radicals joining Labour. Either way, Labour stood to gain most as the party of reasonable reform that would take the Liberals' ground, while, as MacDonald put it, 'the rebel windbag threatens to do for us what the militant suffragist did for the women's suffrage movement'.[58]

But the land campaign illustrated some of the dangers of this strategy for Labour. Its only difference with the Liberals was over the question of subsidies for cottage building and this appeared a minor detail, especially when the Liberal proposals were still in outline. Labour was in danger of submerging its identity in that of the Liberals. Voters might see little point in supporting a party so similar to the Liberals when the two parties clashed at elections. Labour's line on the land campaign might 'but help in the buttressing of Liberalism rather than the strengthening of Socialism'.[59] This, of course, was exactly what the Liberals hoped would occur.

Many in the ILP were acutely aware of this problem and critical of the leadership's attitude. Fenner Brockway warned on 23 October 1913 that 'There is a grave danger that the Labour Party programme will be submerged by the attention given to Mr. Lloyd George's land proposals', or, as Fred Henderson put it, 'The spreading of the Liberal net for the Socialist and Labour vote at the next General Election has begun.'[60] But it proved difficult to formulate an alternative response. Almost all of the left believed that in tackling the question of landownership, Lloyd George was dealing with one of the most powerful 'monopolies' that socialists should be fighting. As

---

55 Box, *Good old days*, 2; Grove, *Sharpen the sickle!*, 148.
56 A. Fox, *A history of the National Union of Boot and Shoe Operatives, 1874–1957*, London 1958, 376–7.
57 *Diary of Beatrice Webb*, iii. 195, entry for 6 Feb. 1914.
58 *Leicester Pioneer*, 17 Apr. 1914.
59 Joseph Duncan in *Forward*, 3 Aug. 1912.
60 *LL*, 23 Oct. 1913; *Clarion*, 24 Oct. 1913.

Snowden said at the June 1912 LNS conference, 'the landowner, by virtue of his land monopoly, drove the people into the slums; the land system was responsible for their narrow streets, their overcrowding, and, in many places, for saying that the people should live in a particular place'.[61] Moreover, all the reforms Lloyd George outlined were good in themselves. 'As palliatives we can support nearly every proposal as tending to restrain the unlimited power of landlordism', T. D. Benson, the ILP treasurer wrote.[62]

Critics were, therefore, forced into more general denunciations of the land campaign. W. C. Anderson claimed that 'The best points in the Report have been commonplaces of Socialist propaganda for years.'[63] This line of attack was not very fruitful, however, as, if it were true, it was difficult to see why Labour should not support the land campaign. More commonly, critics claimed that the Liberal Party could not be sincere in its policies. 'Do they seriously believe that a Party financed by such patrons as these will deal in a fundamental way with the evils of landlordism?', *Labour Leader* rhetorically asked, after listing all the Liberal MPs who were thought to be millionaires.[64] This tactic had its limitations, though, as it was difficult to demonstrate. The cabinet had accepted the land report and the question of its implementation would have to wait until the Home Rule crisis, and probably the 1915 election as well, were over. This only left the claim that the Liberal land policy was inadequate and Labour had a better alternative. As Labour disagreed with only the finer points of the campaign, this meant, in effect, re-emphasising Labour's commitment to the goal of land nationalisation. The ILP drafted a resolution that was accepted by the 1914 Labour conference, outlining a concrete plan for gradual land nationalisation. It proposed a levy on all land of 3s. *per annum* to provide funds to purchase the whole land surface of Britain over the following ninety-nine years.[65]

However, this still involved admitting the validity of Lloyd George's programme in the short term. In addition, the ILP had no clear idea what to do with the land when it was nationalised, or what benefits it would bring, other than ushering in the future (undefined) utopia. This was not a package to impress voters. As *Forward* declared, 'The ordinary voter does not, and never will, go to the poll with any far off divine event in his mind to guide his decision.'[66] This inability to outmanoeuvre Lloyd George was symptomatic of the ILP's failure to deal with the challenge of Liberal welfarism. The ethical emphasis and moral fervour of the pioneers, when it was enough to contrast 'the one-roomed tenement of the labourer who created the wealth with the "mansions of the just" who spent it' provided no guide as to how to deal with

61 *Land and Labour*, June 1912.
62 *LL*, 27 Nov. 1913.
63 Ibid. 16 Oct. 1913.
64 Ibid. 16 Jan. 1913.
65 Ibid. 27 Nov. 1913.
66 *Forward*, 20 Dec. 1913.

Lloyd George's strategy.[67] As evolutionists, the ILP could not reject welfarism out of hand – to them every step away from *laissez-faire* was a victory for socialism. But they could not produce alternative policies to show why the voters should prefer their brand of reformism. Simply to assert that their ultimate goal was different was not enough. This is what Snowden meant when he talked of the ILP being 'checkmated by Lloyd Georgeism'.[68]

The ILP could not look to other groups on the left for a feasible alternative strategy. The 'rebels' grouped around the *Daily Herald* stood only for an instinctive rejection of all that welfarism or the 'servile state' stood for. If anything, the space the paper gave to the single taxers, Lansbury's obsession with land colonies and guild socialist plans to organise the labourers, reinforced the left's attention to land questions without providing any coherent answers.[69] On the land question, as on most political issues, the *Daily Herald* represented an attitude, not a policy, and not a very significant attitude, either, as the derisory results of Jack Scurr, the 'rebel' candidate in 1911–14, show.[70]

The only distinctive alternative on the left to the Liberal land campaign was that articulated by the BSP. They, too, believed that 'there is no matter of more vital importance today from every point of view than this question of the land'.[71] A decaying agriculture was a sign of an effete capitalism and a military weakness. To correct it, the BSP had a distinct land policy dating back to the 1880s – essentially a socialist gloss on the old radical tradition of cultivating waste land to cure unemployment. It also formed a central element in the BSP's plan for a transitional stage to socialism. The land was to be immediately nationalised and the surplus population of the towns compulsorily transferred to the countryside. There they would work on state farms, producing cheap and plentiful food for exchange with municipal enterprises in the towns. This superior method of production would eventually supersede capitalism entirely.[72] Though undoubtedly a distinctive approach, it is difficult to see what appeal it would have for rural labourers, or those forcibly deported to the state farms. It was a sign of the left's difficulties that the BSP's plans were the only scheme they produced that differed significantly from the land campaign.

---

[67] Lord Snell, Men, *movements and myself*, London 1936, 146.

[68] *LL*, 30 Apr. 1914.

[69] See the *Daily Herald*, 14 May 1912, 11 Feb. 1914, for pro-single tax articles; 24 Apr. 1914, for Mellor and Coles on the need to organise the labourers on guild socialist lines; passim, for land colonies.

[70] Scurr's results were Bethnal Green South-West (3.3%), Chesterfield (4.2%), Bethnal Green South-West (5.3%) and Ipswich (3.1%).

[71] *Justice*, 13 July 1912.

[72] Ibid. 25 Oct. 1913, 16, 23 Apr. 1914. See also R. Higgs, *The heart of the social problem*, London 1913.

Labour and housing policy, 1912–14

Labour's response to the land campaign in October 1913 left them in grave danger of being dragged along behind Lloyd George's latest initiative, unable to deny its significance or to produce alternatives. Once again the possibility of outflanking the Liberals on the left was being blocked. However, as the urban side of the land proposals became clearer during 1914, some opportunities for Labour to present a distinct image opened up. This was not the case with all urban land issues. For instance, the moderate site value rating stance adopted in the urban report, and foreshadowed in the budget, had overwhelming Labour support. Labour contained few who believed that land taxation was a panacea – at the national level only George Barnes, who 'came into politics inspired by *Progress and Poverty* and died over eighty years old still faithful to the Gospel' shared this view.[73] There was also considerable friction with the single taxers, exacerbated during by-election conflicts at Hanley, Crewe, Midlothian and Derbyshire North-East.[74] But socialists naturally favoured the taxation of unearned increments, and land taxation was a start in this direction. Thirty-six of the forty-two Labour MPs elected in December 1910 signed the single taxers' land memorandum of 1911, and the principle of site value rating in the 1914 budget was warmly welcomed by Labour.[75] Similarly, the urban report's plan to extend the system of trade boards to cover all low-paid occupations closely coincided with the ILP and Fabian policy of a universal minimum wage.[76]

But Labour might have an opportunity if the urban report could focus attention on the question of working-class housing. Despite its centrality in the report, the approach to housing was oblique, focusing on town planning, land acquisition by local authorities and transit schemes.[77] The subjects of state grants to subsidise house-building, and municipal construction were left unclear. At the national level, Labour was forced to define its attitude on these matters by the series of bills introduced in 1912–14 by the USRC to embarrass the government. At first, Labour MPs were allowed a free vote on these bills, as their proposals for state subsidies to house-building divided the party.[78] Most Labour MPs, including MacDonald and Henderson, were prepared to accept subsidies. But a minority of up to eight MPs, led by George

---

[73] Wedgwood, *Memoirs*, 78.
[74] In all these by-elections, single taxers formed the core of the Liberal campaign against the Labour candidate.
[75] Calculated from the copy in LG C/15/1/4. For Snowden's speech on the budget see *Hansard*, 5th ser., 1914, lxii. 504–17.
[76] Compare *The land*, ii. 159–60, with the Labour plans outlined in the *Daily Citizen*, 12, 21 Oct. 1912.
[77] *The land*, ii. 148–63.
[78] *Hansard*, 5th ser., 1912, xxxv. 1465–7.

Barnes, rejected the principle.[79] Barnes claimed that subsidies would benefit landlords, and would 'perpetuate low rents and therefore low wages'.[80] He also objected strongly to taxpayers subsidising particular towns and families. Fred Jowett was the ablest exponent of the opposite view.[81] He emphasised that better housing stimulated workers to demand higher wages by raising their self-respect and aspirations. Only state aid could achieve any progress on municipal housing. This view gradually prevailed over 1912–14. It was endorsed at the 1914 Labour conference and, on 20 March 1914, George Roberts committed the Labour MPs to back the USRC's bill, as state subsidies were party policy.[82]

By 1914, then, Labour did have a distinctive urban housing policy. It urged that state grants, or very low interest loans, should be available to local authorities to build working-class housing. Potentially, this was of some importance as there were some signs in 1909–14 that urban housing might, for the first time, become a significant election issue. The number of houses built by local authorities was beginning to increase rapidly, though from a very low base. Between 1910 and 1914 the local government board sanctioned loans for 6,780 houses and 112 of the 179 local authorities who constructed houses before 1914 started to do so in this period.[83] Moreover, many towns saw the first tentative steps at using public housing to tackle a general housing shortage rather than merely replacing houses destroyed in slum demolition.[84] The reasons for this rise in municipal building varied according to local circumstances. The 1909 Housing Act made it easier for local authorities to acquire land and loosened the restrictions on local government board loans. There was some concern that the private house-building sector would not be able to meet the future demand for cheap working-class housing.[85] But in some areas, pressure from working-class organisations like trade councils and trade unions was clearly important.[86]

However, most of the local authority schemes started in 1909–14 were very small – often less than one hundred houses – and rents were often beyond all but the most affluent of the working class.[87] The financial crisis in

[79] The eight were J. Parker, J. Pointer, G. Wardle, J. Tyson Wilson, G. Barnes, C. W. Bowerman, C. Duncan and J. Hodge.
[80] *Forward*, 26 Apr. 1913.
[81] *Clarion*, 16 May 1913.
[82] *Hansard*, 5th ser., 1914, lix. 2438.
[83] E. Gauldie, *Cruel habitations*, London 1974, 300–1.
[84] Alexander, *Reading, 1835–1985*, 195–6; M. J. Daunton, *Coal metropolis: Cardiff, 1870–1914*, Leicester 1977, 104–5; H. Hawson, *Sheffield: the growth of a city, 1893–1926*, Sheffield 1968, 111–15. See also *LL*, 4, 18, 25 June 1914, 23 July 1914, for Southampton, Ipswich, Huddersfield and Bristol.
[85] This question was considered in *The land*, ii. 59–66. Differing views on it are expressed in Offer, *Property and politics*, 308–13, and Daunton, *House and home*, 286–307.
[86] An example of this is *ASE Monthly Journal and Report*, Aug. 1914, on the situation in Greenock.
[87] LCC rents were usually between 7s. and 9s. 6d.: Wohl, *Eternal slum*, 263. See Daunton,

local government made councils reluctant to put new burdens on the rates. Housing schemes therefore tended to be very cautious and self-financing – the LCC's Boundary Road estate made the council £2,370 *per annum*.[88] As council housing was built to a high standard most working-class families could not afford the rents. Labour councillors accepted that it would be impossible, and electoral suicide, to propose subsidising council housing from the rates. Labour's losses at Nelson, one of its strongest boroughs, in 1913, were attributed to unwise association with schemes for large-scale house-building.[89] Labour was generally anxious to claim the mantle of financial prudence and show that they would not push up the rates.[90] The most important and popular Labour housing scheme outlined before 1914 was John Wheatley's plan to build 1,000 cottages in Glasgow, to be let at £8 *per annum*. But this would have been financed from the profits of the tramway system and would not have cost the Glasgow ratepayers anything.[91]

For most authorities, though, if they wished to build a substantial number of reasonably priced houses, the only answer was a state subsidy. By associating themselves with this policy, Labour gave themselves a simple and distinct stance on housing with which to challenge the Liberals. At the local level, many towns were beginning to experience the start of debates over public housing provision before 1914. If this had been repeated at a national level in 1914–15 through Liberal advocacy of the urban report's proposals, Labour would have had the chance to distinguish themselves from the Liberals as a party of plausible social reform.

Another possible opportunity for Labour was the rise in rents in many English towns in 1913–14. These provoked a series of ephemeral rent strikes in, for instance, Wolverhampton, Birmingham, Bradford and Leeds.[92] This movement was not very successful and produced severe disagreements inside local Labour parties. But it was a sign of the anger felt against rent rises when most urban working-class incomes were stagnant in real terms. Labour had a possible policy to capitalise on this feeling – fair rent courts. There was no mention of this in the Liberal land reports but it had long been a proposal of various working-class organisations, particularly the Workmen's National

Cardiff, 104–5, for a particularly clear case of the difficulty of building affordable working-class housing.

[88] Wohl, *Eternal slum*, 269.

[89] *LL*, 28 May 1914.

[90] See, for example, R. Wright, 'Liberal Party organisation and politics in Birmingham, Coventry and Wolverhampton, 1886–1914', unpubl. PhD diss. Birmingham 1977, 366–7, for Labour's efforts to avoid charges of municipal extravagance in Birmingham. In some areas Labour councillors were active opponents of more spending: F. Bealey, 'Municipal politics in Newcastle-under-Lyme, 1870–1914', *North Staffordshire Journal of Field Studies* v (1965), 64–73.

[91] I. Maclean, *The legend of Red Clydeside*, Edinburgh 1983, 20; *Forward*, 25 July, 1, 8 Aug. 1914.

[92] D. Englander, *Landlord and tenant in urban Britain, 1838–1918*, Oxford 1983, 143–61.

Housing Council.[93] If it were taken up by Labour at a national level it would give the party another distinct line, popular with those electors whom Labour could hope to wean from the Liberals.

One of the aims of the land campaign was to force Labour to align itself with the Liberals and blur its identity into that of the larger party, as in 1910. It could not perform the role of the constitutional crisis of 1909–10, but its purpose was to convince working-class electors that the Liberals remained a party committed to domestic reform and radicalism, that Labour could only support, and not outbid. In this, during 1913–14, the land campaign was largely successful. The Labour Party found itself lamely echoing the government's plans for land reform. The Liberals could therefore hope that in a general election few voters would be tempted to defect to a party so similar in its outlook. This would prevent the Unionists winning a significant number of three-cornered contests. However, once the urban side of the land campaign was launched, there were indications that Labour would have more opportunities to present itself as a party of distinctive social reform. The Liberal–Labour contest was still in a state of flux in July 1914; but the Liberals continued to hold the initiative.

[93] Wohl, *Eternal slum*, 329.

10

The Strange Death of the Land Issue

When the outbreak of the First World War suspended the party battle the land issue was a central topic of controversy and a crucial dividing line between the two parties. The form that issue had taken had been far from constant. In 1909–10 it had revolved around land taxation and the role of the House of Lords. In 1912–14 Lloyd George had redefined it to mean minimum wages for agricultural labourers and new schemes for housing development in the towns. But underlying these transformations were the themes of Liberalism's hostility to landowners and the party's attempts both to win the political allegiance of agricultural voters and to combine social reform with traditional radicalism. The war was to have a transforming effect on the nature and significance of the land issue precisely because it had such a profound impact on the Liberal Party, the role of landowners and the politics of social reform.

The First World War and the land issue

The importance of agriculture in a country's national life was a commonplace of Edwardian writing. But an overwhelming proportion of the food consumed by the British people was produced abroad and the agricultural sector of the economy had been in long-term relative decline since at least the 1870s. This situation was much-lamented, but few in British public life believed it could be reversed. For better or worse, Britain was an overwhelmingly industrial and urban society by 1914. Both parties claimed that their rural policies would help agriculture. Liberals asserted that smallholdings were better adapted to pursuits like market gardening and dairying where agriculture could meet new urban needs and that a minimum wage was a positive step towards a more highly-skilled workforce. Tories believed tariffs would help agriculture become more efficient and remunerative for all who worked on the land. But neither party was willing to commit itself to the aim of restoring agriculture to its former centrality in the British economy. This idea remained the preserve of a minority of enthusiasts in all parties. Moreover, arguments about efficiency and production were usually justifications for policies that would have been pursued anyway, as both parties sought to use agricultural reform to win over the English counties, or to express deeply-held views about the value of landownership.

The First World War turned this situation on its head. With party strife suspended, both Liberals and Tories halted the promotion of their rival schemes. Instead the productivity of British agriculture became a matter of major concern to all policy-makers. Before 1914 it had been assumed that the superiority of the British navy would ensure that the country could continue to import food from abroad, while blockading the enemy.[1] Campaigns by German U-boats and the unpredictability of foreign harvests soon put an end to this complacency and it was recognised that Britain had to increase its domestic food production, especially of staples like wheat, which had declined dramatically during the agricultural depression.

The weakness of the harvest in Britain and North America in 1916 ensured that food production presented Lloyd George's new government with one of its most testing crises. The prime minister responded with his usual alacrity. A new Food Production Department was set up to oversee war agriculture executive committees in each county, equipped with powers to compel farmers to switch to cereal production. The Corn Production Act of 1917 introduced guaranteed prices for wheat and oats and rewarded labourers with a minimum wage, thus fulfilling the primary purpose of the rural land campaign in rather different circumstances.[2] Effectively, the government was trying to reverse the economic trend of the previous fifty years by increasing domestic cereal production and, incidentally, providing more employment on the land. In the latter stages of the war, German prisoners of war, the Women's Land Army and British soldiers were all used to help with the harvest and there was actually an acute shortage of agricultural labour.

The war seemed to have revealed that Britain needed a bigger agricultural sector for its own safety and that a greater number of men could make a living on the land. This optimism was soon to be shattered by the crash in agricultural prices in the 1920s, but in the short term it had a profound effect on Lloyd George's thinking on the land issue. At the war's end in 1918 he could not have returned to a pre-war type of land campaign, even if he had wanted to do so, as he was in an alliance with the Unionists and they would scarcely have approved an all-out assault on landlordism. But he still believed that land reform could work to his advantage. The first item of domestic policy in the coalition manifesto of 1918 was a promise to provide allotments and smallholdings for returning ex-servicemen. As the manifesto stated

> [the war] has . . . demonstrated that the land of the country, if properly culti-
> vated and used, could have yielded food and other products of the soil to a
> much larger extent. It must be among the first tasks of the new Government to
> repair this error, which added so much to our difficulties in our struggles
> against the submarines of the enemy.[3]

---

1 For the problems of British food production in World War One see L. M. Barrett, *English food policy during the First World War*, London 1985; P. Dewey, *British agriculture in the First World War*, London 1989.
2 E. Whetham, *Agrarian history of England and Wales*, viii, Cambridge 1978, 94–7.
3 F. Craig (ed.), *British general election manifestos, 1900–1974*, London 1975, 28–31.

This emphasis was reproduced in Lloyd George's election campaign in 1918. He made only six public speeches and in the first three – at Wolverhampton on 23 November, Newcastle-upon-Tyne on 29 November and Leeds on 7 December – he dwelt at length on his smallholdings pledge.[4]

This new-found rural revivalism was completely opposed to the aims of the pre-war land campaign, which had been aimed at existing agricultural workers and had downgraded the importance of smallholdings. But it was very much in tune with the lessons that the war seemed to have taught about the importance of agriculture. Moreover, from Lloyd George's point of view, land reform was an excellent form of social reconstruction to highlight. The Tories could hardly object to it, given their past record of promoting allotments and smallholdings. But 'the land' was still an issue that the public associated with Lloyd George and its prominence in the coalition programme seemed to demonstrate his ability to determine the government's future programme. In effect, having already revolutionised the content of the land issue in 1912–14, Lloyd George was doing so once again, transforming it from a programme of anti-landlord social reform into a consensual means of raising agricultural production and rewarding ex-servicemen.

Unfortunately for Lloyd George, he was unable to repeat his pre-war successes. As in the Edwardian era, townsmen were not interested in a life of toil in the countryside and his campaign speeches of 1918 were soon diverted onto the more pressing and exciting topic of the post-war peace settlement. Lloyd George was able to embody his ideas in a Land Settlement (Facilities) Act passed in 1919, but it attracted little attention in the turmoil of the post-war years. The state provided £20 million to subsidise the provision of smallholdings by county councils, thus proving considerably more generous than pre-war schemes. But the act could scarcely have been passed at a less propitious time. Land was bought and equipped in 1919–20 when prices were rocketing in the post-war boom, but the new smallholders started farming just as prices collapsed in 1921–2. Losses to county councils averaged £550 per tenant in the years 1919 to 1924–5.[5] Not surprisingly, purchases of land by councils ground to a halt. Overwhelmed by a myriad of other difficulties at home and abroad in 1919–22, Lloyd George let the land issue slip quietly into the background of politics.

Landowners and politics in the post-war era

However, Lloyd George's miscalculations and many other concerns were not the only reason why the land issue did not return to its pre-war prominence. The driving force behind the interest in 'the land' of all on the left in politics was hostility to landowners. In the years before 1914 it was still possible to

4   K. Morgan, *Consensus and disunity*, Oxford 1979, 39.
5   Whetham, *Agrarian history*, viii. 137–9.

view Britain as a country where landowners wielded significant political power and played a major role in obstructing radical change. Landlords remained prominent in some areas of local government and in the higher echelons of the Tory Party.[6] Crucially, the House of Lords was still an over-whelmingly landed assembly and a real obstacle to change. Its rejection of the 1909 budget made the composition and powers of the Lords central issues in the 1910 elections and the constitutional crisis of 1911. In 1912–14 the Lords were still using their delaying powers to block Irish Home Rule, Welsh Church disestablishment and the abolition of plural voting. It was not surprising that the House of Lords, and by implication the aristocracy as a whole, retained their role in radical demonology.

After 1918 this way of looking at politics rapidly became obsolete. In the new, post-war world landowners looked both less obnoxious and less powerful. As landowners were eager to point out, they had had a 'good' war. The disproportionate number of officer casualties meant that landed families suffered a relatively high toll of fatalities during the conflict – nearly 20 per cent of peers and their sons aged under fifty who served in the armed forces were killed.[7] Moreover, landowners had not been able to make unseemly profits from wartime food shortages because they had generally not been able to raise rents.[8] The war had produced a new bogeyman on whom all radicals and reformers could focus their dislike – the war profiteer, who had made himself rich while others sacrificed their lives.[9] But if landowners were less hateful after 1918, there was also less reason to hate them. The brief boom in agriculture and land prices after the war produced a widely-publicised avalanche of land sales by the aristocracy, as many took the first opportunity since the 1870s to sell agricultural land at an attractive price. It was believed, on fairly good evidence, that up to a quarter of England changed hands in the years 1918 to 1921.[10] Those who retained the confidence and the resources not to sell found themselves the victims of renewed agricultural depression in the 1920s. Increasingly, landowners ceased to be prominent figures in rural English society as they closed up their big houses and withdrew from active leadership of their localities.[11]

The political impact of the aristocracy also waned dramatically. The Fourth Reform Act of 1918 created electorates that were so big, even in rural constituencies, that it seemed unrealistic to suggest that landlord intimida-tion was any longer a significant factor in politics. The management of constituencies and political parties became ever more obviously a matter for

6 Adonis, *Making aristocracy work*, 186–95; Ramsden, *Age of Balfour and Baldwin*, 94–8.
7 G. E. Cockayne, *The complete peerage*, ed. H. V. Gibbs, London 1910–53, viii, appendix F, 759–826.
8 Thompson, *English landed society*, 328.
9 See B. Waites, *A class society at war: England, 1914–18*, Leamington Spa 1987, 68–70, for the introduction of the term 'profiteer' into everyday speech.
10 *Estates Gazette*, 31 Dec. 1921.
11 P. Mandler, *The fall and rise of the stately home*, London 1997, 242–53.

professionals, rather than lordly amateurs. Finally, and most crucially, the importance of the House of Lords as an obstacle to reform declined steeply. This was simply because the Conservative Party became much better at winning elections than it had been before 1914. After 1918 the Lords were still willing and able to cause serious difficulties for radical governments.[12] In 1924 they seriously amended the first Labour government's London Traffic Act and Prevention of Evictions Act. In 1930–1 they forced important changes on some of the second Labour government's major pieces of legislation, including the Unemployment Insurance (no. 2) Act, the Coal Mines Act and the Land Utilisation Act. They also rejected the education (school attendance) bill altogether and would certainly have delayed the representation of the people bill for the maximum of two years if the government had not fallen. But these were rare recurrences of the pre-war political configuration. Apart from 1924 and 1929–31 the Conservatives were continuously in power, either alone or in coalition, from 1918 to 1939 and there was no need for the Lords to act as the last redoubt of conservatism. The chamber's public profile sank accordingly and, to most of those on the left of politics, the enemy of reform became the Tory Party and its ability to win elections and dominate the Commons. The Lords and the landowners retreated into the background.

The last land campaign and the decline of the land issue

Much of the motive force that had made the land issue an important part of politics before 1914 had thus been dissipated. It never regained the centrality it had held in 1909–14. But it did not disappear altogether. Part of the appeal of the land issue to politicians had always been the hope that it could deliver victory in rural England and this still remained an element in the politics of the 1920s. Even after the redistribution of seats and extension of the franchise in 1918 many politicians continued to work on the assumption that agriculture was the determining factor in the political allegiance of many (if not all) of the English counties.[13] As before 1918, this was not entirely irrational. Rural seats were again over-represented after a successful backbench Tory revolt in 1917 had ensured that area as well as population should be taken into account when determining constituency boundaries.[14] Michael Kinnear has calculated, on the basis of the 1921 census figures, that there

---

[12] P. A. Bromhead, *The House of Lords in contemporary politics, 1911–57*, London 1958, 151–6; P. Williamson, 'The Labour Party and the House of Lords, 1918–31', *Parliamentary History* x (1991), 317–41.

[13] Even the Labour Party believed that there were as many as 167 'rural' seats after 1918: C. V. J. Griffiths, 'Labour and the countryside: rural strands in the British labour movement, 1900–39', unpubl. DPhil. diss. Oxford 1996, 17–21.

[14] M. Pugh, *Electoral reform in war and peace, 1906–18*, London 1978, 108–9.

were still 111 English county seats where 20 per cent or over of the population was dependent on agriculture.[15] Moreover, rural seats were still a volatile
element in politics, even under the Fourth Reform Act system. One spectac-
ular example of the rapid turnover of votes in these seats was the fact that the
Liberals won forty-three English agricultural constituencies in 1923 and none
at all in 1924. Rural England remained a 'swing' area that politicians believed
could be won by the production of appropriate policies.

Indeed, rural England became a matter of increasing, rather than
decreasing, concern to the Liberal Party. The 'rise of Labour' between 1918
and 1924 gradually reduced the party's representation in urban England to a
rump, often held in tacit alliance with the Conservatives. Though the
Liberals won twenty-two seats in urban England in 1924, for instance, there
was no Tory opponent in seventeen of them. In contrast, while the Liberals
did not win any agricultural seats in 1924, their situation was actually more
hopeful in rural England because Labour was still too weak in most of these
constituencies to be the major challenger to the Tories. Even in a disastrous
year for the Liberals like 1924, Labour was still in first or second place in only
thirty-one English rural seats. This situation did not escape the attention of
Lloyd George, still the most dynamic and innovative force the Liberals
possessed. In June 1923 he set up a new inquiry into all aspects of the land
issue.[16] Some of its findings were incorporated into the Liberals' 1924 election manifesto, but in a contest dominated by the Zinoviev Letter and
anti-socialism, they largely escaped notice.[17] Lloyd George enlarged and
revamped the inquiry in August 1924 and its conclusions were presented to
the world as the 'Green' and 'Brown' Books, on rural and urban questions,
respectively, in the autumn of 1925.[18]

Lloyd George launched his new land crusade in a speech at Killerton Park
in Devon on 17 September 1925 and a Land and Nation League was set up to
campaign across the country, endowed with £240,000 by the Lloyd George
Fund. These events bore a striking similarity to those of 1912–14. But while
most observers believed that the first rural campaign was a great success, the
second campaign was abandoned by Lloyd George as a failure. Land issues
received only a passing mention in his own election address in 1929 and *Land
News*, the organ of the Land and Nation League, was wound up just before
the election.[19] Instead, Lloyd George campaigned on the slogan 'We Can

15 M. Kinnear, *The British voter*, 2nd edn, London 1981, 119–21.

16 For accounts of Lloyd George's new initiative see J. Campbell, *Lloyd George: the goat in the
wilderness, 1922–31*, London 1977, 120–8; T. Wilson, *The downfall of the Liberal party,
1914–35*, London 1966, 324–7; Douglas, *Land, people and politics*, 190–5; M. Dawson, 'The
Liberal land policy, 1924–9', *TCBH* ii (1991), 272–90.

17 *Election manifestos*, 64–8.

18 *The land and the nation: the rural report of the Liberal land committee, 1923–5*, London 1925;
Towns and the land: the urban report of the Liberal land committee, 1923–5, London 1925.

19 *Election manifestos*, 86–8; Dawson, 'Land policy', 280.

Conquer Unemployment' – something the economists who drew up the strategy thought could be done without reference to the land issue.[20] Ironically, while the Liberals failed to sweep rural England in 1929, they did gain twenty-two English agricultural seats they had not won in 1924, providing their largest bloc of newly-won territory at the election. But nobody was prepared to give the benefit for this modest success to Lloyd George's land policy. After five years of relentless agricultural depression under the Baldwin government, the Liberals were merely the most plausible repository for anti-Tory protest votes.

The abandonment of Lloyd George's second land campaign signalled the demise of the rural land issue as an important factor in British politics, so it is worthwhile pausing to dissect the reasons why the campaign was not a success. First, Lloyd George had considerable problems in convincing his party of the merits of his plans. Two of the Liberals' national figures, Edward Hilton Young and Sir Alfred Mond, defected to the Tories in protest at Lloyd George's schemes and a special NLF conference on 17–19 February 1926 was only persuaded to accept a heavily-modified version of the Green Book after a considerable show of hostility from many Liberal activists.[21] Liberals in some rural areas were deeply hostile to the whole project and local associations in Devon and Cornwall, and even Lloyd George's heartland of Wales, effectively ignored or condemned the new land policy.[22] This opposition stemmed partly from a dislike of any new initiative in the direction of state intervention. Many 'progressive' Liberals had already left the party by the mid-1920s and the remaining stalwarts had been made suspicious of bureaucracy by the state's war-time infringements of civil liberties and the rising tax burden on middle-class voters.[23] But, just as important, the deep divisions of 1916–23 had not healed and many Asquithians were unwilling to accept any initiative from Lloyd George. A particularly embarrassing example of this difficulty occurred at the St Ives by-election of 1928 when the Liberal candidate, Hilda Runciman, the wife of the Asquithian ex-cabinet minister, Walter Runciman, refused to let Lloyd George speak in the division, let alone expound land reform.[24]

But this lack of unity would have been much less important if Lloyd George had been able to use the land issue to propound a vote-winning strategy, as in 1912–14. Unfortunately, this was far from being the case. Some of the policies of the pre-war land campaign were obviously less relevant after 1918. Rent courts, for instance, were of little use to those farmers who had

[20] Campbell, *Goat in the wilderness*, 195.

[21] Dawson, 'Land policy', 278–9.

[22] Ibid. 282–90; J. G. Jones, 'Wales and "the new Liberalism", 1926–9', *National Library of Wales Journal* xxii (1981–2), 323–5.

[23] For these general trends see M. Bentley 'The Liberal response to socialism, 1918–29', in K. D. Brown (ed.), *Essays in anti-labour history*, London 1974, 42–73.

[24] For general Asquithian dislike of Lloyd George's initiative see Campbell, *Goat in the wilderness*, 124–6.

become owner-occupiers in the great wave of land sales in the 1920s.[25] But wages boards were still an issue of some importance in agricultural politics, though it was much harder for the Liberals to capitalise on their significance than it had been before 1914. The statutory minimum wage had been repealed by the coalition in 1921 when guaranteed prices were dropped – a decision for which Lloyd George and his Liberal followers had to accept responsibility. The wages of most agricultural labourers had fallen as a result and there had been a number of bitter strikes in highly-unionised areas like Norfolk.[26] Labour was able to take advantage of the situation and in 1924 the first Labour government's only significant agricultural measure was to introduce a bill to reinstate statutory wages boards. The minister responsible, Noel Buxton, had previously sat as a Liberal for his North Norfolk seat and was an older brother of Roden Buxton, the honorary secretary of the pre-war land enquiry. His second reading speech could have been lifted directly from that era. It condemned low wages as 'a blot on the social state of rural England – probably the most beautiful country in the world – which I think we all admit ought to be removed' and catalogued the inadequacy of labourers' housing and diet.[27]

The Conservatives responded cautiously. They feared the bill's popularity and had themselves operated a wages board system in agriculture in 1917–21. They endorsed the principle of statutory wages boards, but objected to the important role that Buxton had assigned to a Central Wages Board.[28] The Liberal response was led by F. D. Acland. He attempted to steer a middle course, arguing for more independence for local wages boards, but with a central authority retaining some residual powers.[29] This was immensely significant. The wages board issue had been the Liberals' trump card in 1912–14, but Labour's initiative reduced them to playing 'honest broker' between the Tories and Labour.

The bill was heavily amended in committee and emerged as a measure agreed between the parties.[30] It set up local wages boards, but removed most of the powers of the Central Board by providing that disagreements between farmers and labourers would be settled at a local level by independent members of the boards. But though the party leaderships had approved this solution the matter remained controversial. Many Tories, particularly those linked to the NFU, disliked the whole idea of wages boards. The labourers' union was disappointed at the absence of a national minimum figure and Walter Smith the union's president and parliamentary secretary at the

---

[25] S. G. Sturmey, 'Owner-farming in England and Wales, 1900–50', *Manchester School of Economic and Social Studies* xxiii (1955), 246–68.

[26] Howkins, *Poor labouring men*, 130–75.

[27] *Hansard*, 5th ser., 1924, clxxiv. 911–22.

[28] See ibid. clxxiv. 922–33, for the Tory amendment moved by Sir Henry Cautley.

[29] Ibid. clxxiv. 942–54.

[30] See ibid. clxxvi. 1796–802, for Buxton's speech, outlining the new shape of the bill.

ministry of agriculture denounced the Liberals for wrecking the Central Board. The Liberals themselves were divided, as they were on much else in the 1920s. Acland endorsed the bill, but argued that the Central Board should have retained the power to overturn a local award that did not ensure a living wage.[31] But five Liberals had voted for the Tory amendment against a powerful Central Board, while others rose at the third reading debate to denounce the compromise over its powers and the creation of 'an absolutely weak Bill'.[32] This weak and hesitating performance merely confirmed that the minimum wage was no longer available to the Liberals as a means of sweeping the countryside.

Given this background one of the obvious tasks of the Green Book was to allow the Liberals to re-establish their appeal to the labourers. In fact, agricultural labourers and their wages were scarcely mentioned.[33] In obvious contrast to Lloyd George's pre-war schemes, the second land campaign offered the labourer virtually nothing, beyond some vague promises. There was certainly no attempt to make a direct and arresting appeal on the lines of, for instance, a higher minimum wage or more council housing in rural districts. This was not because labourers were no longer a significant feature of rural life. Though their numbers fell by nearly 100,000 in 1911–21, they still made up more than 60 per cent of the agricultural workforce.[34] Nor had rural poverty been eradicated. The Green Book itself pointed out the continuing problems of low wages and poor housing.[35]

The crucial distinction between the pre-war situation and the 1920s was that it was no longer realistic to blame the labourer's plight on the landlord. The discussions on the 1924 Agricultural Wages Act, for instance, had proceeded entirely without reference to landowners. The arguments had focused on the farmer's ability to pay higher wages in difficult economic circumstances. Nobody suggested passing the cost of wage rises on to the landlord through rent reductions. This reflected the impact of the massive land sales of 1918–21, the depressed state of rents in the 1920s and the wartime growth of the NFU to a position whereby it could displace landed representatives as the main spokesman for the agricultural interest.[36] It was notable that the Green Book treated landlords merely as an irrelevance, rather than a force against which a new campaign needed to be launched.[37] Without landowners to blame, rural poverty seemed to most Liberals to be a

---

[31] See ibid. clxxiv. 979–83; clxxvi. 1839–44, 1813–17, for the attitudes of J. Q. Lamb, Walter Smith and F. D. Acland.
[32] The five were Sir Courtenay Mansel, S. Pattinson, J. T. Rees, Sir William Sutherland and Maxwell Thornton. See clxxvi. 1835–6 (Sir Hugh Seely), for one of those who spoke against the compromise.
[33] *The land and the nation* had no separate section on wages, for instance.
[34] Howkins, *Reshaping rural England*, 201, table 8.2.
[35] *The land and the nation*, 14–15.
[36] Whetham, *Agrarian history*, viii. 129–30.
[37] *The land and the nation*, 221–76.

direct result of agricultural depression, just as urban poverty was the outcome of industrial depression.

Faced with these assumptions, most Liberals became much more wary of legislative action to raise labourers' wages – as the debates on the 1924 act showed, Labour had easily been able to outflank them on this issue. Liberals feared that advocating a redistribution of income from labourers to farmers would merely worsen the obvious economic problems of agriculture and place more burdens on hard-pressed farmers. The only solution to rural poverty was to increase the prosperity of agriculture as a whole. As Liberals could hardly advocate tariffs, the party had been at a loss as to how this might be achieved until Lloyd George started to generate new policies. His solution was similar to the ideas he was to propound to solve urban unemployment. The key was to use the state to promote and disseminate greater technical knowledge and better organisational methods.[38] This was to be achieved by effectively nationalising agricultural land and making farmers state tenants on condition of good tenure – a form of landholding dubbed 'cultivating tenure'. Lloyd George had again drastically updated the content of the land issue to centre it on reviving agricultural prosperity.

However 'modern' these proposals were, they were not popular. Not only did they offer nothing to labourers, but it proved impossible to convince farmers of the benefits of bureaucratic management, especially after their experience of the enforced 'ploughing up' of grasslands in World War One and the sudden reversals of state policy under Lloyd George in 1920–1. Local NFU branches were resolutely hostile to the whole idea.[39] This situation was only too obvious to many Liberals and the 1926 NLF conference insisted that 'cultivating tenure' should just be one form of landholding among many.[40] But the 'cultivating tenure' proposal still remained the best-known and most controversial part of the second land campaign, if only because it left the Liberals open to charges of wanting to nationalise the land and because Lloyd George would not stop promoting the idea. Under these circumstances it was no wonder that the second land campaign was quietly wound up before the 1929 election. It may have suited Lloyd George to emphasise technical development and long-term recovery, but such policies were impossible to turn into popular slogans.

What 1925–9 proved was that the Liberals could no longer look to the land issue to deliver the English county seats. However desperately they needed votes in the English countryside they would have to rely on less active initiatives. This was not entirely a counsel of despair. The unpopularity of the Baldwin government alone produced a modest Liberal revival in English agricultural seats in 1929. But without a new initiative there could be no great

---

38 For the Green Book's key proposals see ibid. 297–361.
39 Dawson, 'Land policy', 283.
40 *Land proposals as adopted at the Liberal conference held in the Kingsway Hall, London, February 17th–19th 1926*, London 1926, 7.

Liberal revival in the English counties. In effect, the decline of the rural land issue helped ensure that the Liberals could not regain their status as a major party.

Rural land reform had not just been a Liberal issue, but no other party was prepared to take up the baton dropped by the Liberals. The Conservatives had produced legislation on allotments and smallholdings in the late nineteenth century, but this had been largely tactical, to compete with Liberal initiatives. With the demise of the Liberal Party and its ability to produce an effective policy of rural reform, Conservative interest in the topic waned. Baldwin's government contented itself with a modest Smallholdings Act in 1926 to counter Lloyd George's faltering schemes.[41] It offered to subsidise 75 per cent of county councils' losses on new smallholdings, but envisaged creating only 2,000 new holdings per year for the next four years. Interest in such a minor measure was so low that the second reading debate was nearly suspended for lack of attendance.

The party continued to contain advocates of plans to promote peasant proprietors. Some of them, like Lord Bledisloe, even gained a foothold in the ministry of agriculture in the 1924 Tory government. They pleaded that a solid yeoman class would save England from socialism and revive agriculture. But fears about the danger of state intervention and wasting tax-payers' money were even greater among Conservative leaders than among Liberals.[42] Besides, the depression gave a further boost to most Tories' faith in protectionism. More than ever, the tariff, not land reform, seemed to them the answer to agriculture's problems. As Lloyd George had failed to raise the counties against the Tories, Baldwin could concentrate his fire on Labour and socialism in 1929 with a campaign of 'Safety First'.

The obvious party to take up rural land reform was Labour. The party had largely agreed with the Liberals' pre-war land policies and as the Liberals moved away from championing the labourer's cause this opened up a gap for Labour to make some sort of distinctive appeal in the countryside. In the early 1920s this seemed possible. The labourers' union had aligned itself wholeheartedly with Labour and the party managed to win four agricultural seats in 1923 (North and South Norfolk, Holland and Maldon). Party organisers assured the leadership that only by winning rural seats could Labour gain an overall majority and the act reinstituting wages boards for labourers was one of the party's few achievements in 1924.[43]

But this initiative was never followed up and Labour never gave any prominence to rural land reform in the inter-war period. This was partly because the party was and remained an overwhelmingly urban organisation, interested in urban problems. Once it was clear that landowners were no

---

[41] See *Hansard*, 5th ser., 1926, cxcviii. 779–86, for Walter Guinness's speech outlining the measure.
[42] A. F. Cooper, *British agricultural policy, 1912–36*, Manchester 1989, 69–71.
[43] R. McKibbin, *The evolution of the Labour party, 1910–24*, Oxford 1974, 150–6.

longer a serious threat to the forces of progress, Labour's leaders and activists were unwilling to invest precious time and money in rural England and its difficulties. For instance, the party's first nationwide campaign in rural seats in 1926–8 was allocated no new staff and relied on a grand total of two horse-drawn vans to take its message to the countryside. Conferences on rural policy in 1926 attracted only about thirty activists.[44] Labour may have been willing to put up candidates even in hopeless rural seats but this was largely because the party wished to present itself as a truly national organisation and to inflate the total Labour vote. Most Labour leaders tended to regard rural England as a backward place that would, no doubt, fall to Labour as part of its inevitable march forward. But there was not much interest in it for its own sake. The TUC even managed to organise a centenary commemoration of the Tolpuddle Martyrs in 1934 while scarcely mentioning that they had been agricultural workers.[45]

Given this basic disregard of rural England it was not surprising that policies to appeal to those working in agriculture did not receive much priority. The topic was never given much time at conference, for instance. When the party did pronounce on agriculture it rarely spoke with much conviction. Some announcements were ripostes to initiatives from other parties. The most obvious example was A Labour policy for agriculture (London 1926), which bore a striking resemblance to Lloyd George's schemes, but quickly faded from view as the second land campaign failed to take off. In office, though, Labour tended to agree with the Liberals that only greater efficiency and better organisation of farming could help the labourer. The Agricultural Marketing Act of 1931 was the perfect example of this approach – one that was shared, with modifications, even by many Tories.[46] Labour was simply not interested in producing its own vision of land reform.

The demise of the urban land issue

The fading of the rural land issue was accompanied by the demise of its urban counterpart. Indeed, Lloyd George had given the matter hardly any attention at all in 1925–9, despite the existence of an urban Brown Book of recommendations to accompany the Green Book. This decision was determined by the strategic choices the Liberal Party faced in the mid-1920s. Lloyd George saw the second land campaign as overwhelmingly rural in its emphasis because the countryside was the obvious area where the Liberals could hope to make gains. As he wrote to Frances Stevenson, the aim was 'to strengthen our grasp on the rural districts and the capture of a few towns where Liberalism is still a

[44] Griffiths, 'Labour and the countryside', 98–100, 241–2.
[45] C. V. J. Griffiths, 'Remembering Tolpuddle: rural history and commemoration in the inter-war labour movement', HWJ xliv (1997), 144–69.
[46] Cooper, Agricultural policy, 127–36.

force'.[47] It was not a surprise that the Brown Book had so little impact – it was not meant to.

But the Brown Book did demonstrate the difficulties of constructing a set of policies relevant to town-dwellers in the 1920s under the general heading of land reform. The pre-war land report had blamed housing shortages on landowners who charged inflated prices for development land or prevented it from being used for building altogether. In the 1920s this analysis was no longer realistic. Rent controls and spiralling building costs had drastically slowed the construction of privately-rented accommodation for the working class. New housing for rent came largely from local councils, subsidised by the state. Arguments over housing shortages focused on how many houses councils should build and the degree of state subsidy, not the role of landowners.[48] The Brown Book had nothing to contribute to this discussion. Indeed, it avoided the topic of council housing completely, as this was likely to divide Liberals and directly confront them with the question of whether they were prepared to increase taxes and rates to provide better accommodation for the working class.

The inquiry fell back on calls to make the housing market work more efficiently, in much the same way as the Green Book's proposals promised to restore prosperity to agriculture. In effect this meant a collection of policies on town planning, leasehold reform and site value rating that was not dissimilar to the proposals in the urban report of 1914.[49] Lloyd George clearly did not believe in wasting time in injecting any originality into the urban side of his new campaign, nor did he seem to care that, in the completely different situation of the 1920s, these ideas were simply irrelevant to contemporary debates on the provision of working-class housing. The Brown Book actually marked a retreat from the pre-war urban report. It contained no plans for a minimum wage or increased grants for local authorities and short-hold tenants were offered leasehold enfranchisement, rather than a land court to deal with their grievances. This was a fairly clear sign that social reform was a far more difficult subject for Liberals after 1918 than it had been before the war.

So neglected and marginal a set of ideas as those contained in the Brown Book were hardly likely to revive the urban land issue. The other parties were not forced to make its proposals matters of central political importance, though the Conservatives did produce a landlord and tenant (no. 2) bill in 1927 to improve the position of business tenants, thus quelling any unrest among the ranks of the shopkeepers.[50]

---

[47] Lloyd George to Frances Stevenson, 20 Aug. 1925, in My darling pussy: letters of Lloyd George and Frances Stevenson, 1913–41, ed. A. J. P. Taylor, London 1975, 97–8.
[48] See, for instance, Merrett, State housing, 31–60.
[49] See Towns and the land, 259–68, for a summary of the proposals.
[50] See Hansard, 5th ser., 1927, cciv. 2301–14, for the introduction of the measure by Joynson-Hicks.

Labour's response was more complicated, though. In some ways Labour shared the Tories' lack of interest in the complex of ideas and policies that had made up the urban land question. For all Labour politicians the key issue in the 1920s was the new problem of persistent, large-scale unemployment – the 'intractable million'. In the Edwardian era governments had moved decisively away from the idea that employment on the land could be a remedy for unemployment. The war had briefly appeared to reverse this trend, but its wisdom seemed to be confirmed in the 1920s when the slump in agricultural prices made it difficult for many who were already on the land to make a living from it, let alone any newcomers. The Labour minister of agriculture in 1930, Christopher Addison, concluded that the land was no use as a remedy for unemployment.[51] Even in his agricultural land (utilisation) bill of 1930, which contained proposals to increase the number of allotments and smallholdings, he was cautious about their effect on urban unemployment. Allotments would help the workless only by 'providing them with something to do', while smallholdings were suitable principally for agricultural labourers and only then for some 'men who were born in the country' but had followed other trades.[52]

However, not everyone in the Labour Party was willing to abandon the urban land issue. Most significantly, the party contained a small band of vociferous advocates of land taxation. There had always been some single taxers in the Labour movement, but in the 1920s their number was swollen by the defection of some prominent enthusiasts from the Liberal Party, including Josiah Wedgwood, R. L. Outhwaite, E. G. Hemmerde and Dundas White. They were as great a nuisance for Labour as they had been for the Liberals and provoked a number of open quarrels in the party, most notably at the 1926 conference.[53] To most people in the Labour movement they were merely a set of eccentrics. But this should not obscure the fact that a number of prominent Labour cabinet ministers retained a long-standing commitment to land taxation, albeit in a rather more moderate and less obstreperous fashion than that displayed by the single taxers. This group included George Lansbury, C. P. Trevelyan and, most notably of all, Philip Snowden.[54]

Snowden's continued support for land taxation was crucial. Because he held the post of chancellor of the exchequer in 1924 and 1929–31 he was actually in a position to take some practical steps towards taxing land. Any moves he made in this direction would first have to recover the ground lost after the war. In 1920 the Unionist chancellor of the exchequer, Austen Chamberlain, had abolished the 1909 land taxes on the grounds that they

---

[51] 'Office conference on agricultural policy', 5 June 1930, Addison papers, Bod. Lib., MS dep. c. 164.
[52] For Addison's comments see Hansard, 5th ser., 1930, ccxliv. 1898, 1903.
[53] C. Cline, Recruits to Labour: the British Labour Party, 1914–31, New York 1963, 43–51.
[54] Snowden's first speech when elected to Keighley Borough Council in 1899 was on the taxation of land values: C. Cross, Philip Snowden, London 1966, 45.

were far too complicated and expensive to administer and were yielding very little in revenue. The land valuation had never been completed and had been made obsolete by wartime fluctuations in property prices, so it, too, was abolished.[55] But Snowden remained keen to make a start. In 1924 and in 1929–30 he pressed the cabinet to agree to a new land valuation bill.[56] Most of his colleagues were distinctly unenthusiastic and the bill was squeezed out of the government's programme on both occasions. This attitude was not surprising. Land taxation offered no solution to unemployment, nor any prospect of new sources of revenue in the immediate future, even if a valuation bill could pass the House of Lords, which was highly doubtful. To most Labour leaders the enemy who needed fiscal punishment was the 'war profiteer' and the weapon was the capital levy. Land taxation was merely a cry from the past.

The matter might have remained a footnote in the history of the inter-war Labour governments and a testament to Snowden's fiscal Liberalism. But when the new budget was unveiled on 27 April 1931, it revealed that Snowden had decided to replicate Lloyd George's strategy and include land taxation in the finance bill. He proposed a new land valuation, to take probably two years, after which a tax of 1d./£ on capital land values would be imposed.[57] The reasons behind Snowden's sudden haste to introduce land taxation were largely short-term and tactical and were hinted at in his budget speech.

First, he was eager to steady the markets and preserve the gold standard by introducing substantial cuts in the welfare budget. The May Committee had been set up earlier in the year to achieve this end. As the chancellor said, he anticipated that 'considerable reductions of expenditure will be made during the year'. These would be hard to sell to his party, but the task might be made easier if he could persuade them that the idle rich would be carrying their share of the burden, too. Rentier taxes were notoriously hard to construct, but land taxation might fulfil this role. It might also serve as a medium-term alternative to tariffs, which some of Snowden's colleagues were eager to explore as a new source of revenue, but which the chancellor regarded as anathema. To him, 'A revenue tariff, apart from its Protectionist object, is a means of relieving the well-to-do at the expense of the poor, and is an indirect method of reducing wages' and he would never countenance this option. Finally, land taxation would help to bind the Liberals, and especially Lloyd George, to the support of the minority Labour government; indeed the Liberal leader declared that Snowden's budget 'rejoices my heart'.[58]

There were, therefore, a number of reasons entirely particular to the situation in 1930–1 why Snowden gave such priority to land taxation. His budget did not signal that the inter-war Labour movement was obsessed with the

[55] Douglas, *Land, people and politics*, 179–81.
[56] Ibid. 200–2.
[57] See *Hansard*, 5th ser., 1931, ccli. 1391–411, for Snowden's budget statement.
[58] Ibid. ccli. 1413.

land issue in any form, but rather that land taxation represented to Snowden a way out of a very tight political situation. Ironically, the budget merely served to show how far the Liberals had retreated from their pre-1914 enthusiasm for the taxation of monopolies and the wealthy. While welcoming land taxation in principle, Liberal MPs recoiled from the 'double taxation' of some landowners by income tax and the proposed land tax.[59] In an atmosphere of economic crisis and constant complaints of 'wasteful' expenditure many Liberals were doubtful about any more soaking of the rich, even if they were landowners. Lloyd George was compelled to make a highly embarrassing stand against some aspects of the new taxation that seriously threatened the Liberal–Labour alliance in the Commons, but on 16 June 1931 he was finally able to extract a compromise from Snowden. However, a week later, twelve Liberals voted for a Conservative motion hostile to the land taxes and Sir John Simon chose the issue to make his formal break from the Liberal Party, thus laying the foundations for the creation of the future Liberal National grouping and yet another Liberal split.[60] Land taxation had always been a contentious issue for Liberals, but it was ironic that the issue that Lloyd George had used to such good effect before 1914 should return to deal another blow to his tottering party. By 1931 neither the rural nor urban land issues offered the Liberals any hope of revival.

The 1931 budget was the last, fleeting, manifestation of the land issue as a central factor in British politics. By then, Snowden's interest in 'the land' already seemed archaic to many in politics. As Sir John Simon put it, 'For those of us who were members of the House two-and-twenty years ago, a discussion such as is now beginning on the land clauses in the Finance Bill has something of a reminiscent echo of "far-off things/And battles long ago".'[61]

As Simon suggested, the fight against landlordism made no sense in the new post-war world. Lloyd George may have been anxious to refashion the land issue. But he could not centre it upon social reform, as he had done before 1914. Depression and rising taxation had closed off that route for the Liberals. Instead, he attempted to redefine the land issue once again as a species of economic development. But it was impossible to turn such ideas into the populist slogans of the Edwardian era. By 1931 the land issue's time as an important element in British politics was long over. It faded from the political scene, doomed to be viewed as an irrelevancy, like the Liberal Party with which it had been so closely associated.

[59] See P. Williamson, *National crisis and national government: British politics, the economy and the empire, 1926–32*, Cambridge 1992, 249–51, for this incident.
[60] See *Hansard*, 5th ser., 1931, ccliii. 1709–12, for Snowden's statement on a compromise; ccliv. 571–6, for the Conservative motion.
[61] Ibid. cclii. 1834.

Conclusion

Rural and urban land reform in their English context were certainly important to late nineteenth- and early twentieth-century Liberalism, but only in 1909–14 did the party gain much benefit from them. The Liberal governments of 1892–5 and 1905–8 pursued the land issue without success. Agricultural labourers were not grateful for allotments or interested in smallholdings and rural England continued usually to vote Tory. Urban land reform was discarded as a solution to unemployment, while attempts to use the land question to tackle local government finance and housing were feeble, to say the least. The land issue seemed to be in danger of fading away, when it was rescued by the ingenuity of Lloyd George. By putting land taxation at the forefront of his 1909 budget he created a huge political storm and, for the first time, made the land question a central political issue. Though the quarrel over land taxation was soon subsumed in the wider issue of the role of the House of Lords, the events of 1909–11 had a crucial impact on perceptions of the land issue. The elections of 1910, in particular, convinced many politicians that there was a deep reservoir of anti-landlord feeling in the electorate and that, therefore, the land issue could be used to the Liberals' advantage, if it were handled skilfully.

Lloyd George attempted to tap into these feelings again with his land campaign of 1913–14. But he did not just rely on stimulating traditional radical prejudices. He recognised that the land issue had to be linked to broader themes to be successful. In 1909–11 land taxation had become implicated with the struggle for democracy and the need to raise funds for pensions and defence. In 1913–14 he redefined the land question to focus on minimum wages and housing development. In other words, while Lloyd George's campaign retained the form of a traditional crusade against 'privilege', its content became major social reform. Lloyd George was able to use land reform to construct a bridge between the old and the new Liberalism, to discard failed policies for more popular alternatives and to attempt to correct the Liberals' underperformance in crucial areas in 1910. The ingenuity of this scheme allowed the land issue to become a crucial element in the transformation and revival of Liberalism. Most of the signs that are available suggest that the land campaign had every chance of success when war intervened to transform the political landscape.

After 1918 the land issue, like the Liberal Party, could not be reconstructed in its Edwardian form. The near-universal perception that landowners were no longer a significant force in society and politics deprived it of any relevance for many on the left of politics, whether they were Liberals or socialists. The new issues of agricultural and industrial depression could not be tackled through land reform, or at least not in ways that were either popular or credible. Despite Lloyd George's best efforts to once again reformulate the content of the land question, it flickered out as a major political issue. But this conclusion should not be read back into the pre-1914 period. Land reform mattered, at least between 1909 and 1914, because it offered Liberalism its best chance of successfully combining social reform with traditional radicalism. This situation, however, depended on skilful manipulation of a very specific set of political circumstances. Once these had disappeared, so did the significance of the land issue.

The English land issue may have lacked the depth of feeling and resonance that lay behind the cause of land reform in, say, Ireland, but it was not a product of rural nostalgia or wishful thinking about the beauties of nature. It was rooted in the political conflict of late nineteenth- and early twentieth-century England. Indeed, before 1914 the English countryside was not the location of an unthinking consensus about the superiority of rural life. It was a subject of intense political controversy, in which Liberals sought to portray the countryside as a scene of squalor and misery inflicted by landed oppressors. It was only when these quarrels had faded after the First World War that rural England could be perceived by urban dwellers purely as an amenity – a place of recreation and a break from town life – and the country could be romanticised and prettified, as it was in the guide books of H. V. Morton and S. P. B. Mais, the journalism of J. Robertson Scott and hundreds of paintings of the Cotswolds.[1]

Once alternative views of rural England had lost their political importance the way was open for this picture book idea to become the dominant perception of rural life and once this had occurred the preservation of the landscape could begin to be important, rather than the plight of agricultural labourers. Thus the inter-war years saw the foundation of the Council for the Preservation of Rural England in 1926 and the first serious attempt to restrict urban development with the 1935 Ribbon Act.[2] This was not necessarily a conservative vision of rural England. Indeed it was a vision from which the landowner was largely absent and which could acquire a radical edge when demanding access to beauty spots and footpaths.[3] But it was an ideal that was most successfully appropriated into the rhetoric of 1920s Conservatism.

Baldwin, above all, tapped into the urban dweller's view of the country and helped to entrench the idea of the rural idyll at the heart of Englishness. As he famously put it in a speech of 1924 to the Royal Society of St George:

---

[1]   There is a burgeoning literature on this phenomenon. A particularly good example is A. Potts, ' "Constable country" between the wars', in R. Samuel (ed.), *Patriotism: the making and unmaking of British national identity*, London 1989, iii. 160–86.

[2]   D. N. Jeans, 'Planning and the myth of the English countryside in the interwar period', *Rural History* i (1990), 249–64.

[3]   J. Lowerson, 'Battles for the countryside', in F. Gloversmith (ed.), *Class, culture and social change: a new view of the 1930s*, Brighton 1980, 258–80.

To me, England is the country and the country is England . . . the hammer on the anvil in the country smithy, the corncrake on a dewy morning . . . the sight of a plough team coming over the brow of a hill . . . for centuries the one eternal sight of England.[4]

This sort of imagery won out over ideas about the poverty of rural society or the need to revive agriculture. But it would not have been possible before 1914 to talk about the countryside in this way and to present this vision of England as something on which all reasonable people could agree. In Edwardian England such a speech by Baldwin would have been inconceivable without some mention of the plight of the labourer and the controversy over landowners' role in politics and society. Only when these issues had died away could Englishness be unproblematically assimilated into the idyll of the countryside.

---

[4] S. Baldwin, On England, London 1926, 6–7.

Rural English Constituencies, 1885–1918

Table 1 is derived from N. Blewett, *The peers, the parties and the people: the general elections of 1910*, London 1972, appendix ii, 488–94; M. Kinnear, *The British voter*, 2nd edn, London 1981, 119–21; H. Pelling, *Social geography of British elections, 1885–1910*, London 1967, passim.[1] All use different methods to classify a 'rural' seat. Blewett defined it as one where over 60 per cent of voters lived in areas covered by rural district councils. Pelling relied on local newspaper sources. Kinnear was able to produce more definite estimates, but only for the post-1918 era. As Kenneth Wald found in his analysis of the relationship between census returns and parliamentary boundaries in 1885–1910, while it is possible to correlate some of the borough seats with census figures, this is not possible for county divisions.[2] Every English county, apart from Rutland, was divided into at least two parliamentary seats and the number of agriculturists in each county cannot be accurately broken down into estimates of the numbers in each parliamentary division. Counties had been divided into constituencies in 1885 on the basis of petty session divisions, while census figures referred only to counties and district councils. By 1910 there was little correlation between these areas.[3]

Table 1 is, therefore, no more than an estimate of those seats with an electorally significant number of agriculturists. The table also shows, briefly, the electoral history of each seat and the position in December 1910.

Table 1
Liberal electoral performance in English agricultural seats, 1885–1910

Seat (Total 111)	When Liberal, 1885–1910	Liberal vote Dec. 1910
South-East		
Chelmsford	never	no contest
Epping	never	35.9%
Harwich	1906	43.6%
Maldon	1885, 1892, 1906	46.6%
Hitchin	1906	43.0%

[1] The regions are those defined by Henry Pelling in *Social geography*, 3–4, and they are listed in the order in which Pelling dealt with them. Likewise within each region the consistuencies are listed in the order in which Pelling considered them.

[2] K. Wald, *Crosses on the ballot*, Princeton, NJ 1983, 81–8.

[3] *Census of 1911*, iii: *parliamentary areas*, 1912–13 (Cd. 6343), cxii, pp. iv, vii.

South-East (cont.)

Wokingham	never	no contest
Wycombe	1906	no contest
Guildford	1906	36.3%
Reigate	1906	40.3%
Chichester	never	33.6%
East Grinstead	1906	37.3%
Horsham	never	no contest
Rye	1903 by-election	40.1%
Ashford	never	no contest
Medway	never	no contest
St Augustine's	never	no contest

East Anglia

Chesterton	1892, 1906–	51.9%
Newmarket	1885–95, 1903–Jan.1910, Dec. 1910–13	52.2%
Wisbech	1885, 1891–5, 1900–	52.7%
Saffron Walden	1885–Jan. 1910, Dec. 1910–	50.2%
Ramsey	1906	49.0%
Norfolk East	1892–	57.7%
Mid	1885, 1892–Jan. 1910	49.8% (**P**)
North	1885–	53.6%
North-West	1885, 1892–	55.9%
South	1885, 1898–	59.6%
South-West	1906–	52.7%
Eye	1885–	54.2%
Stowmarket	1885, 1891–5, 1906	49.0% (**P**)
Sudbury	1885, 1906	no contest
Woodbridge	1885, 1892, 1906	47.4% (**P**)

Central

Biggleswade	1885, 1892, 1906–	52.9%
Abingdon	1906	41.6%
Newbury	1906	39.7%
Aylesbury	1885	no contest
Buckingham	1885, 1889–95, 1906–	51.4%
Cirencester	1885, 1892, 1906	45.6%
Huntingdon	1885, 1906	48.3% (**P**)
Northants Mid	1885–95, 1900–	51.0%
North	1906	44.5%
South	1892, 1906	46.9%
Banbury	1885–95, 1906, Dec. 1910–	50.6%
Henley	1906	40.9%

Woodstock	1885, 1892, 1906	47.9% (P)
Devizes	1892, 1906	45.4%
Wessex		
Petersfield	1885	no contest
Andover	never	no contest
New Forest	1906	no contest
Dorset North	1885–92, 1905–Jan. 1910	49.8% (P)
West	never	no contest
Wilton	1885, 1906	46.4%
Bristol		
Tewkesbury	never	48.0% (P)
Thornbury	1885, 1906–	53.9%
Bridgwater	1906	42.3%
Somerset East	1885, 1906	44.9%
South	1885–1911	52.6%
Wellington	1885	no contest
Chippenham	1885, 1906	49.9% (P)
Devon & Cornwall		
Bodmin	1885, 1906–Dec. 1910	49.8% (P)
Launceston	1885–	57.4%
St Ives	1885, 1906–	56.0%
Ashburton	1885–1908, Jan.–Dec. 1910	48.4%
Barnstaple	1885, 1892, 1900–	54.0%
Honiton	never	39.1%
South Molton	1885, 1891–	56.8%
Tavistock	1885, 1892–1900, 1906– Dec. 1910	48.4% (P)
Tiverton	never	40.7%
Totnes	1885	36.7%
West Midlands		
Leominster	1885, 1906	42.7%
Ross	1885, 1906–7	49.4% (P)
Ludlow	1885	no contest
Newport	1885	no contest
Oswestry	1904 by-election	45.9%
Rugby	1885–95, 1900–Jan. 1910	46.4%
Stratford	1885, 1906–9	40.2%
Bewdley	never	no contest
Evesham	never	no contest
East Midlands		
Rutland	never	38.7%
Bassetlaw	1906	49.0% (P)

East Midlands (cont.)

Newark	never	46.0%
Derbyshire West	1885	44.8%
Melton	1906–Dec. 1910	48.7% (**P**)
Leek	1885, 1906, Dec. 1910–	52.7%
Brigg	1885–94, 1895–1907 Jan. 1910–	53.6%
Gainsborough	1885, 1892–1900, 1906–	50.3%
Horncastle	never	47.1%
Louth	1885, 1892–Jan. 1910, Dec. 1910–	50.4%
Sleaford	1906	no contest
Spalding	1887–95, 1900–	51.3%
Stamford	never	48.1% (**P**)

Lancastria

Eddisbury	1906	48.4% (**P**)
Knutsford	1906	43.2%
Chorley	never	39.7%
Lancaster	1886–95, 1900–	50.5%
North Lonsdale	1892	49.5% (**P**)
Ormskirk	never	no contest
Kendal	1906	47.3%

Yorkshire

Barkston Ash	1905 by-election	46.3%
Ripon	1885, 1906	46.0%
Skipton	1885, 1892, 1900–	50.2%
Richmond	1885, 1906	no contest
Thirsk & Malton	never	no contest
Whitby	1905 by-election	47.6%
Buckrose	1892–	51.2%
Holderness	never	48.0%
Howdenshire	never	43.6%

North of England

Berwick	1885–	61.2%
Hexham	1885–92, 1893–	54.2%
Appleby	1900–Jan. 1910	45.1%
Eskdale	1885–1900, 1906–Dec. 1910	47.9% (**P**)
Penrith	1885. Speaker's seat from 1905	no contest

(**P**) Seats identified in both the memorandum by W. A. Gales, n.d. [1917], Steel-Maitland papers, GD/193/202/62, and *LM* xviii (1910), 645, as won by the Unionists only because of the votes of plural voters.

Table 2
Number of seats won by Liberal candidates at general elections in English agricultural seats, 1885–1910

1885	54
1886	16
1892	37
1895	18
1900	24
1906	74
Jan. 1910	30
Dec. 1910	30

Bibliography

Primary sources

Aberystwyth, National Library of Wales
E. W. Davies papers
E. T. John papers
Lloyd George papers

Birmingham, University of Birmingham Library
Joseph Chamberlain papers
Midland Liberal Federation papers

Bristol, University of Bristol Library
National Liberal Club papers

Cambridge University Library
Crewe papers

Edinburgh, National Library of Scotland
Elibank papers
Haldane papers

Edinburgh, Scottish Record Office
Steel-Maitland papers

Hatfield House
4th marquess of Salisbury papers

Keele, University of Keele Library
J. Wedgwood papers

Kew, Public Record Office
Association of Municipal Corporations papers
Board of Education papers
Cabinet papers
Inland Revenue papers
Local Government Board papers
Ramsay MacDonald papers
Ministry of Reconstruction papers
Treasury papers

Leeds, West Yorkshire Archive Service
Barkston Ash Conservative Association papers
Leeds Liberal Federation papers
Yorkshire Liberal Federation papers

Liverpool, City Library
R. Holt papers

London, British Library
Balfour papers
J. Burns papers
Campbell-Bannerman papers
Cecil of Chelwood papers
Dilke papers
H. Gladstone papers
W. Gladstone papers
E. Hamilton papers
Iddlesleigh papers
W. Long papers
Riddell papers
Ripon papers
C. P. Scott papers
J. A. Spender papers

London, British Library of Political and Economic Science
Co-operative Smallholdings Society papers

London, Friends House
T. Cadbury (A. S. Rowntree) papers

London, House of Lords Record Office
Bonar Law papers
Lloyd George papers
H. Samuel papers

London, Labour Party archive (now in Labour History Archive and Study Centre, John Rylands University Library, Manchester)
Labour Party letter files
NEC minutes

Manchester, Central Reference Library
Lancashire, Cheshire and North-Western Liberal Federation papers
Manchester Liberal Federation papers

Newcastle, University of Newcastle Library
Runciman papers
C. P. Trevelyan papers

Oxford, Bodleian Library
Addison papers
Asquith papers
J. Bryce papers
Harcourt papers
Lincolnshire (Carrington) papers (microfilm)
Milner papers
Nathan papers
Selborne papers

Oxford, Nuffield College Library
Emmott papers
Fabian society papers (now in the BLPES)
Gainford (J. Pease) papers

Oxford, Rhodes House Library
C. R. Buxton papers

York, Joseph Rowntree Foundation
B. S. Rowntree papers

York, Joseph Rowntree Reform Trust
J. Rowntree Social Service Trust papers

Primary printed sources

Official papers (in chronological order)
Parliamentary debates (Commons and Lords) 4th and 5th ser.
Instructions to boundary commissioners, PP 1884–5
Board of trade report on agencies and methods for dealing with unemployment, 1893 (C. 7182)
Report of the royal commission on Welsh land, 1896 (C. 8242)
Returns as to the number and size of agricultural holdings in Great Britain, 1895, 1896 (C. 8243)
Report of the departmental committee appointed by the board of agriculture on smallholdings in Great Britain, 1906 (Cd 3277)
Select committee on the housing of the working classes acts amendment bill, 1906 (H of C . 376)
Annual report of proceedings under the Smallholdings and Allotments Act 1908 part 1, smallholdings for 1911 (Cd 5615)
Census of England and Wales, 1911
Report of the departmental committee appointed to inquire into the position of tenant farmers on the occasion of any change in the ownership of their holdings and to consider whether any legislative change is desirable, 1911–12 (Cd 6030)

Newspapers and journals

Daily, national
Daily Chronicle
Daily Citizen
Daily Herald
Daily News
Pall Mall Gazette
Times
Westminster Gazette

Daily, regional
Birmingham Gazette
East Anglian Daily Times
Eastern Daily Press
Glasgow Herald
Liverpool Daily Post
Manchester Guardian
South Wales Daily News
The Sun
Yorkshire Herald

Weekly
British Weekly
Clarion
Forward
Gloucester Journal
The Homeland
Justice
Labour Leader
Leicester Pioneer
Nation (previously *The Speaker*)
New Statesman
Sheffield Guardian
South Bucks Free Press
Taunton Echo
Yorkshire Gazette

Other
ASE Monthly Journal and Report
Dockers Record
Estates Gazette
Fabian News
Government Workers Advocate
Land Nationaliser (previously *Land and Labour*)
Land Values
Liberal Magazine
National Review

Our Flag
Postman's Gazette
Rural World
Typographical Circular
Young Liberal

Contemporary books and articles

Addison, C., *Four and a half years*, London 1934

Adeane, C. and E. Savill, *The land retort*, London 1914

Aldridge, H., *The case for town planning*, London 1915

Anon., *Land values in parliament*, London 1903

Arnold, A., *Free land*, London 1880

Aronson, H., *Our village homes*, London 1913

—— *The land and the labourer*, London 1914

H. H. Asquith: letters to Venetia Stanley, ed. M. Brock and E. Brock, Oxford 1985

Baldwin, S., *On England*, London 1926

Bateman, J., *The great landowners of Great Britain and Ireland*, 4th edn, London 1883

Bathurst, C., *To avoid national starvation*, London 1911

Booth, C., *Life and labour of the people in London*, London 1902

—— *Rates and the housing question in London*, London 1904

Box, S., *The good old days: then and now*, Hereford 1955

Brodrick, G. C., *English land and English landlords*, London 1881

Budget taxes and the building industry (Land Union pamphlet, no. 117), London 1913

Carrington, Lord, 'The land and the labourers', *The Nineteenth Century* xlv (1899), 368–77

Channing, F., *An agricultural policy*, London 1905

—— *Memories of Midland politics, 1885–1910*, London 1918

Churchill, R., *W. S. Churchill: young statesman, 1901–14*, London 1967; companion vols i–iii

Clynes, J. R., *Memoirs*, London 1937

Cockayne, G. E., *The complete peerage*, ed. H. V. Gibbs, London 1910–53

Collings, J., *The colonisation of rural Britain*, London 1914

—— and J. Green, *Life and times of the Right Hon. Jesse Collings*, London 1920

The Crawford papers: the journals of David Lindsay, 27th earl of Crawford and 10th earl of Balcarres, 1871–1940, during the years 1892–1940, ed. J. Vincent, Manchester 1984

The crisis of British Unionism: the domestic political papers of the second earl of Selborne, 1885–1922, ed. G. Boyce, London 1987

The destruction of Lord Rosebery: from the diary of Sir Edward Hamilton, 1894–5, ed. D. Brooks, London 1986

The diary of Beatrice Webb, ed. N. Mackenzie and J. Mackenzie, London 1984

Diggle, J. H., *The creation of smallholdings in Lincolnshire and Norfolk*, King's Lynn 1903

Edwards, G., *From crow-scaring to Westminster*, London 1922

Eighty Club year book, 1914, London 1914

Free Land League, *12th annual report, 1897*, London 1897

Grant, C., *Allotments and smallholdings handbook*, London 1908

Griffith-Boscawen, Sir A., *Memories*, London 1925

Haldane, R. B., *The unearned increment*, London 1892

——— *An autobiography*, London 1929

Harben, H. D., *The rural problem*, London 1913

Heath, R., 'The rural revolution', *Contemporary Review* lxvii (1895), 182–200

Higgs, R., *The heart of the social problem*, London 1913

Hobson, J. A. (ed.), *Co-operative labour on the land*, London 1895

Horsfall, T., *The improvement of the dwellings and surroundings of the people: the example of Germany*, Manchester 1904

Housing the town worker (Central Land and Housing Council leaflet, no. 17), London 1914

Howard, E., *Tomorrow: a peaceful path to real reform*, London 1898

Howarth, E. and M. Wilson, *West Ham: a study in social and industrial problems*, London 1907

Inside Asquith's cabinet: from the diaries of Charles Hobhouse, ed. E. David, London 1977

Irvine, J., 'Forecasting by-election results', *NR* lxiii (1914), 765–74

Jebb, L., *The smallholdings of England*, London 1907

Joseph Arch: the story of his life, told by himself, ed. Frances ['Daisy'] Greville, countess of Warwick, London 1898.

Journals and letters of Reginald, Viscount Esher, ed. M. V. Brett, London 1934–8

The Labour party and the agricultural problem, London 1914

Land Club League, *Land Club convention, 1909*, London 1909

Land Conference, *The land problem*, London 1914

Land enquiry committee, *The land*, i, ii, London 1913, 1914

Land Law Reform Association, *Proceedings of conference, 25 May 1897*, London 1897

——— *14th annual meeting, 1901*, London 1901

——— *17th annual meeting, 1904*, London 1904

——— *19th annual meeting, 1906*, London 1906

The land and the nation: the rural report of the Liberal land committee, 1923–5, London 1925

Land Nationalisation Society, *Annual report, 1909–10*, London 1910

Land proposals as adopted at the Liberal conference held in the Kingsway Hall, London, February 17th–19th 1926, London 1926

Land Tenure Reform Association, *Report of inaugural public meeting, 15 May 1871*, London 1871

Lansbury, G., *My life*, London 1928

Liberal land policy and the shopkeeper (Central Land and Housing Council leaflet, no. 4), London 1914

Liberal Publication Department, *Pamphlets and leaflets, 1908*

——— *Proceedings of the annual meeting of the council of the NLF at Nottingham 21–22 Nov. 1912*, London 1912

——— *Proceedings of the annual meeting of the council of the NLF, 26–7 Nov. 1913*, London 1913

——— *100 points in Liberal policy and of the Liberal record*, London 1914

Lloyd George, D., *The urban land problem: the case of the town tenants*, London 1913

Long, Viscount, *Memories*, London 1923

Marchant, J., J. B. Paton, London 1909

Masterman, C. F. G., W. Hodgson and others, *To colonise England: a plea for a policy*, London 1907

Masterman, L., *C. F. G. Masterman: a biography*, London 1939

Merivale, H., 'Essays on the tenure of land', *Edinburgh Review* cxxxiv (1874), 449–83.

Minutes of the Rainbow Circle, 1894–1924, ed. M. Freeden (Camden 4th ser. xxxviii, 1989)

Moulton, J. F., *The taxation of ground values*, London 1889

My darling pussy: letters of Lloyd George and Frances Stevenson, 1913–41, ed. A. J. P. Taylor, London 1975

National Land and Home League, *Annual report, 1911*, London 1911

————— *Annual report, 1912*, London 1912

————— *Annual report, 1913*, London 1913

Neilson, F., *My life in two worlds*, Appleton, Wisc. 1952–3

Owen, R., *The signs of the times: or the approach of the millennium*, London 1841

Paine, T., *Agrarian justice: opposed to agrarian law and to agrarian monopoly*, London 1797

Parmoor, Lord, *A retrospect*, London 1936

Perks, Sir R. W., *Autobiography*, London 1936

Political diaries of C. P. Scott, 1911–28, ed. T. Wilson, London 1970

Price, M. P., *My three revolutions*, London 1969

Prothero, R. [Lord Ernle], *From Whippingham to Westminster*, London 1938

Raffan, P. W., *The policy of the land values group in the House of Commons*, London 1912

Real old Tory politics: the political diaries of Robert Sanders, Lord Bayford, 1910–35, ed. J. Ramsden, London 1984

Report of proceedings at the 46th Trades Union Congress, London 1913

Riddell, Lord, *More pages from my diary, 1908–14*, London 1934

Rogers, J. E. T., *Six centuries of work and wages*, London 1884

Rowntree, B. S., *Poverty: a study of town life*, London 1901

————— *Land and labour: lessons from Belgium*, London 1911

————— *The labourer and the land*, London 1914

————— and M. Kendall, *How the labourer lives*, London 1913

————— and A. C. Pigou, *Lectures on housing: the Warburton lectures for 1913*, London 1914

Seale-Hayne, C. H., *Agricultural distress: its causes and remedies*, Exeter 1895

Snell, Lord, *Men, movements and myself*, London 1936

Spence, T., *The rights of infants*, London 1797

Spender, J. A., *Life, journalism and politics*, London 1927

Thorold, A., *Life of Labouchere*, London 1913

Town Tenants League, *The town tenants bill*, London 1908

Towns and the land: the urban report of the Liberal land committee, 1923–5, London 1925

The town worker's rent and his wage (Central Land and Housing Council leaflet, no. 18), London 1914

Trevelyan, C. P., *Land taxation and the use of land*, London 1905

Tuckwell, Revd W., *Reminiscences of a radical parson*, London 1905.

Turnor, C., *Land problems and national welfare*, London 1911

United Committee for the Taxation of Land Values, *Annual report, 1911–12*, London 1912

Unwin, R., *Nothing gained by overcrowding*, London 1912

Webb, S., 'The Liberal cabinet: an intercepted letter', *NR* xlvi (1906), 789–802

Wedgwood, J., *Memoirs of a fighting life*, London 1940

Wilkinson, M. (ed.), *E. Richard Cross: a biographical sketch*, London 1917

Winfrey, R., *Leaves from my life*, privately printed, King's Lynn 1936

—— *Great men and others I have met*, Kettering 1943

Zincke, Revd B., 'Peasants of the Limagne', *Fortnightly Review* xxx (1878) 646–60, 821–35

Secondary sources

Acland, A., *A Devon family*, London 1981

Adonis, A., 'Aristocracy, agriculture and Liberalism: the politics, finances and estates of the third Lord Carrington', *HJ* xxxi (1988), 871–97

—— *Making aristocracy work: the peerage and the political system in Britain, 1884–1914*, Oxford 1993

Alexander, A., *Borough government and politics: Reading, 1835–1985*, London 1985

Allfrey, A., *Edward VII and his Jewish court*, London 1991

Ashworth, W., *The genesis of modern British town planning*, London 1954

Barker, M., *Gladstone and Radicalism: the reconstruction of Liberal policy in Britain, 1885–94*, Hassocks 1975

Barrett, L. M., *English food policy during the First World War*, London 1985

Barry, E., *Nationalisation in British politics*, London 1965

Bealey, F., 'Municipal politics in Newcastle-under-Lyme, 1870–1914', *North Staffordshire Journal of Field Studies* v (1965), 64–73

Beavington, F., 'The development of market gardening in Bedfordshire, 1799–1939', *AgHR* xxiii (1975), 23–47

Bebbington, D. W., 'Nonconformity and electoral sociology, 1867–1918', *HJ* xxvii (1984), 633–56

Bellamy, J. and J. Saville, *Dictionary of Labour biography*, London 1972–

Bentley, M., 'The Liberal response to socialism, 1918–29', in K. D. Brown (ed.), *Essays in anti-labour history*, London 1974, 42–73

Bernstein, G., *Liberalism and Liberal politics in Edwardian England*, London 1986

Bew, P., *Land and the national question in Ireland, 1858–82*, Dublin 1978

Biagini, E., *Liberty, retrenchment and reform*, Cambridge 1992

Blackburn, S., 'Ideology and social policy: the origin of the Trade Boards Act', *HJ* xxxiv (1991), 43–64

Blewett, N., 'The franchise in the United Kingdom, 1885–1918', *P&P* xxxii (1965), 27–56

—— *The peers, the parties and the people: the general elections of 1910*, London 1972

Brandon, P., 'A twentieth-century squire in his landscape: Reginald Bray of Shere, Surrey', *Southern History* iv (1982), 191–220

Briggs, A., *Social thought and social action: a study of the work of Seebohm Rowntree*, London 1961

Bromhead, P. A., *The House of Lords in contemporary politics, 1911–57*, London 1958

Brown, J., 'Scottish and English land legislation, 1905–11', *SHR* xlvii (1968), 72–85

Brown, K., *John Burns*, London 1977

Bull, P., *Land, politics and nationalism*, Dublin 1996

Burnett, J., *A social history of housing, 1815–1985*, 2nd edn, London 1986

Cameron, E. A., *Land for the people? The British government and the Scottish Highlands, c. 1880–1925*, East Linton 1996

Campbell, J., *Lloyd George: the goat in the wilderness, 1922–31*, London 1977

Cannadine, D., *The decline and fall of the British aristocracy*, London 1990

Chambers, J. and G. Mingay, *The agricultural revolution*, London 1966

Chase, M., *The people's farm: English radical agrarianism, 1775–1840*, Oxford 1988

Cherry, G., *Factors in the origins of town planning in Britain: the example of Birmingham, 1905–14*, Birmingham 1975

Clarke, P., 'The electoral position of the Liberal and Labour parties, 1910–14', *EHR* lxxxx (1975), 828–36

———— *Liberals and social democrats*, Cambridge 1978

———— and K. Langford, 'Hodge's politics: the agricultural labourers and the Third Reform Act in Suffolk', in Harte and Quinault, *Land and society in Britain*, 119–36

Cline, C., *Recruits to Labour: the British Labour Party, 1914–31*, New York 1963

Collini, S., *Liberalism and sociology: L. T. Hobhouse and political argument in England, 1880–1914*, Cambridge 1979

Cooper, A. F., *British agricultural policy, 1912–36*, Manchester 1989

Cornford, J., 'The transformation of Conservatism in the late nineteenth century', *VS* vii (1963), 35–65

———— 'The parliamentary foundations of the Hotel Cecil', in R. Robson (ed.), *Ideas and institutions in Victorian Britain*, London 1967, 268–311

Cox, J., *The English churches in a secular society: Lambeth, 1870–1930*, Oxford 1982

Cragoe, M., *An Anglican aristocracy: the moral economy of the landed estate in Carmarthenshire, 1832–95*, Oxford 1996

Craig, F., *British parliamentary election results, 1885–1918*, London 1974

———— *British general election manifestos, 1900–74*, London 1975

Creese, W., *The search for environment: the garden city: before and after*, New Haven 1966

Cross, C., *Philip Snowden*, London 1966

Crossick, G., 'The emergence of the lower middle class in Britain: a discussion', in G. Crossick (ed.), *The lower middle class in Britain, 1870–1914*, London 1977, 11–60

Daunton, M. J., *Coal metropolis: Cardiff, 1870–1914*, Leicester 1977

———— *House and home in the Victorian city*, London 1983

———— 'The political economy of death duties: Harcourt's budget of 1894', in Harte and Quinault, *Land and society in Britain*, 137–71

Dawson, M., 'The Liberal land policy, 1924–9', *TCBH* ii (1991), 272–90

de Bunsen, V., *Charles Roden Buxton: a memoir*, London 1948

Dewey, C., 'The rehabilitation of the peasant proprietor in nineteenth-century economic thought', *History of Political Economy* vi (1974), 17–47.

Dewey, P., *British agriculture in the First World War*, London 1989

Douglas, R., *Land, people and politics: a history of the land question in the United Kingdom, 1878–1952*, London 1976

Dunbabin, J. P. D., 'Expectations of the new county councils, and their realisation', *HJ* viii (1965), 353–79

—— 'The rise and fall of agricultural trades unionism in England', in Dunbabin, *Rural discontent*, 62–84

—— 'The Welsh "tithe war" ', in Dunbabin, *Rural discontent*, 211–31

—— (ed.), *Rural discontent in nineteenth-century Britain*, London 1974

Dutton, D., 'His Majesty's loyal opposition': the Unionist Party in opposition, 1905–15, Liverpool 1992

Emy, H. V., *Liberals, Radicals and social politics, 1892–1914*, Cambridge 1973

Englander, D., *Landlord and tenant in urban Britain, 1838–1918*, Oxford 1983

Fels, M., *Joseph Fels: his life and work*, London 1920

Fforde, M., *Conservatism and collectivism, 1886–1914*, Edinburgh 1990

Fisher, J., 'The Farmers Alliance: an agricultural protest movement of the 1880s', *AgHR* xxvi (1978), 15–25

Fox, A., *A history of the National Union of Boot and Shoe Operatives, 1874–1957*, London 1958

Freeden, M., *The new Liberalism: an ideology of social reform*, Oxford 1978

Gailey, A., *Ireland and the death of kindness: the experience of constructive unionism, 1890–1905*, Cork 1987

Gauldie, E., *Cruel habitations*, London 1974

Gilbert, B., 'David Lloyd George: the reform of British landholding and the budget of 1914', *HJ* xxi (1978), 117–41

Gooch, G. P., *Frederic Mackarness: a brief memoir*, privately printed, London 1922

Goodlad, G. D., 'The Liberal Party and Gladstone's land purchase bill of 1886', *HJ* xxxii (1989), 627–41

Gourvish, T. R., 'The standard of living, 1890–1914', in A. O'Day (ed.), *The Edwardian age: conflict and stability, 1900–14*, London 1979, 13–34

Green, B., *Hampstead Garden Suburb, 1907–77: a history*, London 1977

Green, E., *The crisis of Conservatism: the politics, economics and ideology of the British Conservative Party, 1880–1914*, London 1995

Green, F., *The Surrey hills*, London 1915

—— *History of the English agricultural labourer, 1870–1920*, London 1920

Griffiths, C. V. J., 'Remembering Tolpuddle: rural history and commemoration in the inter-war labour movement', *HWJ* xliv (1997), 144–69

Groves, R., *Sharpen the sickle! The history of the Farmworkers Union*, London 1949

Hanham, H. J., *Elections and party management*, London 1959

—— 'The problem of Highland discontent, 1880–5', *TRHS* 5th ser. xix (1969), 21–65

Harris, J., *Unemployment and politics: a study in English social policy, 1886–1914*, Oxford 1972

—— *William Beveridge*, Oxford 1977

Harrison, R., 'The Land and Labour League', *Bulletin of the International Institute of Social History* viii (1953), 169–95

Harte, N. and R. Quinault (eds), *Land and society in Britain, 1700–1914: essays in honour of F. M. L. Thompson*, Manchester 1996

Hawson, H., *Sheffield: the growth of a city, 1893–1926*, Sheffield 1968

Heuston, R., *Lives of the Lord Chancellors, 1885–1940*, Oxford 1964

Hosgood, C., 'A "brave and daring folk"? Shopkeepers and trade associational life in Victorian and Edwardian England', *Journal of Social History* xxvi (1992), 285–308

Howarth, J., 'Politics and society in late Victorian Northamptonshire', *Northamptonshire Past and Present* iv (1970–1), 269–74

Howell, D., *Land and people in nineteenth-century Wales*, London 1978

────── *British workers and the ILP, 1888–1906*, Manchester 1983

Howkins, A., 'Edwardian Liberalism and industrial unrest: a class view of the decline of Liberalism', *HWJ* iv (1977), 143–61

────── *Poor labouring men: rural radicalism in Norfolk, 1870–1923*, London 1985

────── 'The discovery of rural England', in R. Colls and P. Dodd (eds), *Englishness: politics and culture, 1880–1920*, Beckenham 1986, 62–88

────── *Reshaping rural England: a social history, 1850–1925*, London 1991

Hyman, R., *The Workers Union*, Oxford 1971

Jackson, F., *Sir Raymond Unwin*, London 1985

Jay, R., *Joseph Chamberlain: a political study*, Oxford 1981

Jeans, D. N., 'Planning and the myth of the English countryside in the interwar period', *Rural History* i (1990), 249–64

Jenkins, T., *Gladstone, Whiggery and the Liberal Party, 1874–86*, Oxford 1988

────── 'The funding of the Liberal Unionist Party and the honours system', *EHR* cv (1990), 920–38

Jones, A., *The politics of reform, 1884*, Cambridge 1972

Jones, G., 'Further thoughts on the franchise', *P&P* xxxiv (1966), 134–8

Jones, J. G., 'Wales and "the new Liberalism", 1926–9', *National Library of Wales Journal* xxii (1981–2), 321–46

────── 'Select committee or royal commission? Wales and "The land question", 1892', *WHR* xvii (1994), 205–29

Kinnear, M., *The British voter*, 2nd edn, London 1981

Lansbury, G., *The miracle of Fleet Street*, London 1925

Laybourn, K., 'The defence of the "bottom dog": the ILP in local politics', in J. Jowitt and D. Wright (eds), *Victorian Bradford*, Bradford 1982, 223–44

Lowerson, J., 'Battles for the countryside', in F. Gloversmith (ed.), *Class, culture and social change: a new view of the 1930s*, Brighton 1980, 258–80

Lubenow, W. C., *Parliamentary politics and the Home Rule crisis: the British House of Commons in 1886*, Oxford 1988

McBriar, A., *Fabian socialism and English politics, 1884–1918*, Cambridge 1962

McKibbin, R., *The evolution of the Labour Party, 1910–24*, Oxford 1974

Maclean, I., *Keir Hardie*, London 1975

────── *The legend of Red Clydeside*, Edinburgh 1983

Macleod, H., *Class and religion in the late Victorian city*, London 1974

Mandler, P., *The fall and rise of the stately home*, London 1997

Matthew, H. C. G., *The Liberal imperialists: the ideas and politics of a post-Gladstonian elite*, Oxford 1973

────── *Gladstone, 1809–74*, Oxford 1988

────── *Gladstone, 1875–1898*, Oxford 1995

Merrett, S., *State housing in Britain*, London 1979

Mingay, G., *Rural life in Victorian Britain*, Stroud 1990

Morgan, K., *Consensus and disunity*, Oxford 1979

Morley, J., *Life of Richard Cobden*, London 1881

Murray, B., *The people's budget, 1909/10: Lloyd George and Liberal politics*, Oxford 1980

—— 'Lloyd George, the navy estimates and the inclusion of rating reform in the 1914 budget', *WHR* xvi (1990), 56–78

—— ' "Battered and shattered": Lloyd George and the 1914 budget fiasco', *Albion* xxiii (1991), 483–507

O'Callaghan, M., *British high politics and a nationalist Ireland*, Cork 1994

Offer, A., *Property and politics, 1870–1914: landownership, law, ideology and urban development in England*, Cambridge 1981

Olney, R. J., *Lincolnshire politics, 1832–85*, Oxford 1973

Packer, I., 'The Conservatives and the ideology of landownership, 1910–14', in M. Francis and I. Zweiniger-Bargielowska (eds), *The Conservatives and British society, 1880–1990*, Cardiff 1996, 39–57

—— 'The land issue and the future of Scottish Liberalism in 1914', *SHR* lxxv (1996), 52–71

—— 'The Liberal cave and the 1914 budget', *EHR* cxi (1996), 620–35

Parry, J., *The rise and fall of Liberal government in Victorian Britain*, London 1993

Pease, E., *History of the Fabian Society*, 3rd edn, London 1963

Pelling, H., *Social geography of British elections, 1885–1910*, London 1967

Potts, A., ' "Constable country" between the wars', in R. Samuel (ed.), *Patriotism: the making and unmaking of British national identity*, London 1989, iii. 160–86

Pugh, M., *Electoral reform in war and peace, 1906–18*, London 1978

—— *The making of modern British politics, 1867–1939*, Oxford 1982

Ramsden, J., *The age of Balfour and Baldwin, 1902–40*, London 1978

Readman, P., 'The 1895 general election and political change in late Victorian Britain', *HJ* xlii (1999), 467–93

Reed, M., 'The peasantry of nineteenth-century England: a neglected class?', *HWJ* xviii (1984), 53–76

Reeder, D., 'The politics of urban leaseholds in later Victorian Britain', *IRSH* vi (1961), 413–30

Rowland, P., *The last Liberal governments*, London 1968–71

Russell, A. K., *Liberal landslide: the general election of 1906*, Newton Abbot 1973

Searle, G., *The Liberal Party: triumph and disintegration, 1886–1929*, London 1992

Sherington, G., *English education, social change and war, 1911–20*, Manchester 1981

Simon, A., 'Church disestablishment as a factor in the general election of 1885', *HJ* xviii (1975), 791–820

Sinclair, Marjorie, Lady Pentland, *Memoir of Lord Pentland*, London 1928

Smith, N., *Land for the small man: English and Welsh experiments with publicly supported smallholdings, 1860–1937*, New York 1946

Sturmey, S. G., 'Owner-farming in England and Wales, 1900–50', *Manchester School of Economic and Social Studies* xxiii (1955), 246–68

Sutcliffe, A., *Towards the planned city*, Oxford 1981

Swenarton, M., *Homes fit for heroes*, London 1981

Sykes, A., *Tariff reform in British politics, 1903–13*, Oxford 1979

Thompson, F. M. L., *English landed society in the nineteenth century*, London 1963

—— 'Land and politics in England in the nineteenth century', *TRHS* 5th ser. xv (1965), 23–44

Tichelar, M., 'Socialists, Labour and the land: the response of the Labour Party to the land campaign of Lloyd George before the First World War', *TCBH* viii (1997), 127–44

Tsuzuki, C., *H. M. Hyndman and British socialism*, Oxford 1961

Vaughan, W. E., *Landlords and tenants in mid-Victorian Ireland*, Oxford 1994

Waites, B., *A class society at war: England, 1914–18*, Leamington Spa 1987

Wald, K., 'Class and the vote before the First World War', *British Journal of Political Science* viii (1978), 441–57

—————— *Crosses on the ballot*, Princeton, NJ 1983

Waller, P., *Town, city and nation: England, 1850–1914*, Oxford 1983

Weiner, M. J., *English culture and the decline of the industrial spirit*, Cambridge 1981

Whetham, E., *Agrarian history of England and Wales*, viii, Cambridge 1978

Williamson, P., 'The Labour Party and the House of Lords, 1918–31', *Parliamentary History* x (1991), 317–41

—————— *National crisis and national government: British politics, the economy and the empire, 1926–32*, Cambridge 1992

Wohl, A. S., *The eternal slum*, London 1977

Wilson, J., *CB: a life of Sir Henry Campbell-Bannerman*, London 1973

Wilson, T., *The downfall of the Liberal Party, 1914–35*, London 1966

Zangerl, C., 'The social composition of the county magistracy in England and Wales, 1831–87', *JBS* xi (1971), 113–25

Theses

Brooks, D., 'Gladstone's fourth ministry, 1892–4: policies and personalities', PhD diss. Cambridge 1975

Fisher, J. R., 'Public opinion and agriculture, 1875–1900', PhD diss. Hull 1973

Griffiths, C. V. J., 'Labour and the countryside: rural strands in the British labour movement, 1900–39', DPhil. diss. Oxford 1996

Packer I., 'The Liberal land campaign and the land issue, *c*. 1906–14', DPhil. diss. Oxford 1994

Simon, A., 'Joseph Chamberlain and the unauthorised programme', DPhil. diss. Oxford 1970

Ward, S., 'Land reform in England, 1880–1914', PhD diss. Reading 1976

Wright, R., 'Liberal Party organisation and politics in Birmingham, Coventry and Wolverhampton, 1886–1914', PhD diss. Birmingham 1977

Index

Acland, A. H. D., 84–5
Acland, F. D., 185
Acland-Hood, Sir A. F., 62
Addison, C., 89, 127, 141, 191
Agar-Robartes, Hon. T., 40, 128
Agricultural Holdings Acts: (1875), 10;
  (1883), 10; (1906), 40–2
agricultural holdings bill (1895), 24–5, 35,
  40
Agricultural Land Rating Act (1896), 25,
  156
Agricultural Wages Act (1924), 185–6
agriculture, 1–2, 5–6, 8–9, 23–5, 178–9.
  See also farmers
Alden, P., 36, 81
Aldridge, H., 67
allotments, 12–13, 15, 18–25, 33–4,
  156–7, 191
Allotments Act (1887), 19–20, 33
Allotments Extension Act (1882), 12
Allotments Extension Association, 12, 18
Arch, J., 17, 31
Arnold, S., 82, 124
Aronson, H., 168
Ashby, A. K., 86
Ashby St Ledgers, 1st Lord, 128
Asquith, H. H., 3, 51, 55, 58, 60, 69, 76,
  160; and land campaign, 82–4, 96, 112,
  116–20, 123, 134, 139, 145–7
Association of Municipal Corporations,
  56, 70

Balcarres, 10th earl of, 62, 81, 157
Baldwin, S., 188, 195–6
Balfour, A., 19, 33, 40, 43–4, 48, 61, 156
Barnes, G., 163, 170, 174–5
Barnett, H., 67
Barnett, S., 67, 72
Bathurst, C., 88, 92, 130, 159, 188
Beauchamp, 7th earl, 124, 128
Beck, C., 124, 127, 129, 131
Bennett, E. N., 131
Benson, T. D., 172
Bentinck, Lord H., 159
Beveridge, W., 72–3
Black, A. W., 89
Bledisloe, 1st Lord, *see* Bathurst, C.

Blizard, G. P., 168
Bonar Law, A., 130, 159–60
Booth, C., 32, 55, 86
Bray, R., 168
Brett, O., 130
Brett, R. B., *see* Esher, 2nd viscount
British Socialist Party, 142, 173
budgets: (1894), 27; (1909), 2, 51–2,
  60–4, 191–2; (1914), 148–55; proposed
  (1915), 150–1; (1931), 192–3
Burns, J., 42, 58–60, 68–71, 72–3, 89, 119,
  121
Butler, J. G., 142
Buxton, C. R., 36–7, 40, 49, 83, 85–6, 89,
  99, 185
Buxton, N., 128, 185
Buxton, S., 118
by-elections: Ashburton (1908), 49; Brigg
  (1894), 23, (1907), 42–3, 49;
  Buckingham (1891), 19; Chelmsford
  (1908), 49; Crewe (1912), 174;
  Derbyshire, North-East (1914), 174;
  West Dorset (1895), 23; Durham,
  North-West (1914), 143; Evesham
  (1895), 23; Hanley (1912), 96, 174;
  Harborough (1891), 19; Holmfirth
  (1912), 82; Ilkeston (1912), 133;
  Ipswich (1914), 143; Lanarks, South
  (1913), 167; Leith (1914), 162;
  Manchester, South (1912), 79, 81, 133;
  Midlothian (1912), 174; Newmarket
  (1913), 116, 133–4; Newport (1908),
  49; Mid-Norfolk (1895), 23; Norfolk,
  North-West (1912), 81–2, 133;
  Oldham (1911), 162; Reading (1913),
  141–3; Ross (1908), 49; Rutland
  (1907), 49; St Ives (1928), 184;
  Spalding (1887), 18–19; Stowmarket
  (1891), 19; Wisbech (1894), 23;
  Wycombe (1914), 135–6

Cadbury, G., 66–7, 77, 124
Campbell-Bannerman, Sir H., 34, 38–9,
  42, 54, 56–9, 68, 70
Carrington, 1st earl, 37–45, 49, 76, 80, 91,
  124, 128, 135–6, 161, 166

Carter, G. Wallace, 125, 130, 138, 140–1, 147

Carter Jonas, 39

Cavendish, S. C., see Hartington, marquess of

Central Land and Housing Council, 124–5, 127, 135–6, 138, 140–1, 143–4, 147

Central Smallholdings Society, 129

Central Unemployed Body, 72–4

Chamberlain, A., 62, 191–2

Chamberlain, J., 2, 12–15, 33–4, 79, 83, 95, 142, 154

Channing, F., 17, 34–5, 36, 38, 40, 44

Chaplin, H., 19–20

Churchill, W., 73–4, 77–8, 149–52; and land campaign, 83, 97, 117–20, 122–3, 134, 139

Coal Mines Acts: (1912), 77–8, 88; (1930), 182

Cobb, H. P., 17

Cobden, R., 66–7

Collings, J., 11–12, 15, 17–18, 20, 43–4, 92

Congested Districts (Scotland) Act (1897), 10

Co-operative Smallholdings Society, 36–7, 45, 85

Corn Production Act (1917), 179

Cornish Farmers Union, 128

Crawfurd, H. E., 100

Crewe, 1st marquess of, 117, 122–3

Crewe-Milnes, R. O. A., see Crewe, 1st marquess of

Cripps, Sir C. A., see Parmoor, 1st Lord

Crofters' Holdings (Scotland) Act (1886), 9, 22

Crook, W., 130, 138–9, 141

Crooks, W., 166

Cross, E. R., 81, 85, 98–100, 105, 107–11, 147

crown lands, 39–40

Dalmeny, Lord, 40

Davies, E. W., 41, 85

de Forest, Baron, 82, 84–5, 97–8, 115, 165

Denison-Pender, J. C. D., 134

departmental committees: local government finance (1911–14), 148–9; national expenditure (1931), 192; smallholdings (1905–6), 33–4

Devonshire, 8th duke of, see Hartington, marquess of

Dickinson, W. H., 108

Dickson-Poynder, Sir J., 44

Dilke, Sir C., 31, 77

Du Pre, W. B., 135

ecclesiastical commissioners, 39

education, policy, 11, 42, 45, 51, 61, 115, 117–18, 149

Edward VII, 38–40

Edwards, G., 131, 165

Eighty Club, 129

Elibank, master of, 82, 123

Elliott, Sir T., 39

employers liability bill (1893), 22, 27

English Land Colonisation Society, 36

English Land Restoration League, 30

English League for the Taxation of Land Values, 113

Equalisation of Rates Act (1894), 29–30

Esher, 2nd viscount, 80

Evans, B. B., 108–9

Eve, T., 49

evicted tenants bill (1894), 21

Fabian society, 166–9

farmers: land reform, 10–11, 41, 52, 91–4, 131–2, 186–7; political allegiance, 6, 10–11, 34–7, 40–2, 52, 91–2, 132–3, 159. See also landowners

Farmers Alliance, 10–11, 34

Fellowes, A., 46

Fels, J., 72–3, 164

Finnemore, W., 130, 141

Fowler, H. H., 22, 29

Frank, Knight and Rutley, 145

Free Land League, 11, 34

Free Trade in land, 6–7, 9, 11, 12

Free Trade Union, 123, 125

Ganzoni, F. J. C., 143

Gardner, H., 16, 17, 24, 38

Gascoyne-Cecil, J. E. H., see Salisbury, 4th marquess of

Gascoyne-Cecil, R. A. T., see Salisbury, 3rd marquess of

general elections: (1880), 10; (1885), 12–13, 14, 17, 82; (1886), 16; (1892), 20–1, 82; (1895), 24–5; (1900), 25–6, 33; (1906), 42–3, 45, 54, 82; (Jan. 1910), 48–53, 62–3, 82, 162–3; (Dec. 1910), 63, 76; planned (1915), 136–7, 147–8, 161; (1918), 179–80; (1923), 183; (1924), 183; (1929), 184

George, H., 30, 96. See also single taxers

Gladstone, W. E., 6, 9–11, 15, 17–18, 20–1, 24, 26
Glebe Lands Act (1888), 20
Gooch. G. P., 36, 142–3
Grant, C., 45
Grey, Sir E., 3, 78, 83, 118–19, 123
Griffith-Boscawen, Sir A., 159
Ground Game Act (1880), 10
Guest, I. C., *see* Ashby St Ledgers, 1st Lord

Haldane, R. B., 31, 83, 117–19
Harben, H. D., 167–8
Harcourt, L., 27, 43–4
Harcourt, Sir W., 10, 22, 27, 29
Hardie, J. K., 32, 164
Harmsworth, C., 123
Harper, E., 51, 98
Harris, J. E., *see* Malmesbury, 5th earl of
Hartington, marquess of, 8–9, 11, 22
Harvey, A. G. C., 154
Heath, J. St G., 86, 96, 100, 107, 109–11
Hely, E., 130, 158
Hemmerde, E. G., 81, 83, 85, 96–7, 191
Henderson, A., 163, 169, 174
Henderson, R. B., 86
Henry, Sir C., 112, 127
Herbert, A. T., *see* Lucas, 8th Lord
Hirst, F. W., 127
Hobhouse, Sir C., 78, 118–19
Hobhouse, L. T., 57, 81, 88, 127
Hobson, J. A., 35, 57, 81, 127
Holt, R., 154–5
Home Rule Council, 123, 125
Hope, J. F., 158
Horsfall, T. C., 67
House of Lords, 5, 16, 21–3, 26–7, 41–4, 61–3, 115, 152–3, 156–7, 160, 181–2
housing, 31, 40, 64–6, 68–9, 190; and land campaign, 89–90, 101–6, 120–2, 174–7
Housing Acts: (1890), 31; (1909), 68–71, 175–6
Howard, E., 66
Hughes, C., 130
Hyder, J., 167

Illingworth, P., 119, 123–4
Independent Labour Party, 142, 164, 166, 169–72
Irish councils bill (1907), 43
Irish Home Rule, 15–17, 19–21, 26–7, 79–80, 115–16, 123, 143, 158–60, 181
Irish Land Acts: (1870), 6, 9; (1881), 9
Isaacs, Sir R., 82, 141

Jebb, L., 37
Jowett, F., 164, 175

Kimberley, 1st earl of, 15

Labouchere, H. 13, 31
Labour Party: housing, 165, 169, 174–7; Labour land enquiry, 163–6; and land campaign, 82, 169–73, 176–7; and land reform, 164–5, 172, 174, 185–6, 191–3; and Liberal Party, 162–3, 165–6, 171–3, 176–7; and rural England, 182–3, 188–9
labourers, agricultural: elections, 11–14, 16–17, 45–52, 132–4, 156, 181–3, 185–7; land campaign, 77–80, 120–2, 130–1; trade unions, 11, 46, 88, 130–1, 164–5, 170–1, 185–6. *See also* housing, farmers
Lambert, G., 24–5, 34, 128
land campaign: cabinet, 116–23, 139; land commissioners, 118–19; legislation, 121–2; Lloyd George speeches, 118, 122–3; organisation, 124–6; timing, 115–16
land campaign (rural): electoral impact, 130–7; farmers, 128, 131–2; housing, 120–2; labourers, agricultural, 130–1; Liberal Party, 126–30; Unionist Party, 130, 133, 156–61
land campaign (urban): budget (1914), 148–55; cabinet, 146–8; delays, 138–40; electoral impact, 138–43; housing, 146–8; land taxation, 146, 148–55; leaseholders, 139, 144–6; Lloyd George speeches, 100, 105–6, 110, 140, 145; minimum wage, 147
land campaign (1925–9), 183–90
Land Clauses Consolidation Act (1845), 106
Land Club League, 129
land colonies, 32, 72–5
land enquiry: delays, 98–100; land acquisition, 95, 106–7; land taxation, 96–7, 99–100, 110–13; organisation, 83–7, 95–100; origins, 77–83; Scotland and Wales, 84–5; town planning, 95; Unionist Party, 86–7; urban enquiry, 85, 95–100
land enquiry (1923–5), 183–4, 186–7, 189–90
Land and Labour League, 8, 31
Land Law Reform Association, 34, 40, 69
Land ministry (proposed), 119–20

Land and Nation League, 183
land nationalisation, 97–8, 107, 164–5
Land Nationalisation Society, 107, 164
land purchase, 9–10, 35, 42, 44, 48–9,
    91–2
land report (rural): housing, 89–90; land
    courts, 92–4; minimum wage, 87–9;
    part V, 94; rating system, 94; schedules,
    86–7; security of tenure, 93–4;
    smallholdings, 90–1
land report (urban): de Forset
    memorandum, 97–8; housing, 101–6;
    land acquisition, 95, 106–7; land
    nationalisation, 107; land taxation,
    109–14; leaseholds, 95, 107–9;
    minimum wage, 104–6; town planning,
    95, 102–4
Land Settlement (Facilities) Act (1919),
    180
land taxation, 2, 3–4, 28–30, 51–2, 54–64,
    148–55. See also land enquiry, land
    report (urban)
Land Tenure Reform Association, 4, 7
Land Utilisation Act (1931), 181, 191
land values (Scotland) bills (1907–8),
    59–61
landlord and tenant (no. 2) bill (1927),
    190
landowners, 2–3, 4–6, 16–17, 25, 28–31,
    42, 50–1, 79–80, 92, 106, 110–11
    156–61, 180–2, 184–7,
Lansbury, G., 72–3, 164, 191
Lansdowne, 5th marquess of, 157, 160–1
Lasker, B., 131–2
Leasehold Enfranchisement Association,
    30–1, 34
leasehold system, 28–31, 107–9, 144–6
Lees-Smith, H. B., 131
Lever, W. H., 66–7, 82, 84, 124
Liberal Party: land reform, 29–31, 84,
    112–13, 126–30, 153–5, 184–6, 193;
    rural England, 10, 12–14, 16–18, 21,
    23–6, 45, 47–53, 81–2, 183, 187–8
Liberal Unionists, 15–16, 17–18, 19, 22–3
licensing reform, 22, 61, 63
light railways bill (1895), 24
Lilford, 5th Lord, 131
Lincolnshire, 1st marquess of, see
    Carrington, 1st earl
Lindsay, D. A. E., see Balcarres, 10th earl
    of
Lloyd George, D.: budgets (1909), 51,
    60–2, (1914), 148–5, (1931), 192–3;
    cabinet, 116–21, 139; coalition

government (1918–22), 179–80; land
    campaign (1925–9), 183–90; land
    courts, 79, 93; land enquiry, 81–7; land
    taxation, 96–7, 110–14; leaseholds, 95,
    107–9; Marconi, 116; minimum wage,
    77–80, 87–8, 104–5, 147; rural
    housing, 89–90; rural land campaign,
    122–6, 128, 134; speeches, 100, 105–6,
    110, 118, 122–3, 140, 145;
    unemployment, 73–4; urban land
    campaign, 138–41
Lloyd-Greame, P., 159
Local Government Acts: (1888), 18;
    (1894), 22–5, 26, 33, 35
Logan, J. W., 24
London County Council, 29–31, 55, 65
Long, W., 43, 72, 145, 159–61
Lough, T., 155
Lucas, 8th Lord, 128
Lumley, A., 98
Luttrell, H. C. F., 34
Lygon, W., see Beauchamp, 7th earl

McCurdy, C. A., 131
MacDonald, J. R., 166, 169, 171, 174
Mackarness, F., 69
McKenna, R., 118–19
Macnamara, T. J., 58
Macpherson, I., 85
Macrosty, H. W., 169
Malmesbury, 5th earl of, 161
Massingham, H. W., 81–2
Masterman, C. F. G., 35–6, 44–6, 58, 68,
    71, 80–2, 143, 168
Mathias, Sir R., 127
Middleton, J., 163
Mill, J. S., 4, 7
Mond, Sir A., 82, 184
Money, L. G. C., 127
Montagu, E. S., 39, 50, 123
Morley, A., 19
Morley, J., 19, 78
Morrell, P., 47, 50–1
Mosley, T., 135
Munro-Ferguson, R., 41
Murray, A. C., 112–13
Murray, A. W. C. O., see Elibank, master
    of

Nathan, Sir M., 151
National Farmers Union, 132, 185–7
National Housing Reform Council, 67–8
National Insurance Act (1911), 77, 80,
    115, 134, 141–3

National Insurance Committee, 123
National Land and Home League, 85–6, 88–9, 129–30, 159, 166, 168–9
National Liberal Federation, 16, 19–20, 26, 29, 45, 84, 112, 126, 184, 187
navy, 149–52, 154
Nettlefold, J. S., 67–8, 70, 104
Nicholls, G., 46, 134
Nicholson, Sir C., 127, 154
Nonconformity, 22, 45, 51, 117–18
Northcote, Sir S., 10–11
Nunnelly, E. M., 128

Onslow, 4th earl of, 19, 33
Onslow, W. H., see Onslow, 4th earl of
Orr, J., 98
Outhwaite, R. L., 50, 96, 191

parish councils, 18–21, 22–3, 24–5
Parker, B., 66
Parker, J., 163
Parmoor, 1st Lord, 161
Parnell, C. S., 17, 19
Paton, J. B., 36
Paulton, J. M., 41
Pease, E., 167–9
Pease, J., 78, 117–18, 123
Pease, M., 167–9
Perks, R. W., 45, 51, 129
Petty-Fitzmaurice, H. C. K., see Lansdowne, 5th marquess of
plural voting, 61, 115, 136–7, 181
Poor Law reform, 11, 22, 23–4
Powys, J., see Lilford, 5th Lord
Price, P., 128
Price, Sir R., 127
Primrose, A. E. H. M. A., see Dalmeny, Lord
Prothero, R., 158
Public Health Act (1875), 65

Radford, G. H., 155
Raffan, P. W., 150
Raphael, H. H., 112, 155
Reform Acts: (1884), 11–12; (1918), 181–2
Reiss, R. L., 86, 89, 132, 140
revenue bill (1914), 122, 153
Riddell, Sir G., 78–80, 84, 107, 149, 151
Ripon, 1st marquess of, 17, 19–20, 42
Roberts, G., 163, 166, 169–70, 175
Robinson, G. F. S., see Ripon, 1st marquess of
Robson, Sir W., 60

Rosebery, 5th earl of, 27, 38, 40–1
Rosebery, 6th earl of, see Dalmeny, Lord
Rowntree, A., 81
Rowntree, B. S.: land campaign, 124–5, 136, 139–40, 146–7, 160; land enquiry, 81, 85–6, 88–9, 91, 94, 103–6, 111, 116
Rowntree, J., 66, 81, 84, 98, 124
royal commissions: aged poor (1893–5), 24; agriculture (1893–7), 24, 34; housing (1884–5), 31; Welsh land (1893–7), 9, 21–2, 37
Runciman, H., 184
Runciman, W., 58, 76–7, 118–22, 139, 184
Runciman, Sir W., 127
Rural League, 164

Salisbury, 3rd marquess of, 18, 22, 25, 26–7, 31
Salisbury, 4th marquess of, 50, 62, 160–1
Salvation Army, 32, 72
Samuel, H., 3, 17, 79, 146–7
Sanders, R., 130, 133, 158
Saunders, W., 30, 57
Saye and Sele, 18th Lord, 128
Schuster, G., 128
Scotland, land reform, 1–2, 9–10, 22, 38, 41–4, 58–9, 113
Scott, C. P., 82, 91, 123
Scottish Land Restoration League, 30
Scottish small landholders bills: (1907–8), 43–4
Scurr, J., 143, 173
Seale-Hayne, C. H., 17, 34
select committees: Haversham committee (1911–12), 92; leaseholds (1886–9), 30, 108; rural housing (1906), 68–9, 90; smallholdings (1888–90), 20
Settled Estates Act (1882), 9, 11
Shaw-Lefevre, G., 29
Shove, G., 86, 98
Simon, Sir J., 123, 193
Sinclair, J., 38, 43–4
single taxers, 30, 56, 60, 81, 96–7, 112–13, 174, 191
smallholdings: elections, 45–6, 48–50, 179–80; Liberal Party, 8, 20, 33–48, 50, 52, 76–7, 90–1; Unionist Party, 20, 33–4, 43–4, 48–9, 156–8, 188
Smallholdings Acts: (1892), 20, 33, 35, 37, 46, 48; (1907), 41–8, 52, 76–7; (1926), 188
Smith, W., 185–6
Snowden, P., 166, 171–2, 173, 191–3

Soames, A. W., 127
Soares, E. J., 34
Spencer, 5th earl, 15
Spender, J. A., 51, 57, 85
Stansfeld, J., 18
Steel-Maitland, A., 130, 157, 160–1
Stevens, C., 86
Stewart, H., 19
Storey, H., 130, 158
Strachey, Sir E., 76, 89, 127
Strachie, 1st Lord, see Strachey, Sir E.
Strutt, E., 88
Stuart, J., 29
Surveyors Institution, 70, 99–100

Tariff Reform, 8, 11–12, 33–4, 45–6, 73–4, 159, 178, 188, 192
Tariff Reform League, 83, 123
Thompson, W., 67–8
town planning, 65–71, 95, 102–4
Town Tenants League, 108–9, 145
Trade Boards Act (1909), 77–8, 88, 117, 146–7, 166
Trades Union Congress, 164–5, 170–1, 189
Trevelyan, C. P., 56–7, 60, 191
Turnor, C., 92, 159, 167
Twistleton-Wykeham-Fiennes, G. C., see Saye and Sele, 18th Lord

Unemployed Workmen Act (1905), 72
unemployment, 8, 31–2, 72–5, 191–2
Unemployment Insurance (no. 2) Act (1930), 182
Unionist Party, 22–3, 25, 35, 48–52, 55–6, 62–4, 181–2, 185–6; and land campaign, 86–7, 91–2, 130, 133, 156–61. See also farmers, smallholdings

Unionist Social Reform Committee, 89, 121–2, 158–9, 161, 174–5
Unwin, R., 66–7, 104
Ure, A., 56, 59

Verney, Sir H., 123
Verney, R. G., see Willoughby de Broke, 19th Lord

Wales, land reform, 1–2, 9, 21–2
Wallop, Hon. J. F., 132
Walls, P., 163
Warner, Sir C., 127
Webb, B., 167, 169, 171
Webb, S., 167, 169
Wedgwood, J., 56, 96, 98, 113, 167, 191
Welsh Church disestablishment, 21–2, 79–80, 115, 181
Wheatley, J., 176
White, Sir L., 128
Williams, A., 143
Williams, L., 44
Willoughby de Broke, 19th Lord, 160
Wilson, L. O., 141–2
Wilson, P. W., 70, 77, 82
Winfrey, R., 37, 39, 45–7, 82–3, 85
Wodehouse, J., see Kimberley, 1st earl of
Workmens National Housing Council, 176–7
Wynn-Carrington, C. R., see Carrington, 1st earl

Young, Edward Hilton, 184